CONNECTED STRUGGLES

Connected Struggles

*Catholics, Nationalists,
and Transnational Relations between
Mexico and Quebec, 1917–1945*

MAURICE DEMERS

McGill-Queen's University Press
Montreal & Kingston · London · Ithaca

© McGill-Queen's University Press 2014

ISBN 978-0-7735-4356-0 (cloth)
ISBN 978-0-7735-4357-7 (paper)
ISBN 978-0-7735-9198-1 (ePDF)
ISBN 978-0-7735-9199-8 (ePUB)

Legal deposit third quarter 2014
Bibliothèque nationale du Québec

Printed in Canada on acid-free paper that is 100% ancient forest free
(100% post-consumer recycled), processed chlorine free

This book has been published with the help of a grant from the Canadian
Federation for the Humanities and Social Sciences, through the Awards
to Scholarly Publications Program, using funds provided by the Social
Sciences and Humanities Research Council of Canada. Funding has also
been received from the Université de Sherbrooke's Faculté des lettres
et sciences humaines as well as the Université de Sherbrooke's programme
d'Appui aux activités de création et d'édition savant.

McGill-Queen's University Press acknowledges the support of the
Canada Council for the Arts for our publishing program. We also
acknowledge the financial support of the Government of Canada through
the Canada Book Fund for our publishing activities.

Library and Archives Canada Cataloguing in Publication

Demers, Maurice, 1977–, author
     Connected struggles: Catholics, nationalists, and transnational relations
     between Mexico and Quebec, 1917–1945 / Maurice Demers.

     Based on thesis (doctoral) – York University, 2010, under title:
     Pan-Americanism re-invented in Uncle Sam's backyard: Catholic
     and Latin identity in French Canada and Mexico in the first half
     of the 20th century.
     Includes bibliographical references and index.
     Issued in print and electronic formats.
     ISBN 978-0-7735-4356-0 (bound). – ISBN 978-0-7735-4357-7 (pbk.). –
     ISBN 978-0-7735-9198-1 (ePDF). – ISBN 978-0-7735-9199-8 (ePUB)

     1. Religion and international relations – Québec (Province) – History –
     20th century. 2. Religion and international relations – Mexico – History –
     20th century. 3. Catholics – Québec (Province) – History – 20th century.
     4. Catholics – Mexico – History – 20th century. 5. Canadians, French-
     speaking – Québec (Province) – History – 20th century. 6. Nationalists –
     Québec (Province) – History – 20th century. 7. Nationalism – Québec
     (Province) – History – 20th century. 8. Québec (Province) – Relations –
     Mexico – History – 20th century. 9. Mexico – Relations – Québec
     (Province) – History – 20th century. 10. Canada – Relations – Mexico –
     History – 20th century. 11. Mexico – Relations – Canada – History –
     20th century. I. Title.

     BL65.I55D44 2014   201'.727   C2014-901232-2
                                                 C2014-901233-0

This book was typeset by Interscript in 10.5/13 Sabon.

À Christian Demers

Contents

Figures

Acknowledgments

This project is the result of many years of work and has benefited from the help and guidance of many people, the financial support of various institutions, and the encouragement of friends and family. Let me state at the outset that I am indebted to their questions, suggestions, and support, which played a significant role in my ability to carry through with the production of this book. I am especially grateful to my PhD supervisors Anne Rubenstein and Roberto Perin for their assistance and guidance during my doctoral studies. I wish to recognize, in particular, the helpful advice and suggestions of Marcel Martel and Catherine LeGrand who both have provided valuable recommendations throughout the process of writing this book. I want to thank Jean-François Côté, Patrick Dramé, Romana Falcón, Mathieu Lapointe, Marc Lessage, Alex Major, Gillian McGillivray, Lorenzo Meyer, Andrea Mutolo, Michel Nareau, Carolyn Podruchny, Franco Savarino, Bradley Skopyk, María Fernanda Vázquez Vela, and Jean-Philippe Warren for their valuable help, comments, and observations on different aspects of my research. I am very grateful for the insights and support of many colleagues at the history departments of York University and Université de Sherbrooke, at the meetings of the Toronto Latin American Research Group and the Groupe interdisciplinaire de recherche sur les Amériques, at conferences organized on the religious history of Mexico, and at the congresses of the Société canadienne d'histoire de l'Église catholique. The assistance of my graduate students Myriam Alarie and Mauricio Correa with the latest revisions of the manuscript was deeply appreciated. I would like to extend a special thank you to Gratia O'Leary and Eugenia Loaeza de Manhes for sharing

their memories and experiences with me. This project greatly bene-
fited from the helpful comments of outside reviewers and the help of
Kyla Madden, Jessica Howarth, Helen Hajnoczky, Darren Hunter,
Kaarla Sundström, Ryan Van Huijstee and the rest of the staff at
McGill-Queen's University Press.

Various governmental and academic programs funded my research
and the publication of this book. First, this book has been published
with the help of a grant from the Federation of the Humanities and
Social Sciences through the Awards to Scholarly Publications
Program, using funds provided by the Social Sciences and Humanities
Research Council of Canada. Université de Sherbrooke (through
funds granted by the Programme d'Appui aux activités de création
et d'édition savante and by the Faculté des lettres et sciences
humaines) also funded the publication of this book. I was able to
conduct research in Canadian and Mexican archives with the help of
grants received from the Social Sciences and Humanities Research
Council of Canada, the Ontario Graduate Scholarship, and different
York University fellowships. The archivists and the staff at the
Archivo de la Acción Católica Mexicana at Universidad
Iberoamericana, the Archivo General de la Nación, the Acervo
Histórico Diplomático de la Secretaría de Relaciones Exteriores de
México, the Archives du Centre de recherche Lionel-Groulx, Library
and Archives Canada, the archives of the archdioceses of Quebec
and Mexico City, and the historical archives of Universidad Nacional
Autónoma de México, Université Laval, and Université de Montréal
all contributed to the successful completion of this book and I am
sincerely thankful for their help.

In the end, I owe a debt of gratitude to my parents, my wife Karine,
my son Léo, and my newborn Émilien. My parents have always
encouraged me to explore new horizons and Karine's presence
throughout my academic career and her unwavering support during
the process of writing this book were essential to its successful completion. And as for my kids, they (usually) help me unwind.

CONNECTED STRUGGLES

Introduction

Located roughly one hundred kilometres south of Quebec City, in the undulating landscape of the Appalachians, La Guadeloupe stands out as a village with an unusual name. Exoticism is not often associated with rural Quebec's place names. Most municipalities took their French names from the Catholic parishes with which they share borders and Beauce's toponymy is no exception, apart from a few English names present on the region's map (mainly referring to the *cantons* or towns along the old railway line). The name Notre-Dame-de-la-Guadeloupe may come from its parish, but no other town in Quebec honours the Virgin Mary's 1531 appearance to Juan Diego, an *Indio* from Mexico. On the face of it, this fact seems inconsequential. And in many ways, it is. But the events that brought about this namesake – the emergence of transnational connections between French Canadian nationalists and devout Catholics in Mexico in the first half of the twentieth century – nonetheless discloses revealing aspects of power relations in Canada and Mexico.

Who knew nationalists from Quebec and Catholic militants from Mexico once shared a common cause, a cause that influenced the international relations of their respective countries? The field of transnational studies is flourishing and has produced significant breakthroughs, revaluating the history of Latin American nations in light of their global interactions. Nevertheless, scholars have largely shied away from exploring Canadian-Latin American relations in the twentieth century through that lens. Many scholars would argue that the foreign ministries in Ottawa and Latin America have always conceived the connections between their countries, first and foremost, in economic and political terms. Yet, this perspective does not tell the whole story about North-South interactions involving Canadians and Latin Americans. This book questions the premises of this long-held view in academia. Indeed, the following five chapters offer a unique perspective on the subject by highlighting how civilian actors from the French-speaking province had developed an important web of sociocultural connections in Latin America in the first part of the twentieth century; it also shows that Mexican Catholics established good connections with co-religionists from Canada at the same time. Using the case of Mexican-French Canadian transnational relations to demonstrate these points, my book puts forward the argument that Catholics in both nations saw their struggles over cultural identity as interconnected and used their expressions of solidarity as political capital. This camaraderie, when analyzed, helps us understand the process by which identity politics influenced the history of Canada and Mexico's diplomacy in the Americas and created lasting networks of solidarity. The North-South connections largely initiated by the Québécois took shape before the creation of the Canadian International Development Agency (CIDA) or the intensification of Catholic missionary efforts in the region in the 1960s. Catholic nationalists in French Canada and Mexico laid the bases for particular ties between Quebec and Latin America by making mutually supportive gestures in favour of their cultural struggles at a time when the World Wars in Canada and the Revolution in Mexico marginalized voices of dissent. La Guadeloupe is a reminder of that North-South solidarity.

There are lots of parishes devoted to the Virgin of Guadalupe outside of Mexico. Most of them are in Latin America and the old sphere of Spanish influence in the world (e.g. the Philippines), but some were also created following the trail of migrants north of the Rio Grande in the twentieth century. This is not the case for La Guadeloupe in Quebec. When the parish was established by Jean-Marie-Rodrigue Cardinal Villeneuve in 1946 – one year after his resounding welcome in Mexico as papal legate for the Marian celebrations – Latin American immigration to Canada was still insignificant. Official diplomatic relations with Mexico had barely been established, and economic exchanges were minimal. Yet, the creation of this parish was meaningful for those interested in closer Canadian-Mexican relations because it was perceived as a gesture indicating the feelings of solidarity uniting French Canadians and devout Catholics in Mexico. Many French Canadians wished for a concrete socio-political rapprochement with Mexico during the Second World

o.1 Façade of Notre-Dame-de-la-Guadeloupe's Church. This distinctive image of the Virgin of Guadalupe decorates the façade of the church in Beauce. Following Notre-Dame-de-la-Guadeloupe's foundation, two groups of Latin American students accompanied by dignitaries visited it to pray. The creation of the parish also inspired people to travel to Mexico. La Guadeloupe's first priest, Évariste Roy, went with a group of villagers on a pilgrimage to the original basilica on the Tepeyac. It is reported that Roy hoped miracles would result from this connection. (Comité de l'album, ed., *Notre-Dame-de-la-Guadeloupe*, 43–4. The picture is from Maurice Demers' private collection)

War (a time, it has to be said, when Latin American music came into vogue in Quebec). For some, the circumstances explaining the creation of La Guadeloupe indicated that a pan-Americanism more favourable to "Latin"[1] cultures might be possible in North America. Mexican Catholics appreciated gestures like this, as they used the political weight of their co-religionists from Canada and the United States to negotiate better conditions for the Church in post-revolutionary Mexico. Indeed, political significance permeated Catholic symbolism and discourses of identity at the turn of the 1940s, and competing stakeholders tried to make the most of it. But why did apparently unrelated situations come to be perceived as connected by civilian actors in Mexico and Quebec? That is what I try to understand in this study, focusing on how and why some attempted to give a special meaning to French Canadian-Mexican linkages during the Second World War and what the implications of this endeavour were in Canada and Mexico's political contexts.

In order to accomplish this, I organized my argumentation along a narrative structure, exploring various episodes of contact and collaboration between French Canadian and Mexican groups and bringing together two distinct transnational histories that intersected during the Second World War (one articulated mainly by French Canadians, the other by Mexicans). Accordingly, this research could be read differently by specialists of Québécois / Canadian history and Mexicanists – the former can observe in the following five chapters an attempt by nationalist leaders to secure a French Canadian voice in international relations by aligning Quebec with the other Latin cultures of the Americas, while the latter can perceive at first how Catholic groups in Mexico sought to use their transnational connections to denounce the persecution of the Catholic Church in the 1920s and 30s, and again in the 1940s to safeguard the fragile *modus vivendi* with the revolutionary government. In both instances, the State kept an eye on the situation, with the government in Ottawa trying to control how francophones broadcast their country's identity abroad, and Mexico City, after its conflictive attitude during the bitter anticlerical campaign, trying to use North American Catholic connections to gain wider diplomatic respectability. Combining these stories unveils how distinct objectives overlapped along the way and were expressed using a common discourse of identity that focused on their Latin culture.

While cultural points of convergence between French Canadians and Mexicans were decades in the making, the swift rapprochement experienced at the beginning of the Second World War has to be understood as part of a particular *zeitgeist*. The US's Good Neighbor policy toward Latin America certainly stimulated Canadian-Mexican diplomatic ties – and the war effort accelerated these developments.[2] Yet, I am arguing that other factors related to Quebec and Mexico's political cultures were more important in explaining the sudden rapprochement of French-speaking and Spanish-speaking groups at the turn of the decade. The foremost proponents of Canada-Mexico relations during the war were conservative scholars and influential Catholic spokespersons in Mexico and nationalist groups in Quebec; I argue that the transnational ties these proponents worked toward were attempts to make the most of the international context in order to improve their standing at home. Those who lobbied for a rapprochement were able to build broad alliances despite wartime restrictions in part because they were able to display their privileged connections with international dignitaries at a time when a new world order was in the balance. At the end of the day, French Canadian nationalists and Catholic militants in Mexico were successful, to a certain extent, in defending an autonomous space to express a distinctive identity in the Americas. But their internationalist stance during the war is also informative about long-term trends emerging at the turn of the 1940s concerning their relations with the State. Therefore, the main questions I investigate in this study are: can we consider the cultural linkages established between French Canadian nationalists and Mexican Catholic militants as attempts to alter their countries' internal balances of power? Was crafting an imagined community that reached across national borders an effective strategy to prop up local demands? Did it really influence diplomatic dealings or did the authorities use it as an opportunity to grant symbolic concessions to political outsiders?

IDENTITY POLITICS AND FOREIGN RELATIONS

The prism of identity politics has been successfully used by scholars to analyze Quebec-Canada political disputes.[3] The same could be said regarding the disagreement between fervent Catholics and the revolutionary State in Mexico.[4] But what is unique about the history of identity politics in this study is that the transnational collaboration I have been tracing reveals an attempt on both sides to contextualize their cultural struggles into a broader geopolitical framework with implications for their countries' foreign relations. In order to evaluate the role specific groups from civil society played in the formation of diplomatic relations between Canada and Mexico during the Second World War, I found it necessary to analyze their "*prise de parole*" [capture of speech], to use Michel de Certeau's concept.[5] Part of the rhetoric used at the time to explain the special bonds uniting French Canadian Catholics with their Mexican brethren can sound strange these days, but I argue it is symptomatic of a strategic positioning that came to dominate national politics later on. The *Histoire des apparitions de Notre-Dame-de-la-Guadeloupe*, a book published in Quebec a few years after Villeneuve's visit to Mexico, provides a good example of this positioning and establishes clear lineage between the two groups. Its author claims that "*Canadiens*[6] and Mexicans have to act like brothers because we are related in many ways. We belong to the same Latin American family. We are bound together by our blood, our culture, our customs, and our spirituality; but above all, we share the same Catholic religion."[7] If this language of direct filiation seems overblown nowadays – as I think most people would have considered it back then too – it was nonetheless often used to lobby decision-makers in Ottawa and Mexico City. I am arguing these discursive stances carried weight during the war and enabled those who were using them to take the floor in pan-American affairs.

In recent years, the way past cultural policies supported nation-building projects as normative and as symbolic schemes has informed the works of historians. Some have seen the contestation and subsequent negotiations of cultural policies as a symbolic space where the authority of the State was negotiated. For example, the different essays in Gilbert Joseph and Daniel Nugent's seminal work *Everyday Forms of State Formation* suggest that governmental engagement with popular cultures and grassroots groups created a space where the negotiation of rule could be mediated.[8] The literature on foreign relations has been influenced by this approach. Yet, the influence civil society had on international dealings, and the way authorities used symbolic politics to respond to that influence, remains on the margins of this historiographical corpus.[9] The literature on Canadian-Mexican relations is no exception. My research makes a contribution to that historiographical debate.

Although I am analyzing how identity politics intersected with the history of Canadian and Mexican foreign relations, I am doing so with a twist. What interests me is how the transnational bonds created by Quebec and Mexico's civil societies and religious communities influenced the establishment of official diplomatic linkages. In that way, this study proposes a complete reinterpretation of North-South collaboration in the Americas, showing not only the Catholic origins of solidarity, but its conservative – even reactionary – roots as well. Highlighting the common Latin identity (based on the similarities of language and common Roman Catholicism) that united French-speaking and Spanish-speaking transnational associations and organizing cultural events showcasing dignitaries from the other nation became strategies used by French Canadian and Mexican Catholics to curb feelings of being marginalized in their own countries. These encounters were also used as political capital to carve up a space for their organizers to play a role in international affairs. The ins and outs of this rapprochement in the first half of the twentieth century and why the foreign ministries of Canada and Mexico both used and denounced these linkages at times are the focus of this book. What remains at the centre of my attention is the meaning of cultural self-representation in international affairs, in other words, how key participants formulated and legitimized their actions, along with the local consequences transnational alliances have for groups considered to be political dissidents.

Catholic militants in post-revolutionary Mexico and French Canadian nationalists in Canada were, at some point, marginalized in their respective countries; despite the numerical weight of the communities their representatives claimed to speak for, they remained relatively isolated from their countries' decision-making centres. In Mexico, the government adopted staunch anti-clerical measures that provoked right-wing Catholic reaction following the Mexican Revolution (1910–20). This turn of events, and the ratification of the 1917 Constitution, marginalized practicing Catholics from politics until the 1940s. In Canada, francophones felt isolated from power after various measures limiting education in French were adopted in Canadian provinces at the turn of the century, measures that sharply polarized the two main linguistic communities of this country and led to the marginalization of Quebec members of Parliament from the Union government formed by Sir Robert Borden in 1917. This sentiment of isolation deepened with the conscription crises that rocked the country during the two world wars. Considering this outlook, only the economic elites of both countries seemed to be able to successfully connect Canada and Mexico. After all, the informal imperialism facilitating big business in the Americas (whether British or American) connected entrepreneurs from the North with business partners from the South, which is why many Montreal companies were active in Latin America at the turn of the twentieth century. But the economic elites running those companies in Montreal tended to be Anglophone and Protestant. The economic crisis in the 1930s exacerbated the resentment against the advance of Anglo-Saxon capitalism in Quebec and Mexico; nationalist groups and the Catholic petite-bourgeoisie of both places complained about the social transformation brought by this "foreign" influence. Moreover, with the separation of Church and State in France in 1905 and in Spain in 1931, the Catholic clergy in French Canada and Mexico had the impression (along with many conservative citizens) that the fundamental principles of Catholic civilization were endangered.

The community of interests analyzed in this study – favouring the cooperation of the Latin peoples of the Americas – emerged out of this context.

This resistance sometimes took a violent turn, but the collaborative effort I am studying was rather peaceful. True, some of the main actors who established the first cultural connections between French Canada and Mexico were associated with a radical nationalist ideology in Quebec or with the 1920s and the 1930s religious violence in Mexico. Yet, when analyzing the actions of "nationalists" and "Catholic militants," I am using a loose definition of those terms because most people I am studying espoused moderate positions.[10] In any case, the Second World War forced radicals to change their tune if they wanted to achieve their goals, but this transition remained a controversial balancing act; detractors in both countries were prone to denouncing French Canadian nationalists and Mexican Catholic militants as hiding behind semantic ruses to embrace "counter-revolutionary sectarianism."[11] They were seldom officially recognized as having an influence on the establishment of diplomatic ties with foreign countries.[12]

It has to be said, however, that the course of action taken by French Canadian nationalists and devout Catholics in Mexico was not equally polarizing in the 1940s. While controversies surrounding the undue influence of the Catholic Church on the political process are resurfacing in Mexico nowadays, the history I examine here is one of cautious collaboration and rapprochement between Catholic groups and Manuel Ávila Camacho's administration, an informal cooperation meant to strengthen the *modus vivendi* between the government and the Church crafted at the end of Lázaro Cárdenas's presidency – a mutual tolerance that contrasted with the bitter tensions of the 1920s and 1930s.[13] In contrast, the transnational project supported by nationalists and members of the clergy in Quebec proved to be more divisive during the Second World War, not because of the influence the Catholic Church had over the process (something French Canadian critics of clericalism could have pointed out), but because it apparently contrasted with the modernization of Canada's international relations. I argue that representatives of the Canadian government criticized the Québécois' inroads in Mexico because it was perceived as an assertion of an independent French Canadian voice on the world stage, an early example of a praxis that still polarizes federal-provincial relations to this day.

THE NATURE OF FRENCH CANADIAN NATIONALISM
BEFORE THE QUIET REVOLUTION

The French Canadian voice in Mexico was mostly secured by Catholic networking and the initiatives taken by right-leaning nationalist groups. Ottawa opposed those inroads after it came to the conclusion that their organizers broadcasted French Canadian nationalism abroad, something that they thought could have a negative impact on the country's foreign relations. Of course, the war made transnational relations a sensitive issue, even with an allied country. But there was more to it than this wartime caution; some Canadian Liberal reformers saw French Canadian nationalism as retrograde (and paralyzed by too much clerical influence), a force that should not impact the modernization of Canadian foreign relations. Whether French Canada was characterized as a modern Catholic nation or denounced as a backward priest-ridden society depended on an individual's standpoint and intellectual inclinations. Certainly, during the second administration of Maurice Duplessis – which lasted fifteen years – the modernization of the Canadian State clashed with the stern anti-statist and anti-union positions of Quebec's Premier, his traditionalist views on social assistance, and his opportunistic use of French Canadian nationalism to rally support in opposition to Ottawa's progressive social programs. Duplessis' conservatism was increasingly being contested by a new generation of Québécois nationalists who also wanted to modernize the province's institutions and social programs. Nevertheless, the Premier's stance reinforced the opinion of Liberal reformers in Canada's capital who saw French Canadian nationalism as a reactionary and sectarian force that could hardly benefit the country's larger interests. This outlook tainted perceptions of nationalists' aspirations to express a French Canadian voice on the world stage. Pierre Elliott Trudeau wrote about the open-mindedness of the ideological movement: "The truth is that the separatist counter-revolution is the work of a powerless *petit-bourgeois* minority afraid of being left behind by the twentieth-century revolution. Rather than carving themselves out a place in it by ability, they want to make the whole tribe return to the wigwams by declaring its independence. That, of course, will not prevent the world outside from progressing by giant's stride; it will not change the rules and the facts of history, nor the real power relationship in North America."[14] While this diatribe

was directly addressed to *separatists* (who still represented a minority in the nationalist camp in the 1960s), political stakeholders in
Quebec City felt compelled to go up against these kinds of allegations. From Paul Sauvé's "*désormais*" and Jean Lesage's election in
1960, the provincial administration pushed for the modernization of
the apparatus of government and adopted a pro-active attitude in
deploying *Québécois* culture as a diplomatic device. Québécois
nationalists then effectively used foreign relations as bargaining
chips to strengthen their position vis-a-vis the government in Ottawa.

The historiography of Quebec's international relations under-
scores the importance of this international maneuvering, especially
considering the weight cultural exchanges had in securing the assertion of a French Canadian voice abroad. Scholarly literature on the
subject locates this push for transnational linkages as coinciding
with the establishment of cultural connections with France (at the
turn of the 1960s) and the beginning of Quebec's Quiet Revolution.[15]
Initiating a coordinated effort by the government of Quebec and
interested stakeholders was indeed very difficult prior to the 1960s,
for it wasn't until 1965 that the Gérin-Lajoie Doctrine proclaimed
that the French-speaking province had the authority to act internationally in its fields of constitutional competence. Yet, I argue, as
early as the 1940s, we can find an attempt to change this state of
affairs by establishing cultural linkages with Mexico, a project
devised to auspiciously position French Canadians as mediators of
"the real power relationship in North America."[16] The actions of the
nationalist leadership in Montreal within the Union des Latins
d'Amérique (ULA) – the main transnational association I am analyzing in this book – and the governmental support it received from
Quebec City hinted at a paradigm shift that entailed the modernization of the State of Quebec and the reconfiguration of its international persona, an endeavour that would only materialize later
during the Quiet Revolution. The historiography does not directly
take into consideration the ins and outs of this attempt.

The few studies examining Quebec's connections with Latin
America use the Quiet Revolution as the genuine turning point that
lay the foundations of a rapprochement.[17] Still, some scholars have
recognized that "from the 1920s to the 1950s, the interest for Latin
America was reflected by the wealth of publications celebrating
'the affinities of race, religion, and culture' between the heirs of a
Latin spiritual tradition in the Americas."[18] Yet, this corpus does not

explain why this interest peaked during the Second World War, nor does it account for discussions of Mexican nationalism as an inspiring model for the French Canadian nation. Following the example of Daniel Gay's momentous study of Quebec's elite discourses on Latin America from 1959 to 1973, studies tend to portray the preceding period as one characterized by an apolitical and instrumental sympathy for Latin America which reinforced a sentiment of cultural (and racial) superiority.[19] Not completely discarding this image, my analysis reveals a textured portrayal of the motivations prompting nationalists to establish ties with Mexico at the time, shedding light along the way on divergent motives that need to be properly contextualized to be understood.

The mere mention of cultural ties established between Quebec and Mexico in the first half of the twentieth century might come as a surprise to some. Most specialists would agree with Gérard Bouchard's statement that in the century following the defeat of the Patriotes' project to seek independence for their colony (from the 1840s to the 1940s), "the history of Quebec diverges from the history of Mexico and the rest of Latin America."[20] French Canada retained a sense of national identity, which made Quebec its central homeland after the defeat of the Patriotes. However, this nationalism was redesigned to respect the contingencies of the era, shunning political independence as a guiding principle and social reforms contradicting Catholic doctrine.[21] Indeed, it seems as though that deeply religious province had little in common with the officially secular republic that was Mexico. In fact, if I were writing a comparative history, I could draw sharp contrasts between Quebec and Mexico. This can seem paradoxical. After all, 96.6 per cent of Mexico's population claimed to be Catholic in the 1940 census, while 86.8 per cent of the population of Quebec identified as such in Canada's 1941 census (the Protestant population of the province representing a very influential minority).[22] However, the climate of opinion among Quebec and Mexico's political elites was very different at the time. The following examples demonstrate that point: while Plutarco Elías Calles aggressively called for a renewed emphasis on eliminating the social influence of the Catholic clergy in his famous 1934 *Grito de Guadalajara*, Maurice Duplessis agreed to prominently display the crucifix in Quebec's legislature in 1937. Indeed, in the first half of the twentieth century, the political culture in Quebec was very different from that of Mexico.

A comparison with Southern Cone societies could highlight more convincingly the points of convergence uniting French Canadian and Latin American cultures, something literary scholars have taken the lead in showing.[23] As for drawing cultural parallels between Latin America and Canada at large, an interesting literature comparing the prairies and the pampas already exists, and scholars of the Italian, Japanese, and Jewish diasporas have also appraised the matching experiences of immigrant communities in the Southern Cone and Canada.[24] But the leads these works provide do not help in clearing up the increasing interest French Canadian nationalists had for establishing cultural and political ties with Mexico and Latin America during the Second World War.

To a certain extent, Mexico and Latin America became common references in Quebec's popular culture during this period because of the popularity of Latin American music, the growth of tourism in the region, and reports on the French Canadian missionary effort (which had sent roughly 2,000 people to Latin America over the years).[25] Serge Granger's fascinating study of the work French Canadian missionaries did in China demonstrates how this religious endeavour has helped shape Quebec's attitudes about foreign affairs and transnational collaboration – an endeavour dependent on a certain sense of cultural imperialism.[26] The missionary effort is worth assessing in order to study Quebec and Canada's first connections with Latin America (and I do present an overview of this venture in chapter one).[27] However, as far as French Canadian-Mexican relations are concerned, this angle is problematic because French Canadian missionaries were not officially present and working in this country before the 1960s. The fascination for Mexican culture at the turn of the 1940s cannot be explained by missionary ventures alone.

There might be much validity in Bouchard's claim that *modern, secular* Quebec (read post-Quiet Revolution) has more in common with Mexico and Latin America than the *traditional, religious* society it used to be before the 1960s. But it is nevertheless in institutions controlled by the Catholic Church during Quebec's so-called *Grande noirceur* that transnational connections with Mexico were conceived and established by right-leaning nationalist groups. National politics has to be taken into consideration in order to understand this interest in transnational collaboration. Since the recognition of a sense of cultural belonging to the Americas apparently made Quebec's French-speaking elite uncomfortable in the first half of the twentieth century, this type of continental collaboration can be surprising. Indeed, the Manitoba School Question, which restricted French and Catholic education, and Ontario's Regulation 17, which imposed harsh restrictions on education in French, seriously antagonized French Canadians and brought the country to the brink of division during the First World War. The increasing stake of US capitalists in Quebec's economy and the rapid cultural assimilation of French-speaking migrants in New England completed this grim outlook for the survival of French Canadian culture on this continent. As a result, part of the francophone petite-bourgeoisie adopted a nationalist posture that did regard continental dealings with suspicion. Was it possible for nationalist leaders to reverse this defensive stance before the Quiet Revolution, spearheading rather than resisting continental relations? Before answering this question, we have to consider whether French Canadian nationalism could constitute a force for change or whether it was doomed to inconsequential symbolic stances.

The debate associated with this issue is important to take into consideration because the discourses of identity in the 1930s and 40s – which propelled nationalists like Dostaler O'Leary, Walter O'Leary, and Paul Bouchard to establish ties with Mexican conservative scholars and Catholic groups – also found a hearing in Premier Maurice Duplessis' administrations (1936–39 and 1944–59).[28] Whether the symbolic politics associated with the establishment of cultural relations with Mexico constituted an attempt by nationalist leaders to influence Canada's political landscape or whether these linkages constituted, instead, an entertaining apolitical distraction depends on how interwar French Canadian nationalism is understood.[29] The works of two historians can be used to highlight what is at stake here. According to André-J. Bélanger, the nationalist groups who proposed radical options in the 1930s were caught in an apolitical ideological shell that thwarted real political change. He argues that the likes of O'Leary and Bouchard were doomed to stay outside the fray of real political struggles.[30] In contrast, Robert Comeau stresses that the groups of young nationalists influenced by Canon Lionel Groulx were trying to organize a concrete political alternative.[31] Although the attempts to set up a nationalist political party ultimately failed in this decade, "they wanted to translate [Groulx's] national doctrine of the French State into a separatist and corporatist programme of political action."[32] Comeau explains that if these individuals toned down their radicalism at the beginning of the war – deciding, among other things, to opt for autonomy rather than separatism – it is because they could no longer accept being condemned to political marginality.[33] My analysis of the endeavours of the Union des Latins tally with Comeau's assessment. Scholars have noted that a clear political upshot of this 1930s nationalist movement came with the formation of the Bloc populaire in 1942, which constituted a genuine attempt to have an impact on the political process by proposing a nationalist alternative for Québécois voters at provincial and federal elections during the Second World War.[34] Dostaler O'Leary's U L A – which was established in Montreal in 1940 – has to be understood along the same lines. In this case, his association used cultural diplomacy to make sure French Canada would not be spoken for in international relations, and they employed symbolic rather than parliamentary politics as a means to achieve this goal. By mobilizing *latinité* as a meaningful discourse of identity for francophones, the U L A tried to locate French Canada at the crux of Canadian-Latin American diplomatic relations, thus improving the grim outlook for the survival of its culture on this continent.

This political positioning implied accepting Quebec's *américanité*, which was not a given during the *Grande noirceur*. The academic literature assessing Quebec's identity during this period associated the recognition of cultural belonging to North America with French Canada's acculturation to an Anglo-Saxon way of life (or Americanization); scholars preferred to stress French Canada's exceptionalism instead. Louis Dupont argues that writers, literary scholars, and artists like Robert Charlebois were the first to significantly take into consideration the American component of Quebec's identity during the 1960s and 1970s.[35] Geographers, political scientists, and historians soon followed, especially after the State of Quebec changed its approach on foreign affairs.[36] They started to problematize Quebec's *américanité* and to analyze the province's historical openness to the world, comparing its socio-economic evolution with other countries in the Americas.[37] Gérard Bouchard's paradigm of "new communities" [*collectivités neuves*] helped to shed light on the similar development of nations in the Americas, using the conceptual tools of comparative historical sociology to draw parallels between societies that emerged from European colonization (including Quebec and Mexico).[38] He also collaborated with Yvan Lamonde to revisit Quebec's history in a comparative light and survey the various American cultural influences that transformed French Canadian culture in the nineteenth and twentieth centuries.[39] Continuing to re-evaluate Quebec's foreign heritage in the 1990s and 2000s, Lamonde used the concept of *américanité* in order to underline the continental influences on its identity and to invite social scientists to look beyond Paris and Rome for cultural models influencing French Canada.[40]

Various scholars continued to explore Quebec's history in a comparative or transnational light in order to put its development in perspective.[41] While those works were helpful in assessing how cultural transfers renewed French Canadian traditional culture, the historiographical trend that Lamonde influenced with his take on the concept of *américanité* tended to focus heavily on the cultural influence the US enjoyed in Quebec – especially as a consequence of the modernization of the province – and generally omitted Latin American influences. Critics were prone to stating that by focusing on the "normalcy" of American identity, the trend naturalized Anglo-Saxon forms of modernization.[42] Joseph Yvon Thériault writes that the "concept of *américanité* [was] borrowed from the Latin American tradition *americanidad*," which was used there to distinguish how the American experience of the Spanish and Portuguese-speaking cultures diverged from the North American experience. Thériault continues, stating that in contrast, "as a concept, Quebec's *américanité* is based on the analysis of likeness, similarities, and integration."[43] He also argues that "for the supporters of Quebec's *américanité*, our history and our identity are more technically oriented than defined by cultural markers."[44] My research shows a different picture, giving its full meaning to the concept *américanité* by taking into consideration how Mexican culture influenced French Canada in the first half of the twentieth century, and by explaining how – for the likes of O'Leary in the 1940s – "cultural markers" defined French Canada's *américanité*. In this way, my approach is inspired by the works of sociologists and literary scholars – most of whom collaborate with the Groupe interdisciplinaire de recherche sur les Amériques (G I R A) – who have analyzed the history of representations in the Americas and have compared Quebec's literature with Brazil and Argentina's, assessing the cultural transfers between the southern and northern parts of the Americas.[45] However, my research reveals that French Canadian intellectuals argued about the need for French Canada to embrace its own *américanité* as early as the 1940s.

Actually, promoting the recognition of Quebec's cultural belonging to the Americas was an important objective of the ULA during the Second World War. According to its representatives, this recognition was not antithetical to safeguarding Quebec's European cultural heritage. They argued that stronger linkages with Mexico and Latin America could actually strengthen this heritage. Even though the Creole elite that fought for independence from Spain at the beginning of the nineteenth century generally promoted an economic, political, and cultural break from the mother country, the nation building that followed decolonization did not significantly alter the social fabric of the new American republics. Therefore, if Mexican and Latin American nationalism came to mobilize prehispanic symbols to mark the new nations' differences with Spain, the Latin American elite continued to value European cultural models; Paris and London, rather than Madrid, became the new centres of reference that the elite tried to emulate. Moreover, conservative groups kept Catholic social and cultural influences alive, even in Mexico, making it an essential component of their own *américanité*. Independence was not antithetical to preserving Hispanic-Catholic traditions (despite huge disagreements between liberals and conservatives over the role of the Catholic Church in the new republics). After all, didn't Father Miguel Hidalgo y Costilla, who launched the struggle for independence in Mexico, use an image of the Virgin of Guadalupe on the banner representing his revolutionary movement? Néstor García Canclini writes that "Latin American countries are currently the result of the sedimentation, juxtaposition, and inter-weaving of indigenous traditions (above all in the Mesoamerican and Andean areas), of Catholic colonial Hispanism, and of modern political, educational, and communicational actions. Despite attempts to give elite culture a modern profile, isolating the indigenous and the colonial in the popular sectors, an interclass mixing has generated hybrid formations in all social strata. The secularizing and renovating impulses of modernity were more effective in the "cultured" groups, but certain elites preserve their roots in Hispanic-Catholic traditions, and also in indigenous traditions in agrarian zones, as resources for justifying privileges of the old order challenged by the expansion of mass culture."[46] In the 1940s, the mix of tradition and modernity that came to constitute the hybrid cultures of Latin America became appealing to some French Canadians. Their catholic elites, in particular, and nationalist leaders were viewed with respect in Quebec. The representatives of the U L A claimed that collaboration with Latin American Catholics could facilitate the acceptance of French Canada's continental character and improve the geopolitical position of its distinctive culture. The actions of the U L A's nationalist leadership were clearly designed to position themselves as knowledge-brokers of Canada's pan-American affairs. In order to convince decision-makers in Ottawa, they had to build a coalition in Quebec and convince Latin American diplomats to support this plan. Mexico's wish to officialize diplomatic relations with Canada facilitated this course of action during the war.

THE MEXICAN CHURCH-STATE CONFLICT
IN THE TWENTIETH CENTURY

Carlos Calderón, the Mexican consul general in Montreal in the early 1940s, established ties with Canada's business community and cultural associations in order to strengthen links with his country. He collaborated with Dostaler O'Leary and the U L A, giving critical legitimacy to an association Ottawa had doubts about. He also facilitated exchanges between Quebec's Catholic universities and Universidad Nacional Autónoma de México (U N A M), actions that could be interpreted in Mexico as a gesture of good will by a civil servant toward Catholic groups. Yet, it has to be said that the interest for Mexican culture was greater in French Canada than vice versa. Cultural and political ties with French Canada only acquired new meaning in Mexico in the context of the Second World War when links with Catholic groups in Europe were severed. From a Mexican point of view, Canada was valuable for two strategic reasons: the State could use it to re-establish its severed links with the British Empire in the wake of oil nationalization; and the Catholic Church could also strengthen its nationalist credentials by welcoming dignitaries from the province of Quebec in Mexico City, an endeavour that helped it to stabilize the *modus vivendi* with the Mexican government. Rodulfo Brito Foucher, the rector of U N A M during most of the Second World War, also hoped to solidify the international relations of its institution by promoting connections with the French-speaking province. Therefore, French Canada became a convenient example used by Catholic groups and conservative scholars in very particular contexts. Understanding how and why this example surfaced in Mexico at the turn of the 1940s is revealing of the evolution of power relations in the country and the consolidation of the Church-State détente.

Analyzing this issue entails addressing two specific historiographical debates: Mexico's foreign relations at the turn of the 1940s and the relaxation of the twentieth century Church-State conflict. Historians have largely overlooked Mexico's relations with Canada at that time, and Catholic connections between both countries have also been neglected. This is not surprising: it seems that everything separates the history of the Catholic Church in Quebec and in Mexico from the 1840s onward. During this period, while Church privileges were declining in Mexico, they were expanding in Quebec. To begin with, Mexico experienced a series of fierce debates over the role of religion in political life that resulted in civil wars and foreign interventions during the nineteenth century. The desire to finally abolish the Catholic Church's *fueros* – or privileges exonerating it from paying taxes and its clergy from standing trial in civil courts – motivated the Liberal Reforms of 1855–57. The secularization of Mexico then provoked a serious conservative backlash that found its first expression in the War of the Reforms (1858–61), and then in the support for the French occupation of the country (1862–67). Reformers would not forgive the Catholic Church for its support of foreign invasion. The political climate surrounding the Catholic Church's autonomy was permanently affected by this *faux-pas*, and generations of reformers (whether liberal or revolutionary) made curbing the power of this institution their top priority.

Tensions over secularization never provoked comparable violent backlashes in Quebec. Actually, after the Patriotes' downfall, the Catholic Church enjoyed a long period of social ascendency that saw its institutional presence increase greatly in the province. After experiencing the effects of the British Industrial Revolution, Montreal was transformed by the ultramontane Ignace Bourget, its second Catholic bishop, who sought to bring Canada's metropolis into line with Rome.[47] In many ways, this cultural imprint lasted for a whole century. Canada did experience its own controversies over the separation of the spiritual and temporal spheres during the nineteenth century, but these tensions never boiled over into violence like in Mexico. When all was said and done, the Canadian Catholic Church enjoyed a position of authority over the social realm (especially in Quebec) that the Mexican Church could not aspire to.

Yet, the history of the Church in Mexico offers vantage points from which we can relate the experience of Mexican and French Canadian Catholics. As I mentioned above, Hispanic-Catholic traditions in Mexico and Catholicism in Canada were preserved despite violent conflicts. Quebec and Mexico both experienced a Catholic revival in the second half of the nineteenth century. And at the end of that century, the archbishop of Mexico City, Pelagio Antonio de Labastida y Dávalos, adopted a course of action in order to uphold the social standing of the Church that was similar to Bourget's reforms a few decades earlier. Finally, the social encyclicals equally transformed Quebec and Mexico's civil society, as associational life was revitalized in the decades following the publication of *Rerum novarum* in 1891.[48] French Catholic religious communities even settled in Mexico at the beginning of the twentieth century, helping to re-organize religious education in the country.[49] This Catholic impulse survived the Revolution, and helped to re-configure Catholic organizations along the lines of Catholic Action, which in turn became a significant counter-weight to governmental hegemonic control of Mexico's civil society.[50] Finally, the historiography of the Cristiada identified how Mexican Catholics sought the support of foreign co-religionists to influence the balance of power in Mexico.[51] However, wide connections with Catholics from Quebec took a while to get established. At the beginning of the twentieth century, French-speaking Catholics were entangled in their own conflict over education, although it was language that marginalized them, not religion.

Still, French Canadian Catholics extensively discussed the situation of their co-religionists during the Mexican Revolution (1910–20) and the Cristero War (1926–29).[52] These conflicts provided an opportunity for Mexican Catholics to establish a network of support in North America.[53] Jean Meyer convincingly demonstrated the crucial role played by US ambassador Dwight Morrow in convincing President Plutarco Elías Calles to stop supporting a violent course of action against the Catholic Church.[54] In the closing stages of these protracted civil wars, the government tried to eliminate the Church as a competing social and ideological actor on the national scene. The Calles administration went to great lengths to achieve this goal.[55] Church properties were confiscated, public religious ceremonies were prohibited, and restrictions were imposed on wearing religious garb in public. Still, with the help of American diplomacy and the Vatican's desire to settle this dispute, the 1929 *arreglos* were ratified, officially putting an end to military conflict.

Nevertheless, this official peace accord did not prevent Jacobin radicalism from continuing to prevail in some states, such as Tomás Garrido Canabal's Tabasco, where strict limits were imposed on the number of priests allowed in the territory.[56] Garrido Canabal's harsh anticlericalism in the southeastern state radicalized Catholic groups and individuals like Rodulfo Brito Foucher, who actively encouraged radical actions to defend their positions in Mexico.[57] The case of the 400th anniversary celebrations of the Virgin of Guadalupe's apparition, which provoked a violent backlash in 1931, demonstrates the fact that public celebrations were also motives to reignite anticlerical confrontations with Catholic militants.[58] But above all, education became a sticking point that led to direct confrontation and a second wave of religious violence in the 1930s. President from 1924 to 1928, Plutarco Elías Calles still dominated Mexico's political life in July 1934 when he poured oil on the fire by calling for renewed cultural hostilities in his famous *Grito de Guadalajara* where he exposed why Mexico's children had to be shielded from Catholic education. Indeed, the government tried to secularize schooling in the 1920s and impose socialist education in the 1930s.[59] It took over a decade to completely bring an end to the violence that ensued. I argue that the Québécois Jesuit Antorio Dragon's books on Cristero Martyr Miguel Agustín Pro and his publications on the second wave of religious persecution also contributed to this process by drawing international attention to the situation in Mexico. In fact, Dragon's publications were described by the Jesuits in Mexico in the 1930s as the best propaganda for their cause.[60] In the second half of Lázaro Cárdenas's *sexenio*, reacting to international pressure, the president planned a way out of confrontation with Catholic militants, using symbolic politics to secure an appeasement. The support of the Catholic Church's authorities for Cárdenas's nationalization of oil companies, in 1938, helped to change Church-State relations.[61] The *modus vivendi* that was crafted at the time was founded on Catholic support for Mexican nationalism. But as Roberto Blancarte mentions, obstacles and pitfalls still stood in the way of a real ideological rapprochement.[62]

The episodes of collaboration between French Canadian and Mexican Catholic groups can serve as informative case studies to illustrate how the Catholic Church and the Mexican State countered these obstacles and pitfalls at the beginning of the 1940s. Mexican historiography identifies the 1940 election of Manuel Ávila Camacho as a significant turning point in Mexico's political history, a "convenient historical signpost of the shift in revolutionary politics away from Cárdenas's radical redistribution of wealth toward Ávila Camacho's policy of intensive capital accumulation."[63] The disagreements over the nationalization of oil companies, conflicts with conservative groups at UNAM, and the Church-State *modus vivendi* finally came to a long-lasting peaceful resolution during Camacho's presidency despite the fact that major changes had started to take shape during Cárdenas's presidency. The negotiations surrounding these issues impinged on the country's foreign relations, especially with Washington, a factor that Catholic groups tried to benefit from by using their network of support abroad as leverage to negotiate favourable treatment at home. The weight of international support increased with the world conflict, because it "brought Mexico into a much closer relationship, both culturally and economically, with the United States."[64] Building on the literature of Mexican-US cultural and political relations, I argue that ties with Canada played a complementary role in this process during the Second World War, as Mexican conservative scholars and Catholic groups used these circumstances to show off their good connections with Canadian dignitaries in order to strengthen their position at home. The Camacho administration used these opportunities to grant them symbolic concessions, rallying the nation around the president's national unity campaign.

The Second World War has long been sidelined as a germane contextual factor in the consolidation of power in Mexico. Still, scholars have recognized that its advent played an indirect role in forcing the US to accept oil nationalization, changing bilateral relations between both countries. Cárdenas's bold move in 1938 did not force Washington to accept nationalization simply because it was a fait accompli. Peter H. Smith explains that "it was the fall of France in mid-1940 that ultimately led the United States to accept the Mexican position."[65] The war also had a huge impact on Mexican socio-economic dynamics. "Even though Mexico was only marginally involved in the military aspects of the Second World War, that country tied a significant share of its economic output to the war effort," notes Stephen R. Niblo.[66] This overarching context influenced the rapid urbanization of the country – and increasing importance of Mexico City – considering that worker relocation to the nation's economic centre was attributable to external demand for industrialized products.

Recent studies of the early 1940s have emphasized the central importance of the world conflict in explaining these socioeconomic consequences in Mexico. They argue that wartime propaganda smoothed the progress of uniting the nation under President Camacho and the Partido de la Revolución Mexicana (PRM) while moving forward its intensive program of economic moderniza-tion.[67] Monica Rankin mentions that "Government rhetoric and the position of the press moved the country even closer to an alli-ance with the United States without presenting it as such. Instead, the government justified its actions in nationalistic terms of sover-eignty and security."[68] Indeed, a few months after his election, Camacho declared that Mexico would support the Allied war effort. The Conservative press gradually supported this shift by changing its attitude about Mexico's northern neighbours. I argue that cover-age about Canada and cultural activities organized with dignitaries from this country during the war facilitated Mexican conservatives' adaptation to the new pan-American state of affairs. The example of French Canada was used to highlight that a Catholic nation – whose clergy had supported General Franco – could still be at the forefront of the war against Nazi Germany. Moreover, conservative groups at UNAM and representatives of Mexico City's archdiocese invited French Canadian dignitaries to their country and used Quebec's example during their stay to demonstrate how the Catholic Church could play a social role supporting economic modernization – even in a Latin society. The media coverage of student exchanges and Cardinal Villeneuve's 1945 visit to Mexico were also occasions to showcase Catholic groups' good relations with Canada, a coun-try which officialized its diplomatic relations with Mexico at the same time. This might constitute only a minor chapter in the history of North American relations, but it is one that sheds new light on the process of national consolidation and unification during Camacho's *sexenio*, a process in which Catholic stakeholders played a role. Whether latinity (as a discourse of identity) and transna-tional Catholic connections could be used as effective points of leverage is a hypothesis to be tested against the events unfolding in the early 1940s.

SOURCES, CONCEPTS, AND BRIEF OVERVIEW
OF CHAPTERS

The ways that political outsiders cast themselves as knowledge brokers for central authorities in international affairs, with some using religious imagery as symbolic capital to gain concessions from them, are usually judged as theatrical acts of little importance. I think, on the contrary, that these constitute valuable cases to scrutinize how groups of citizens and representatives of the Catholic Church acted on the national and international scene; in turn, they offer a unique vantage point from which to observe how power relations were shaped and contested in Canada and Mexico. Since Joseph Nye and Robert Keohane have explained how nonstate entities and transnational actors can create "new myths, symbols, and norms to provide legitimacy" for their transactions abroad and therefore influence international relations, scholars have paid serious attention to how companies and actors from the civil society can sway the international politics of their country.[69] Historians and social scientists studying migration and border communities, the circulation of ideas across borders, the transnational nature of religious movements, N G O's and other social movements with global reach, have all expanded our ways of understanding the significance of the international connections and interactions of members of the civil society. Peggy Levitt and Sanjeev Khagram note that these types of exchanges and influences "create a space to imagine options for social transformation that are obscured when borders, boundaries, and the structures, processes, and actors within them are taken as given."[70] This transnational approach is useful in analyzing how some Mexican and French Canadian Catholics formed a community of interests, after their first contacts and interactions, and came to express support for each other's particular causes. In doing so, they both expected to draw benefits leading to some kind of social transformation from their collaboration – whether legitimizing the expression of a French Canadian voice on the world stage or safeguarding the Mexican Catholic Church's capacity to have a significant impact in the cultural and social spheres.

I do not need to recover a hidden subaltern voice in the documentation in order to analyze and assess the significance of this community of interests. The main participants of these transnational connections tended to be prominent citizens, and they left plenty of documentary evidence behind that can be examined "working 'along the grain' of political rationalities."[71] Many of the primary sources I analyze were published at the time (as newspaper articles, memoirs, or reports). The main transnational association I study also left a significant amount of documentation in Quebec. I consulted their archives at the Centre de recherche Lionel-Groulx and read the Royal Canadian Mounted Police (RCMP) surveillance reports of the association. In addition, I consulted various other centres to gather information for this book: the archives of the archdioceses of Quebec and Mexico City, along with those of Catholic Action housed at Universidad Iberoamericana; the archives of UNAM, Université Laval, and Université de Montréal; and, finally, governmental documentation in various archives in Canada and Mexico (including the Acervo Histórico Diplomático de la Secretaría de Relaciones Exteriores de México).

Part of my analysis goes beyond working "along the grain," and makes an allowance for the symbolic value of the opinions expressed and the actions taken. Borrowing from Clifford Geertz's symbolic anthropology, Robert Darnton opened up new ways to practice cultural history with the publication of *The Great Cat Massacre*.[72] Despite the controversy that followed, many historians were inspired by his approach and that of others using the theoretical frame of the new cultural history.[73] This innovation has implications for my study, as the cultural history I am writing seeks to understand the textuality of the identity politics deployed by French Canadian and Mexican Catholics during the Second World War, and seeks to interpret the symbolism associated with their transnational collaboration. That is why my study follows a narrative structure, paying particular attention to the storytelling of cultural and religious interactions and evaluating how this was used as a tactic to influence politics.

Analyzing student exchanges as tropes, giving credibility to latinity as a meaningful discourse of identity, and equating the image of the Virgin of Guadalupe with symbolic capital require further clarifications about the theoretical framework of this study. Although my analysis does not adhere to a fixed theory, it is nonetheless inspired by different insights. Pierre Bourdieu's work on symbolic power informs some of the assumptions I make about the significance of using religious symbolism in Mexico's public sphere, and the expressions of Latin affinities in Montreal during the war. I borrow from him the ideas that language and power are intimately linked and that political stakeholders constantly have to discursively (re)produce and legitimate their social position in order to have the privilege of taking the floor in affairs of State.[74] Michel Foucault's reflections on the intertwined relationship between structures of power and the production of knowledge also inspire some of the points I make. In various studies, he proposed a method to investigate the correlation between these two fields of action.[75] Foucault underlines the importance of establishing a "genealogy" of discursive constructions ordering society. Contrary to a search for origins, implying causality, Foucault's use of genealogy entails taking into account the "accidents" of history for making sense of the past.[76] To a large extent, the emergence of transnational connections between French Canadian nationalists and devout Catholics in Mexico can be categorized as accidental in nature. His insights therefore inform a significant part of my investigation of these linkages.

Despite clear correlations with Bourdieu and Foucault's works, the two concepts I use the most in this study (symbolic politics and *prise de parole*) were developed by other social scientists. Therefore, I will clarify my comprehension of these concepts. I understand symbolic politics in a straightforward manner as political gestures undertaken for their theatrical effect on political stakeholders, a way to express contentious positions by other means than strict legislative measures or direct political demands. This take on the concept is informed by the works of Murray Edelman and other political scientists.[77] I use the concept of *prise de parole* as a complement to symbolic politics. In many ways, marginalized groups from the civil society cannot expect to directly influence a political process that labels them as outsiders without trying first to reposition themselves as key actors. They can attempt to do so by occupying a discursive field neglected by central authorities. Michel de Certeau explains that in certain circumstances, a discursive stand has to be considered an action in itself since it enables its perpetrators to "take the floor in the public sphere, and aspire to a modest seizure of power."[78] That's exactly what the nationalists of the Union des Latins had in mind when they founded the association. Many founding members were prominent citizens of Quebec, but their political positions were not well received by decision-makers in Ottawa. As for Mexican Catholics, they did not so much need to legitimize their voice in religious matters, but the Catholic Church and the revolutionary State had to use symbolic politics to express and sustain a rapprochement that could not be officialized. How and why these historical trajectories crossed in the first half of the twentieth century is the subject of this book.

All the chapters roughly deal with the same time frame, with the exception of the first chapter, which surveys the cultural, economic, and political factors that shaped Canadian-Mexican relations. Since I am weaving together two distinct transnational histories that intersected in the early 1940s, it is necessary to contextualize the structuring factors that enabled a rapprochement during the Second World War. Therefore, the first chapter is divided into two sections: the cultural influences and contacts shaped by the Catholic Church and the pre-existing neo-colonial connections and structures. This presentation sheds light on the reason why Canada and Mexico did not establish strong connections beforehand.

The second chapter entitled "Conflicts, Political Upheavals, and Catholic Mutual Interests, 1917–1939" explains why Mexican and French Canadian Catholics felt politically marginalized in their respective countries in the 1910s. The subsequent radicalization of certain nationalist and reactionary movements in the interwar period provided the appropriate context for a rapprochement between groups feeling culturally threatened by the rapid modernization of their nations and the political schemes to side-line them. The chapter is divided into three sections in order to analyze why unrelated events were perceived as connected by civilian actors in Mexico and Quebec: the transnational dimensions of the Cristero War in Mexico at the turn of the 1930s (using Antonio Dragon's publications as a case study), the emergence of latinity as a cultural reference in Quebec at the same time, and the formation in Mexico of the Unión Cultural México-Canadá Francés in 1939. These sections set the stage for understanding the political rationalities of transnational relations between the key actors proposing a rapprochement during the war. In doing so, I also review how *latinité* emerged as a significant discourse of identity in French Canada and I assess the reasons why Mexican diplomats tried, by various means, to secure direct ambassadorial representation with Canada in the 1930s.

The third chapter directly builds on this overview to provide a detailed analysis of the role played by the Union des Latins d'Amérique (ULA) in laying the foundations of a cultural and political rapprochement between Mexico and French Canada. It is divided into two sections, the first describing the context surrounding the formation of the association in Montreal and revealing why highly placed officials in Ottawa had reservations concerning the leadership of the ULA in Quebec and its use of latinity as a discourse of identity to give meaning to Canadian-Mexican relations. In the second section, I thoroughly analyze the way ULA spokespersons framed Quebec's *américanité*, using latinity as an alternative discourse to safeguard the survival of French Canadian culture on the continent. I also assess how Mexico, following this logic, was presented in their gatherings as an edifying cultural model for Quebec.

Chapter four, "The Poetics of Student Exchanges," examines the ULA's most important achievement in the 1940s: the organization of student exchanges between universities in Mexico and Quebec. But before I proceed with this, I introduce the conflicts that divided UNAM for decades, since the French Canadians who went to Mexico found themselves in an educational institution that was considered a conservative bastion at the time (particularly when Rodulfo Brito Foucher was rector). The point here is to understand the violence that happened during the 1944 visit, a case study I use to appraise the "poetics" of student exchanges. In this way, the chapter is genuinely located at the junction of the third and fifth chapters, continuing the reflection started in the previous chapter, "The Union des Latins d'Amérique." It largely brings to a close the examination of the ways *latinité* succeeded (and fell short) in tracing a way out of forced *Americanization* by establishing networks of solidarity with Mexico and the rest of Latin America. At the same time, it introduces the main rationale behind Catholic Mexico's transnational project.

The last chapter of this book focuses on the reasons why Mexican Catholics still sought the support of foreign co-religionists to influence their dealings with the revolutionary State during the Second World War. In "The Virgin and the Cardinal," I take as a case in point the 1945 celebrations held in Mexico City for the fiftieth anniversary of the Virgin of Guadalupe's crowning as queen of Mexico and empress of the Americas. I argue that the golden jubilee represented a cathartic moment of reconciliation between the Catholic Church and the revolutionary State. As with previous chapters, I start this one by explaining the historical context that made this event noteworthy: the Virgin of Guadalupe's past significance in Mexico and the role symbolic politics played in achieving a *modus vivendi* between the revolutionary government and the Catholic Church in the aftermath of the Cristiada. I then proceed with a detailed analysis of the festivities and the context in which they took place. I conclude by taking into consideration the importance of Cardinal Villeneuve's role as papal legate for the celebrations, and I explore how the example of French Canada was used in public speeches.

The Cultural, Economic, and Political Factors that Shaped Canadian-Mexican Relations

During the spring of 1944, the first Mexican ambassador to Canada, Francisco del Río Cañedo, sent a letter to President Manuel Ávila Camacho's secretarial staff to grumble about his style of life in Ottawa. He complained that life in the Canadian capital was harsh for someone of his social standing. Among other things, he feared the food served at the hotel where he was still residing would make him sick. Worse, Ottawa was boring: "Life in general is quiet – no clubs exist – and Sundays here are entirely devoted to religious duties; cinemas are not even open. You will see my angel wings when I come back."[1] Setting up formal ambassadorial representation between Canada and Mexico was relatively intricate, and judging from Río Cañedo's comments, it appears that it was tedious as well.

The historiography surrounding the official establishment of embassies relate a history that could be compared to a cold business deal imposed by the Second World War. Judging from this literature, it seems that interest in socio-cultural collaboration did not stir up much enthusiasm on the Canadian-Mexican diplomatic circuit. It has to be said that Canada only acquired its full sovereignty in foreign relations in 1931, and that before the Canadian Citizenship Act came into effect in 1947, many English-speaking Canadians saw themselves as British citizens first. Consequently, Ottawa's political class still had reservations about having a fully independent foreign policy toward Latin America. As for Mexican diplomacy, Canada seemed to have been merely an appendage of the British Empire, at best a very modest counter-weight to the hegemony of the United States over Latin America. Yet, below the radar of official diplomacy, contacts between Canada and Mexico acquired a powerful significance for certain groups in both countries at the turn of the 1940s. French Canadian nationalists saw Mexico as their best ally to defend their Latin culture in North America in view of the fact that cultural ties with France were cut during the war; Mexican Catholic militants saw Quebec as a providential model of harmonious Church-State relations, a potential point of leverage for them to support the imbrications of President Manuel Ávila Camacho's national unity campaign with North American collaboration during the war. These groups passionately defended their transnational connections throughout the 1940s. The Mexican State attempted to make the most of these links through a shrewd usage of symbolic politics, while the Canadian government flip-flopped on the same issue, granting its support to their endeavours when it appeared the Empire could benefit from them or withdrawing governmental approval when they felt the symbolism associated with it could backfire. Explaining how a *sensibilité commune* came about to link French Canadian nationalists and Mexican Catholic activists is the point of this chapter.[2] I do so by analyzing two sets of factors that formed the underpinnings of this rapprochement: Catholic universalism and neo-colonial competition. But first, I need to assess the direct reasons given to justify the establishment of official diplomatic relations, which should help us put the underlying structuring factors in perspective.

A NEW MOMENTUM? MEXICO'S ATTEMPTS TO RESTORE ITS LINKS WITH THE BRITISH EMPIRE AND CONTRIBUTE TO CONTINENTAL DEFENCE DURING THE WAR

Mexico City was the initiator of the Second World War rapprochement, but a series of factors had to fall into place before their request could be heard in Ottawa. Of course, both countries had some form of diplomatic connections before then. Canada had had economic relations with Mexico since the end of the nineteenth century; Canadian business promoters even played an important role in the Mexican utility sector at that time.[3] Yet, Ottawa essentially relied on London for political representation in Mexico up until the war. The Mexican government attempted to initiate a bilateral rapprochement in the 1930s by inviting the Dominion to join the Pan American Union (PAU) and set up formal diplomatic relations as sovereign

North American states. These invitations fell on deaf ears since Ottawa's political class judged this move could end up contradicting imperial policies. Moreover, the lukewarmness of the majority of Canada's population toward Latin America helps to explain why Ottawa was in no hurry to set up an independent network of ambassadorial representatives there. Three events changed this state of affairs: the nationalization of oil by the government of Lázaro Cárdenas in 1938, the fall of France to Nazi Germany in 1940, and the US's declaration of war at the end of 1941.

When London severed its linkages with the Cárdenas administration over the nationalization of oil in 1938, Mexico sought to re-establish its connection with the British Empire through Canada. The Mexican diplomatic corps renewed its campaign to normalize diplomatic relations with this country, envisioning later improvements with imperial authorities. For example, the minister plenipotentiary of Mexico's embassy in Washington, Luis Quintanilla, asked the Canadian chargé d'affaires in the US capital, Merchant Mahoney, whether London's breaking off of diplomatic relations with Mexico included Canada. In a January 1941 memo by Mahoney to the Canadian under-secretary of state for External Affairs, O.D. Skelton, it is mentioned that "Dr Quintanilla asserted that the present Minister of Foreign Relations of Mexico is decidedly pro-British and that it is his understanding that negotiations are either under way or are to be pursued shortly with a view to resumption of full diplomatic relations between the United Kingdom and Mexico. He advanced the theory that if diplomatic relations could be established collaterally with Canada it would have a psychological effect to the extent that Mexico is in accord with the efforts of Canada and the British Commonwealth to overthrow totalitarianism."[4] Mexico tried to use the context of the war to sway Canada. At the moment, Canada was the only country in the hemisphere directly involved in the world conflict and had its attention entirely devoted to the war effort. So Quintanilla and other Mexican diplomats were unsuccessful. Yet, the context of the Second World War provided the necessary incentives for Ottawa finally to accept the Mexican request at the end of the conflict.

It is true, in hindsight, that the war's consequences forced Canada to play a new role in the international community and face up to the continental state of affairs. The indisputable hemispheric hegemony of the US along with the collapse of British influence in the

Americas tipped the balance in favour of the establishment of
Canadian diplomatic relations with the region.[5] But it took time
before politicians in Ottawa fully accepted these geopolitical facts.
For sure, at the beginning of the conflict, Canada ratified the
Ogdensburg Agreement and approved the Hyde Park Declaration,
which were bilateral military and economic arrangements with the
US to defend North America.[6] In the same vein, Mexico's bilateral
ties to the US were transformed after military and economic arrangements were signed in 1941, one enabling the US army to use
Mexico's air bases, another – the Douglas-Weichers Agreement –
securing the exportation of Mexico's strategic economic output to
the US.[7] The true turning point, however, came with the US's entry
in the war. As James Rochlin mentions, after the attack on Pearl
Harbor "its crusading zeal quickly became Napoleonic."[8] This zeal
included rallying every American nation to the cause. From then on,
Canada had to acknowledge US wishes in continental affairs.
President Roosevelt had a certain effect among Canadian politicians when he exhorted the country to enhance its diplomatic efforts
in Latin America, which gave weight to the Mexican request in due
course. Mexico was particularly important for US officials; Julio
Moreno explains why: "Extensive research findings on Mexican
public opinion shocked American government officials during
World War II. Nelson Rockefeller reported that public opinion surveys conducted in 1940 and 1941 showed that Mexicans were pre-
dominantly anti-American and in many cases supported Germany.
Alarmed at these findings, Rockefeller's OIAA [Office of Inter-
American Affairs] set out to radically innovate Mexico's communi-
cation industry; censor (with the cooperation of the Mexican
government) pro-German advertising; and devise pro-American
content in audio, visual, and textual publicity."[9] Canadian culture
could be of assistance in this endeavour. By the end of the war,
Canada finally agreed to setting up embassies in many Latin
American countries, including Mexico, but that diplomatic effort
fell short of joining the PAU.[10]

My findings tally with this version of the beginning of diplomatic
relations between Canada and Mexico. Still, by taking into consideration the destabilizing effects the fall of France had on Quebec's
civil society, I introduce a different angle to consider how the context of the war swayed Canadian authorities. This event deeply
affected the French Canadians' cultural prospects. Going back

to Quintanilla and Roosevelt's arguments, it can be said that the exigencies of the world conflict made them persuasive. Nevertheless, Canada still delayed its approval of the Mexican request for a while. To be sure, Mexico ranked low in Prime Minister William Lyon Mackenzie King's list of continental concerns. The Department of External Affairs actually gave precedence to Argentina and Brazil in developing new relations in Latin America.[11] The joint North American war effort might have played a vital part in reaching an agreement to exchange ambassadors, but it was the contingencies associated with French Canadian nationalists' acute interest in Mexico and their acquaintance with Latin American diplomats that acted as a catalyst to finalize this process.

Mexican diplomats learned little by little that they could establish substantial linkages with Canadian groups if they moved away from the capital. Montreal was a more fertile ground than Ottawa to build bridges between countries and cultures during the war. Throughout the 1940s, the province of Quebec hosted numerous cultural and political activities promoting stronger linkages with Latin America. This was largely due to the Union des Latins d'Amérique (ULA), a transnational organization that invoked Quebec's *latinité* as an alternative starting point for a rapprochement between Canada and Latin America. The Mexican consul general in Montreal, Carlos Calderón, collaborated with the association and facilitated their comings and goings despite the strong nationalist overtones of its French Canadian organizing committee, a leadership Ottawa distrusted. This informal diplomacy with nationalists in Quebec put some pressure on Canada. Moreover, the transnational connections with Catholic groups from the province also propped up President Camacho's conciliatory image in Mexico, a factor contributing to the stabilization of the *modus vivendi* with Catholic groups there. The following chapters will clarify how symbolic actions affected these cultural and political dynamics in the context of the war.

But making these symbolic gestures meaningful during the war was decades in the making. They only had an impact because they played on sentiments of alienation deeply embedded in the collective psyche of French Canadian nationalists and devout Catholics in Mexico. The need to offset the dictates of governing authorities forced them to seek foreign allies and made them perceive their cultural struggles as interconnected along the way. Overall, the transnational connections established between civil society groups involved a dialectical process of resistance and integration with formal diplomacy; letting political outsiders consolidate their connections with a foreign country constituted both a threat and an opportunity for governing authorities. On the one hand, these groups could obviously use these continental connections for leverage to pressure their own governments. On the other, those cultural linkages could be used by the Canadian and Mexican regimes either as an entry point to relations with a foreign nation or as a relatively inconsequential symbolic concession to pacify political outsiders at home. The cultural underpinnings of this dialectical relation constitute the focal point of my study. At this point, it is imperative to survey the factors that structured the Canadian-Mexican rapprochement in order to understand that dynamic in the following chapters.

EARLY CONTACTS SHAPED
BY THE CATHOLIC CHURCH

As noted in the introduction, it seems that if Catholic French Canada wanted to forge cultural relations with Latin America, Mexico was a peculiar place to start. On the one hand, it is true, Mexico City was "the undisputed cultural center of the Spanish-speaking world between 1938 and 1948."[12] But on the other, conservative Quebec and revolutionary Mexico were on divergent paths and could have been put at the opposite ends of the cultural and political spectrum on many levels. Nonetheless, it is in Mexico that the Unión Cultural México-Canadá Francés (UCMCF) – the forerunner of the ULA – saw the light of day in 1939 and it is the Mexican consul general in Montreal who gave critical legitimacy to an association Ottawa wanted neutralized.[13] It is also in Mexico that the power of French Canadian Catholicism was first widely publicized for a Latin American audience when Cardinal Villeneuve served as papal legate for the 1945 golden jubilee of the coronation of the Virgin of Guadalupe as Queen of Mexico and Empress of the Americas. Mexicans and French Canadians shared cultural affinities after all. The transnational *imaginaire* of nationalists in Quebec and Catholics in Mexico interconnected during the 1940s to produce lasting ties; an original discourse of kindred interests based on a common cultural heritage emerged at that time. Latin identity became the symbolic nexus of their mutual agendas.

Republican Nationalism and Ultramontane Religiosity

It took a while for nationalists from Quebec and Catholic militants from Mexico to realize they shared common objectives. Notwithstanding the historical similarities between these two Catholic societies outlined in the introduction, it is safe to say that almost everything else distinguished Quebec from Mexico culturally – at least from the perspective of their political elites. A markedly non-violent political culture, the lack of widespread militant anti-clericalism (especially after the downfall of the Rouges' radical liberalism in the last third of the nineteenth century),[14] and above all, a dissimilar attitude toward racial and cultural miscegenation were only the most striking points differentiating them. According to French Canada's "defining elites," this nation was Catholic and French, and its foreign identity markers were staunchly European.[15] The appropriation of the North American territory during the colonial era (with its lasting commercial and cultural relationships with native groups), the mass migration of a substantial part of the French Canadian population to New England before the Great Depression, and the extensive cultural linkages resulting from an ethnic identity that spread across political borders, did not alter the European outlook of French Canadian elite culture. The popular classes' adaptation to the continent was undeniable, but the petit-bourgeoisie perceived that a straightforward recognition of being *Américain* was a threat, since Quebec's immediate surroundings were peopled by Anglo-Protestants.[16] Linguistic assimilation was relatively rapid for people settling outside the province; considering that language and faith were intertwined in the minds of many conservatives, Anglo North America looked like a place of perdition.

This has not always been the case, even for prominent citizens. At the beginning of the nineteenth century, when Quebec was known as Lower Canada, the political turmoil rocking the Americas (including the War of 1812 opposing the British Empire to the United States and the beginning of the wars of independence in Spanish America), favoured the circulation of republican ideas in the colony.[17] French

Canadians started to voice their appreciation for the new American nations' political independence. A text published in 1824 by François Blanchet, a member of the House of Assembly, illustrates the extent of this influence:

> The American continent is fundamentally different from the Old Continent in almost all respects... The people there have also been modified differently, and to want them to find good in America what they find good in Europe is completely absurd. The result is that despite all the efforts of despotism, both civil and religious, to maintain European institutions in South America, nothing has succeeded, and a system of government is going to be established there that is very different from that of Europe. The very people who were raised in Europe are the most opposed to its institutions: we could cite, for example, Bolivar, the liberator, the current president of the Republic of Colombia. Does one believe that when public opinion in the whole vast Continent of America is in favour of representative governments, that it would be very easy to establish and maintain a degenerate nobility in Canada. The idea is really most ridiculous.[18]

Yvan Lamonde explains that Blanchet's interventions "initiated a tradition that would be taken up by Papineau and Parent, among others, denouncing British attempts to establish an aristocracy in Lower Canada... and legitimize a Legislative Council like the House of Lords."[19] American and Latin American revolutionary rhetoric and republican ideas found a sympathetic hearing in the Parti canadien (which became the Parti patriote in 1826), the political party through which Francophones voiced their demands for political rights. The tensions opposing the French-speaking population (the vast majority of the inhabitants in Lower Canada were French Canadians) to the British administration and loyalist settlers resulted in a political crisis at the turn of the 1830s, with the Parti patriote openly militating in favour of responsible government and republicanism. Their 92 Resolutions proposed in February 1834 to address French Canadians' decades-old grievances are a good example of that.

The proposals drafted by the Parti patriote were received coldly by the British administration, a fact that worsened the political crisis. This mirrored the attitude government officials and British settlers had toward the French-speaking majority; their numerical weight imposed toleration, but complete cultural assimilation was preferable. French Canadians vigorously resisted British assimilationist plans. This situation helps to explain why, as Lamonde notes, "From 1815 to 1837, the newspapers were filled with information on the military and political situation, in particular in Argentina, Chile, Peru, Venezuela, Colombia, Ecuador, and Mexico. The names of the major figures – Bolivar, San Martín, O'Donnell, O'Higgins – circulated, and there were biographies and speeches of Bolivar, information on decisive events such as the Congress of Tucuman on 9 July 1816, which declared the independence of the provinces of Rio de la Plata, and numerous proclamations by military and political leaders."[20] Latin American republicanism interested the Patriotes of Lower Canada; they did not consider the anticlericalism of liberal reformers in Latin America anathema to their agenda. After the 1837 Russell Resolutions imposed an ultimatum on the Patriotes, the political gridlock degenerated into violence. The Patriotes fought the British army and their allies in 1837–38; the Catholic Church condemned the insurrection. This might be the reason why, when the Patriotes promulgated a Declaration of Independence of Lower Canada in 1838, the fourth article of the text declared the separation of Church and State. The Patriotes' revolutionary movement was defeated by the British authorities, a turn of events that changed the prospects of imposing republicanism and a radical liberal agenda in Quebec. Notwithstanding the fact the declaration of independence never went into effect, it nonetheless shows that the tensions opposing Mexican liberals and conservatives over the role of the Catholic Church during the first fifty years after independence, also polarized Quebec in the 1830s.

The downfall of the Patriotes in 1838 and the reorganization of political life in the wake of this defeat reduced the impact of Latin American news published in the Quebec press. Cultural survival, rather than republicanism and political independence, became the central concern of the French Canadian political class. After having effectively defeated the Patriotes' dream of establishing an independent republic on the banks of the St Laurence River, the British mandated John George Lambton, the Earl of Durham, to report on the 1837–38 rebellions in Lower Canada. His account of the conflict

noted as root cause of the civil war a visceral hatred between the
Canadiens and the British settlers. Since he asserted the French
Canadians formed a people "without history and literature," he
argued assimilation was the best way to improve their lives and
ensure stability in Canada: "The language, the laws and the character of the North American continent are English, and every other
race than the English race is in a state of inferiority. It is in order to
release them from this inferiority that I wish to give the Canadians
our English character."[21] Assuring the protection of the Catholic
faith and the preservation of French Canadian culture became crucial priorities for francophones in Lower Canada. French Canada
had to assert its existence! A people "without history and without
literature" that would gradually abandon its identity, thought
Lord Durham; French Canadians had to find ways to prove him
wrong. The method designed to assimilate the population of the
colony – the union of the two Canadas into a single British administrative entity – was a momentous challenge to the survival of a francophone people in North America. With the consequent unification
of political parties and the deep divisions between French-speaking
and English-speaking liberals, the balance of power shifted toward
the conservatives in the colony. Collaboration with anglophones
within party structure was the only way to gain back the civil rights
abolished by the 1840 Act of Union. In the end, as Roberto Perin
demonstrates, the Catholic Church remained the last bulwark capable of institutionalizing an independent national culture in French
Canada.[22] This realignment had profound consequences on the
future of transnational relations in North America. With the establishment of the Orange Order in Canada in the 1830s – who
staunchly fought Catholics in the country – and the new geopolitical
reality imposed on French Canadians, priorities changed; radical
anticlericalism was progressively abandoned. When the separation
of Church and State was officialized in Mexico's 1857 Constitution,
French Canadian society had changed; reducing the social influence
of the Catholic Church in Quebec seemed undesirable to most French-
speakers at that time.

The French Canadian nation survived London's assimilationist
scheme. It even pulled through by adapting its society to the contingencies of the era.[23] The religious revival that animated French
Canada's renewal produced a unique North American society. Based
on a conservative nationalism of cultural survival in Quebec and on

international networks of Catholic kinship, French Canada had the "providential mission of maintaining and spreading the Kingdom of God in the New World."[24] The second bishop of Montreal, the ultramontane Ignace Bourget, tirelessly worked to redraw Montreal's cultural outlook, dominated at the time by Protestant social and economic establishments. He facilitated this process by attracting French religious communities, Romanizing the Catholic Church, and launching a massive campaign of architectural expansion of Catholic institutions in his diocese to counter the dominance of the Anglo bourgeoisie.[25] In some way, Lord Durham's Report and the political disenfranchisement of francophones in the new political entity did not only spark this revival, but it also set the stage for the anti-imperialist sympathies with Latin America that would be expressed by French-Canadians later on. Roberto Perin writes that "centuries before United States sociologist Everett Hughes wrote his classic work, *French Canada in Transition* (1943), Durham represented French Canada as a kind of '*folk society*,' that is, an undifferentiated social mass at the head of which was a traditional petty bourgeoisie."[26] Hughes was influenced by Robert Redfield's works on Mexico to claim that French Canada was also a "folk society." It is therefore not surprising that Catholics defending this model of society in both Quebec and Mexico came to express a form of Latin solidarity against the modernization of their societies based exclusively on liberal and capitalist values.

The course of action taken by Mgr Bourget in order to defend the social position of the Catholic Church in nineteenth-century Quebec – which also aimed to counter Anglo-Protestant dominance and crush radical liberalism – favoured the emergence of an alternative model of society. This stance by the ultramontain bishop constitutes a point of convergence with conservatives in Mexico, since the Catholic hierarchy there also welcomed foreign ideological and material support to oppose a liberal reformist agenda at home. Indeed, the Catholic clergy in Quebec and Mexico both tirelessly militated against the ideas of the French Revolution from the 1820s on and tried to oppose secularization and anticlericalism as much as possible.[27] As I mentioned above, the role of religion and the influence enjoyed by the Catholic clergy sharply divided conservatives and liberals in Mexico after Agustín de Iturbide proclaimed independence in 1821. The reign of the military and political leader up until 1823 (he became the constitutional Emperor of the new country

and ruled as Agustín I of Mexico) produced fierce debates and
violent political struggles between the political leaders supporting
Iturbide's authoritarian rule and those in favour of representative
government. The proclamation of the Republic in 1824 did not ease
tensions between liberals and conservatives as nation-building projects divided the political elite, a situation that produced political
upheavals and resulted in civil wars and foreign interventions. The
four decades following independence were particularly chaotic, as
Mexico was governed by more than thirty different heads of state,
some like Anastasio Bustamente or Antonio López de Santa Anna
heading the country many times. By the 1850s, however, the liberals
started to have the upper hand and imposed their agenda. The desire
to abolish privileges exonerating the Catholic Church from paying
taxes and those absolving its clergy from standing trial in civil courts
motivated the Liberal Reforms of the late 1850s. The 1857
Constitution confirmed those reforms and proclaimed the separation of Church and State. The implementation of this agenda provoked a serious conservative backlash that found its first expression
in the War of the Reforms (1858–61) and then in the support for the
French occupation of the country (1862–67). The Mexican Catholic
clergy supported this foreign intervention in the 1860s as a means to
uproot radical liberalism from the country – a political doctrine
denounced by Pope Pius XI in his *Syllabus of Errors* in 1864. It also
has to be said that Maximilian's reign facilitated the "reorganisation
of the Catholic Church" and the foundation of new lay associations.[28] As a symbol of Mexican and Quebec Catholics' converging
interests, conservative reporters and adventurers from the French-
speaking territory also supported foreign intervention south of
the Rio Grande, while the Union and the Confederate States tore one
another to pieces during the American Civil War. This constitutes
the second moment when the French Canadian press seriously took
into consideration what was happening in Mexico before the twentieth century. Of course, Mexico was then invaded by France, a
country that was slowly restabilizing commercial and cultural connections with its previous colony.

Emperor Napoleon III of France sent troops to Mexico in 1862,
after the government of Benito Juárez stopped loan repayments
to foreign creditors. The French intervention did not exclusively
have financial motives: the emperor thought an intervention at that
time could help extend his power and influence, ultimately building

a Latin empire in the Americas under the influence of France that would counter Anglo-Protestant sway in the Western Hemisphere. The occupation of the country did enable France to re-establish a monarchy in Mexico. The Austrian noble Maximilian of Habsburg was named emperor of the Second Mexican Empire and landed in Mexico in 1864 to rule the country. Not surprisingly, conservative chroniclers in the francophone press were sympathetic to the reign of Maximilian (1864–1867), while liberals favoured the government of Benito Juárez.[29] Some argued the French invasion represented a providential opportunity to overturn the separation of Church and State proclaimed by the Liberal Reforms and balance out Protestant hegemony on the continent through its establishment of a Latin (and Catholic) empire directly south of the United States. A few French Canadians even participated as mercenaries, like Honoré Beaugrand (an ex-student at the Catholic Séminaire de Joliette who became Mayor of Montreal and published a short story about his involvement with French troops south of the Rio Grande), Narcisse-Henri-Édouard Faucher de Saint-Maurice (who studied at the Séminaire de Québec and published two books on his experience in Mexico), Arthur Taschereau (a lawyer who studied at the École militaire de Québec), and Alphonse Têtu (an ex-Papal Zouaves who studied at the Séminaire de Québec).[30] Their appraisal of Mexican culture was negative and they regarded Benito Juárez's liberal troops as brutes. In their minds, the cause of civilization was at stake and France intervened to re-establish order in an unruly country.[31]

The short story written by Beaugrand and the books written by Faucher de Saint-Maurice, in which they explain their involvement with French troops in Mexico in the mid-1860s through fiction and travel narratives, are a good example of this. For example, Beaugrand explains in his memoirs *Anita: souvenirs d'un contre-guérillas* that honour made him refuse integration with the Mexican troops after his capture (as he tried to join his Mexican *novia*). His subsequent imprisonment made him fear the worst because "Mexicans, with rare exceptions, treated their prisoners like the Indians of the western plains. With them it was slavery, with all the attendant abuse suggested by these brigand-soldiers' savage and vindictive nature."[32] In his short story, Beaugrand said he was saved, but never met again his "black-eyed" girlfriend.[33] Faucher's account of his collaboration with French troops is more factual than Beaugrand's story. But it still has to be said that his narration of the events has to be analyzed with caution. As Pierre Rajotte explains, his account represents an "opportunity to construct a page of justification in the autobiography of a rewarding life in the military."[34] He is also often quoting other authors and his interpretations seem to "depend on a pre-existing vision" of the facts.[35] Finally, Faucher's descriptions of the landscape, the people and their cultural practices – which are mostly negative, unlike in Beaugrand's account – often rely on the works published by other travellers.[36] But Faucher also takes into consideration his audience of readers in French Canada. For example, he quotes Samuel de Champlain's description of the beauty of Mexico City (which he says was still true 275 years later);[37] explains how Maximilian's rule promoted the dissemination of books about Canada in Mexico and facilitated the business of a Montrealer living in Puebla;[38] relates how the son of Emperor Agustín de Iturbide enjoyed telling him memories of his trip to Quebec City (they both stayed at the same hotel for a month);[39] and elaborates improbable theories to explain the similarities between native peoples in Quebec and Mexico.[40] Despite shallow comments about Mexican culture and biased descriptions of the country's recent history, Faucher's texts are interesting to take into consideration because it puts forward a clear representation of the ideas and values defended by the supporters of this war of occupation in which he participated as a "subaltern officer."[41]

Considering his role in the war, it is not surprising to note that he presents a one-sided account that is staunchly pro-Maximilian. He mentions proudly that he had the chance to personally meet the Emperor when he was made Chevalier de l'Ordre de la Guadeloupe in recognition of his feats.[42] He also writes that "ineffable goodness and mercy characterized [Maximilian's] reign," and claims that in the difficult and violent battles he had to fight, "all the French [were] brave."[43] His account mentions various times how living conditions have improved in Mexico under the rule of Maximilian. Conversely, the liberal regime that governed the country in the late 1850s and the guerillas backed by the United States who were fighting the French in the 1860s are presented very negatively. Juárez's liberal troops are described as cowards, bandits, and ruthless killers. He describes with a lot of details the cruelties against foreign soldiers but also the massacres of the local population and the abuses against the Catholic clergy committed by the liberal revolutionaries.[44] Porfirio Díaz, who was then a distinguished general who played a crucial role in the French defeat at Puebla on 5 May 1862, is demonized by the French Canadian who had to battle his troops in Oaxaca.[45] The liberal victory in Mexico is seen by him as the result of the "demon of the revolution" overtaking the country.[46] Maximilian was abandoned by the French and executed by Mexican authorities.[47] As a result of this turn of events, Faucher claims the Mexican nation will have to "bear the stigma of shame and opprobrium" for years to come.[48] All in all, Faucher de St-Maurice's memoirs show how some conservative French Canadians backed the French imperialist effort in the mid-nineteenth century and how they failed to empathize with the difficult situation post-colonial Mexico was in.

Despite the military feats Faucher de St-Maurice describes in his account, the Mexican liberal troops won decisive victories in 1866 and 1867 and claimed back their country. In the end, hope that a return of a French presence on the continent would give more weight to francophones in North America proved to be short-lived. As Faucher wrote, "with Maximilian's death, the American population located between Louisiana and Guatemala witnessed the end of Hippolyte Castille's dream. Castille stated in 1856 that France's duty is to uphold the blossoming of the Latin race as far as Mexico and the Southern States, re-establishing there as in Europe the rightful balance between the Anglo-Saxon Germanic race and the Latin race."[49] If French Canada had a providential mission in the Americas – as some clerics claimed – it had to accomplish it without the help of France and that of political authorities from Canada. From Confederation to the Quiet Revolution, the provincial government of Quebec could not offset this situation since the political mechanisms to uphold an international project like that had not been developed yet. French Canadians drew most of their national pride from their deep devotion to their faith, the strength of Catholic institutions, and the international contribution of its clergy in spreading the precepts of the Church.

CATHOLIC CONNECTIONS BETWEEN QUEBEC AND LATIN AMERICA

During the period between Confederation and the Quiet Revolution (1867–1960), a period where the Catholic Church came to play a dominant social role in Quebec, the image of Latin America – and

Mexico – experienced a radical transformation in the French-speaking province. It has to be said that French Canadian adventurers were not the only ones writing about Latin America. At the turn of the century, ultramontane authors proposed a different view of the essentialist narratives produced by the adventurers. After all, the Catholic Church had established the first connections between the Americas at the beginning of colonization, providing an institutional structure for shared experiences between the Catholic hierarchy and religious orders working in various colonies. The influence South American Jesuit reductions had on similar experiments in Canada and the uses of the image of the Saint Catherine Tekakwitha in Mexico, constitute two good examples of this.[50] If these connections remained limited until the late nineteenth century, they nonetheless established a significant precedent for the formation of transnational bonds between Quebec and Latin America.

Since 1853, when missionaries from Montreal landed in Chile, the Catholic Church of Quebec has had emissaries in Latin America. Considering French Canada's subordination to the British Empire and federal authorities in Ottawa, Catholic missionaries played the role of Quebec's first ambassadors. These missionaries first arrived in Latin America by accident. Five Sisters of Providence, otherwise known as the Filles de la Charité Servantes des Pauvres, landed there in 1853. They had embarked on a perilous journey back to Canada by boat through Cape Horn, Chile, after returning from a failed mission in Mgr Modeste Demers' ecclesiastical province in Oregon. They never made it. The group landed in Valparaiso, Chile, on 17 June 1853.[51] The archbishop of Santiago, Mgr Valdivieso, saw it as a unique opportunity to infuse new vitality to the Church in his country. He sent a letter to Montreal asking Bishop Ignace Bourget if the Sisters could stay in Chile and help with the organization of an orphanage in Santiago. Bourget agreed, seeing divine intervention in this misadventure.[52]

During the next five decades, other Quebec communities were established in Peru, Bolivia, Colombia, and Ecuador.[53] The missionaries there communicated information about the countries of their mission to their Quebec supervisors, providing them with special knowledge of Latin America. The last country mentioned in the list of new French Canadian missions in Latin America had a special meaning for the bishop of Montreal, since he was answering the call of a Latin American leader he admired, President Gabriel García Moreno.[54]

Mgr Ignace Bourget lauded the President of Ecuador; it is not hard to imagine why. The dictator was not only an ultramontane Catholic himself, but he was also a francophile. At one point, Moreno even asked Napoleon III to establish a protectorate over Ecuador.[55] Bourget certainly shared Moreno's Catholicism and probably endorsed his authoritarian administration. He was not the only one. In fact, Jules-Paul Tardivel, journalist and editor of the journal *La vérité* (Truth) which promoted an ultramontane, Catholic, and French-Canadian State in the late nineteenth century, modeled his proposed "Catholic republic" on García Moreno's Ecuador.[56]

If ultramontane authors despised liberal revolutionaries, they nevertheless expressed respect for their Catholic brethren in Latin America. French Canadians were sensitive to some difficulties affecting Latin American societies, perhaps because they also experienced cultural and social marginalization in their country. A neo-colonial mindset of spiritual re-conquest prompted the first encounters, but respect for national differences was part of the missionary effort. When a second group of the Sisters of Providence left for Chile, Bourget allegedly told them: "You will conform to the established customs of the country as much as possible. Love Canada in all your heart; but avoid unfavourable comparisons that could hurt national susceptibilities when you speak about it."[57] Contrary to other mission countries in Africa, Asia, or North-Western Canada, the Church in Latin America was operating in nominally Catholic societies where its institutional presence had been established a long time before Quebec. The people being evangelized were already an integral part of their Christian family. For missionaries, if Latin American societies were economically poorer, they were certainly not backward (in a cultural and social sense). Their social arrangements did not need complete overhaul to bring peace and progress, as modernizers argued (even though many gradually realized that a better redistribution of wealth was necessary to bring social justice).[58]

Still, at first, no ideological middle ground could be found with the "twin heirs of the Enlightenment" (liberal reformers and social revolutionaries) since both attempted to curb religious authority.[59] This was especially true for Mexico, where a law sanctioning the separation of Church and State was adopted in the middle of the nineteenth century. Support for the French intervention was in direct reaction to the Liberal Reforms promulgated in the 1857 Constitution. Religious establishments had been very powerful in the social, cultural, and economic realms until these reforms. Dioceses and monasteries owned a substantial part of the land in the republic and constituted important lending institutions for the Mexican population. Altering their corporate privileges was a priority for all reformers. As expected, the demise of Maximilian meant a strict enforcement of these reforms. Some were successful in curbing the power of the Catholic Church, but the dictatorship of Porfirio Díaz loosened many of those restrictions at the turn of the century.[60]

Religious communities claimed back part of their influence in the social sphere during the Porfiriato, particularly in relation to education.[61] Many individuals – even from the president's inner circles – took advantage of the situation to petition French religious communities to cross the Atlantic and help organize schooling in the country. A few communities migrated to Mexico after a law separating Church and State was passed in France in 1904. Four Lassalian Brothers arrived in Veracruz in the wake of this law to organize private schools; the Marist Brothers, the Brothers of St-Jean-de-Lyon, and the Brothers of Christian Instruction followed them shortly thereafter.[62] A similar process transformed French Canadian schooling. Guy Laperrière mentions that fifty French congregations crossed the Atlantic to settle in Quebec from the time of the election of the republican government of Jules Ferry in 1880 to the First World War.[63] He explains that due to the Law of Associations (1901), enforced by the government of Émile Combes in 1904, which prohibited religious personnel from teaching, about 1,265 members of religious orders left France to settle in Quebec. The French congregations had a considerable impact not only on religious life, but also on the development of the school system and health services, those social services being administered in great majority by religious communities in Quebec until the 1960s. Therefore, the anticlerical laws in France had the remarkable effect of guaranteeing that students in private Catholic institutions in Mexico and Quebec received a similar education, crafting an incipient *sensibilité commune*. Years later, Jean-Paul Trudel argued at a ULA meeting that the Greco-Latin culture and Catholic faith taught in those schools were the foundations of French Canada and Latin America's common culture. He also said: "The Mediterranean people – France, Italy, Spain and Portugal – upheld this Greco-Latin civilization and brought it to the New World with the crucifix. Sadly, the war now threatens to annihilate that civilization. This war brought the Americas closer together, and favoured connections between French Canadians and Ibero-Americans. Our task is to bring back the world to faith, to the Christian spirit of the Middle Ages, and the Humanism of Ancient Greece and Rome."[64] Trudel identified the geopolitical motivation bolstering north-south relations. He also shed light on the values universally shared by the Catholic world, values that constituted the cultural underpinnings of a French Canadian-Mexican rapprochement during the war. But what he failed to mention is that the competition between neo-colonial networks, juxtaposed with Canada and Mexico's situation within those systems, also coloured the cultural foundations of this rapprochement.

BRITISH AND AMERICAN ECONOMIC POWER IN LATIN AMERICA

Catholicism might have shaped an incipient *sensibilité commune* linking French Canada and Mexico in the nineteenth century, but it did not establish direct connections, with one exception. Louis-Nazaire Bégin, archbishop of Quebec City, visited Mexico City in 1895 for the crowning of the Virgin of Guadalupe as Queen of Mexico. Bégin was invited along with other foreign Catholic dignitaries – mostly from the US – to the highly symbolic festivities surrounding this event. These celebrations (which I analyze in more detail in chapter five) figuratively expressed the Church's satisfaction with Porfirian tolerance. Catholic authorities invited North American dignitaries for a reason, namely to show their good relations with Mexico's northern neighbours, connections that were important for the Porfirian administration. Bégin was not invited so much for the model the Canadian Catholic Church represented but because of the increasing economic connections between the British Dominion and Mexico. Consequently, it is essential to survey how British informal imperialism in Latin America facilitated economic linkages between Canadian and Mexican entrepreneurs at the turn of the twentieth century. Because political independence had long-lasting consequences that influenced some of Canada and Mexico's political inclinations with regard to continental dealings, the process by which they secured sovereignty needs to be assessed as well.

National Sovereignty and Continental Diplomatic Relations

How political independence was secured in Mexico and Canada shaped their approaches to continental affairs. While Mexico proudly self-identified as an independent American nation, Canada was much more reluctant to embrace this continental character. Of course, it achieved sovereignty gradually and peacefully, while remaining part of the British Empire, unlike the violent experiences of other American nations.[65] The majority of the Dominion's inhabitants envisioned their future as citizens of the British Empire well into the Second World War. Canada viewed interactions with other American republics accordingly. With the exception of its relations with the US – which Ottawa claimed to administer independently from London – Canada expected British authorities to oversee diplomatic linkages with Latin America, hoping to benefit from its informal imperialism.[66] In doing so, Ottawa approached relations with Spanish and Portuguese-speaking countries as an integral part of the British Empire, a central rather than peripheral nation.

In contrast, Mexico had to fend for itself after independence from Spain in 1821. This had two direct consequences for its dealings with other American countries. First, Mexican elites began to assert and argue about a national identity early on – or at least a feeling of *Mexicanidad*.[67] They might have mostly referred to themselves as *Americanos* rather than *Mexicanos* at first, but this name, along with the visual symbols of the eagle on a nopal cactus and the representation of the Virgin of Guadalupe, provided identity markers that distinguished the new nation from Europe.[68] This is one of the reasons why Benedict Anderson writes that the sentiment of nationalism originated in Spanish America during late colonial times.[69] Whether he is right or not, it can be said that the fragmentation of Spanish America into a series of smaller nations, and the consequent economic ascendency of neo-colonial powers like Great Britain and the US, shaped nation-building projects. At various points throughout the nineteenth century, the inherently unequal relationships with the world's dominant powers put Mexico in a difficult situation. The country not only lost half of its territory to its northern neighbour in the thirty years following independence, but it had to fight Spain once and the French twice.[70] As a result, the second consequence of Mexico's tough transition to independence was the early recognition that some form of collaboration with the forces of international capitalism was necessary to safeguard the nascent republic. Mexico tried to keep all diplomatic options on the table and attempted to play neo-colonial powers against one another in order to get some room to manoeuvre in international dealings. That meant accepting British influence at the same time as US pan-Americanism.

Mexico City and Washington's Pan-Americanism

Notwithstanding the French Imperial dream in Mexico, formal colonialism had lost its shine in the Americas against the more effective model of British informal imperialism. The dominant capitalist powers mostly adopted it as a strategy in their dealings with the independent republics of this hemisphere. Since the Monroe doctrine (1823), the US tried to claim the whole hemisphere as its private backyard. Washington attempted to circumvent Britain's continued economic and political influence, formalizing hemispheric dealings through its own neo-colonial system, the Pan American Union.

The integration of Latin America into the world capitalist system throughout the nineteenth century structured its geopolitical evolution. From the 1880s to the 1930s, most Latin American republics followed an export-led model of economic development sustained ideologically by laissez-faire liberalism and put into practice by co-optative democracy or dictatorship. Despite Washington's expanding sway in its immediate "backyard," Great Britain remained the main underwriter of this neo-colonial arrangement until the First World War.[71] Capitalist competition therefore propelled US interests in forging alliances in the Americas with the objective of coordinating economic integration and redesigning the system in its favour.

In 1890, the US organized the first International Conference of American States, which was held in Washington. This emerging arrangement was welcomed by Latin America's political class, but it also generated anxieties. The results of this gathering were in line with expectations. On the one hand, an agreement to resolve international disputes in the hemisphere was signed and the first pan-American organization, the Commercial Bureau of American Republics, was created.[72] On the other, observers judged the conference to be a failure because none of the eleven republics which designed the treaty later ratified it.[73] Nevertheless, these incipient talks and the resulting accord launched a new era of partnership in the Americas based on the premise of Europe's exclusion. The

American project followed its course in a series of conferences at the
turn of the century. At the fourth gathering held in Buenos Aires,
in 1910, the Commercial Bureau changed its name to the Pan
American Union (PAU).[74] As the balance of power tipped in North
America's favour at the end of the Great War, the Western hemisphere
largely escaped the grip of European metropolises. Washington's
decade-old project of a Pan American Union replaced London's economic ascendancy in the interwar period.[75] That became especially
true for Mexico, which had seen its upper-class citizens identify ever
more closely with the United States during the long dictatorship of
Porfirio Díaz.[76]

The Mexican Revolution did not completely alter this development. Many articles of the 1917 Constitution tightly restricted foreign ownership in the Republic, actions particularly directed toward
combating US economic dominance in the country. Yet, despite this
bravado, the revolutionary government knew it had to come to
terms with its creditors. It realized after the Revolution that the US
was more flexible in its negotiations than other neo-colonial powers.[77] Since economic development remained a priority of the succeeding revolutionary administrations, collaboration with Uncle
Sam and its pan-American scheme continued in formal and informal
ways. The situation nonetheless remained tense until the early 1930s
when President Roosevelt's inaugural address indicated the US's
Good Neighbor policy would be strengthened, describing "his foreign policy as the 'policy of the good neighbor' who respected the
rights of others."[78] Latin American administrations mostly welcomed this statement as an overture, although some still remained
wary. As for Mexico's reaction, Friedrich Schuler writes: "From the
Mexican perspective, Roosevelt's expansion of Hoover's policy idea
of the Good Neighbor – at its center the pledge of non-intervention,
as well as respect for national self-determination and territorial sovereignty – was finally giving Mexico the customary respect that
international law required and increasingly replacing confrontation
with dialogue."[79] With that new attitude in Washington, Mexican
bureaucrats became active participants in the PAU. They solidified
the position of Revolutionary Mexico on the world scene by ably
creating a network of international relations that simultaneously put
the US at the centre of foreign affairs while leaving Mexico some
margin to build counter-balancing alliances with other countries. It
is with the intention of gaining ever more leverage with the US that

Mexico tried to get Canada (still under the mantle of the British Empire) to join the Pan American Union in the 1930s.[80] In many ways, the invitation made to Canada was an extension of Mexico's cultural diplomacy with Latin America: a symbolic gesture meant to improve its strategic positioning on the scene of pan-American affairs.[81] But the British foreign office did not see collaboration with the PAU as a move the US would appreciate. So Canada, unwilling to contradict British imperial interests, decided to ignore the Mexican invitation and keep London as arbiter of its diplomatic dealings with Latin American nations.[82]

Canadian and British Informal Imperialism in Latin America

The British Dominions of this hemisphere were, understandably, cautious about the US-sponsored process of pan-American integration, and abstained from attending the conferences.[83] They could hardly be eager to strengthen their main competitor's ties to markets and raw materials in the Americas. The Dominion of Canada was also suspicious of US intentions for another reason. John Humphrey (a Canadian who was the principal author of the United Nations' Universal Declaration of Human Rights) described this reticence during the Second World War: "Most Canadians believed that the Pan American Conferences were nothing more than a cloak for United States hegemony in Latin America. The Pan American Union looked suspiciously like a colonial office. It is not surprising that, in the circumstances, a country whose greatest fear was annexation should have preferred to leave the twenty-second chair severely alone."[84] Canada had a privileged relationship with London, which had been the financial capital of the world, and was in no hurry to join the PAU as a completely independent country. Moreover, Canada's population was ten times smaller than its southern neighbour, and much like Latin American countries, Canada's economy depended on foreign investments and the export of raw materials.[85] To stand alone in this organization controlled by the US was perceived as a move with potentially lethal consequences for Canada's sovereignty. Many politicians indeed feared that joining the US's neo-colonial network would ultimately weaken Canada's British identity, opening the door to annexation. The PAU, as a platform for hemispheric connections, did not significantly contribute to a Canadian-Mexican rapprochement.

Canadians may have looked suspiciously at US-sponsored continental integration, but their own ideas about hemispheric collaboration still implied a neo-colonial mindset. Before the Allies' war effort in the 1940s, Ottawa only agreed with the economic dimension of continental relations.[86] Direct governmental relations between Canada and Mexico remained virtually non-existent until the establishment of formal ambassadorial representation during the Second World War. Before then, Ottawa had only sent two official trade missions south of the Rio Grande – one in 1865 and another one in 1930 – to assess potential economic outlets.[87] The Canadian Department of Trade and Commerce also produced a survey of economic activity between both countries in 1911, when some form of North American commercial association was discussed. However, no political arrangement resulted from these commercial and financial linkages beyond the exchange of trade representatives.

Although the dominant characteristics of Canada's economy remained similar to Mexico's, some entrepreneurs were very active south of the Rio Grande at the turn of the century.[88] In their work on Canadian promoters in Latin America, Christopher Armstrong and H.V. Nelles describe how the very nature of these commercial ventures help to explain the failure of this *southern exposure* to result in full diplomatic relations. The case of Mexico is especially revealing. From the end of the Porfiriato until the Great Depression, Canadian utility groups controlled $122,717,646 in power and transportation facilities in Mexico.[89] The Canadian Eagle Oil Company, the Northern Mexico Power and Development Company, and the Mexico Tramways Company were among the most prominent corporations operating in this sector of the Mexican economy during this period. These corporations also controlled an important number of subsidiary companies, like Mexican Light and Power Company, demonstrating the importance of Canadian investment in Mexico before the Second World War. The Bank of Montreal and the Canadian Bank of Commerce served as financial intermediaries for these ventures.[90]

But if Canadian capitalists found a niche in the sector of urban public utilities, the nationality of the companies operating these transnational ventures should not be given excessive importance. Armstrong and Nelles remind us that although Canadian entrepreneurs might have been "strategically positioned" between British "capital surplus" and US "technological dynamism," the Canadian financial community nonetheless remained on the periphery of the World's dominant capitalist powers.[91] Moreover, the Canadian government itself did virtually nothing to promote foreign investment and "maintained no formal relationship with them and vice versa."[92] From the capital used to the personnel employed, these Canadian companies rapidly became truly international enterprises.[93] The authors explain this evolution: "The Canadian character of these utilities had, of course, been notional almost from the outset. The place of domicile of most of the founding entrepreneurs and the laxity of company law alone make them Canadian. Within a very few years all but the smallest of the utilities had outgrown the capacity of the capital markets in Canada to provide the necessary funds for investment and expansion. Thereafter control quickly switched to Europe where the money had been raised."[94] This is crucial in explaining the attitude of Canadian promoters in times of trouble. The stakeholders of these ventures relied mainly on European connections to protect their assets, other times even calling on the US for assistance.

Canadian promoters were taken aback when the Mexican Revolution swept away the regime of Porfirio Díaz, turning the previous economic system upside down and replacing it with new policies motivated by economic nationalism. Throughout the military conflict, Canadian stakeholders relied on the severely flawed British analysis of the situation to decide upon a course of action.[95] London's confusion about the situation – made worse by its racial prejudices and stereotypes about Latin America – led the Empire to support counterrevolutionary leaders to the detriment of its own commercial interests.[96] When Canada finally decided to speak out to abet its entrepreneurs and make an official complaint about the situation during the Conference of Versailles in 1919, Prime Minister Borden called upon the president of the United States to stop the "anarchy" in Mexico and close ranks with the British hard liners.[97] The US rejected this demand and dealt with revolutionary leaders their own way. They proved to be more successful at it than Great Britain.[98] Canadian promoters tried to use the malleability of their national identity to their own advantage. Constitutionally British and geographically North American, Canadian promoters played both cultural cards depending on the occasion.[99] This served their interests well, as their companies re-emerged from the Revolution bruised but still better off than British corporations.[100]

CONCLUSION

This chapter exposed the structuring factors enabling a French Canadian-Mexican rapprochement in the interwar period. First, I underlined how Catholic education in Quebec and Mexico instilled humanist values constituting points of convergence that encouraged cultural interaction. Second, I surveyed the opportunities and constraints offered by British and American informal imperialism in Latin America, providing economic and political networks to connect Canada and Mexico together. In the end, however, Mexico's rocky political evolution revealed the Canadian inability – or unwillingness – to imagine a truly independent stance from the two main foreign powers intervening in Mexican affairs.[101] It would take closer Catholic collaboration and the emergence of a new discourse of identity in Quebec to stimulate this kind of thinking. Political turmoil in Mexico and Quebec during the interwar period favoured this outcome.

2

Conflicts, Political Upheavals, and
Catholic Mutual Interests, 1917–1939

The 1910s, 1920s, and 1930s increased the sentiment of alienation felt by French Canadians in Canada and devout Catholics in Mexico. The Revolution and the Cristiada in Mexico and the political turmoil in Quebec enticed Catholic authors from both regions to pay attention to the situation of the other. Sympathetic representations of Latin America emerged in Quebec during the First World War, while religious publications in Mexico started to discuss the envious situation the Canadian Catholic Church was enjoying during the conflict between the Cristeros and the Revolutionary State. These representations laid the foundations of a community of interests expressing shared objectives for French and Spanish-speaking Catholics in North America: resistance to political marginalization and opposition to what they saw as the harmful effects of rapid socio-cultural modernization.

French Canadians felt marginalized by the political process in many ways at the turn of the twentieth century. This was not a new sentiment, considering they had been resisting cultural assimilation throughout most of the nineteenth century, but Confederation had raised expectations for more cordial relations between French and English-speakers in the British Dominion. Nevertheless, at the end of the nineteenth century, the hanging of French-speaking métis leader Louis Riel – which brought tens of thousands of people in the streets of Montreal to protest his execution – and the English Canadians' support for British imperial wars in Africa reawakened tensions, as French-speaking politicians and journalists vigorously expressed their opposition to providing assistance to this type of empire-building. The setbacks imposed on French language education in several Canadian provinces at the turn of the twentieth century worsened the situation. The laws limiting education in French in New Brunswick, Manitoba, and Ontario, which were attempts to assimilate French Canadians there and reduce their political weight in the country, were vigorously opposed by nationalists in Quebec who militated against the dominance of the English language and opposed Canada's endorsement and support of British imperialism. Henri Bourassa became the leading oppositional voice on these issues.

Bourassa's publications, public speeches, and political actions were aimed at combating French Canadian marginalization and British imperialist undertakings. His resignation as a Liberal member of parliament in 1899 (in opposition to Prime Minister Laurier's position on the Boer War), his subsequent political career (pushing a Canadian nationalist agenda aimed at demanding more autonomy from London), and the foundation of the newspaper *Le Devoir* in 1910, contributed to his fame. But as Guy Laperrière mentions, Bourassa made his most famous speech during the 1910 International Eucharistic Congress of Montreal.[1] This Congress, the first one to be held in the Americas, helped to broadcast how much Quebec constituted a Catholic society. The successful hosting of the event supported this view; half a million faithful attended or participated in the Sunday procession. Lomer Gouin, Liberal Premier of Quebec, took part in the Congress and affirmed that the event was "a valuable testimony of the cordial relationship, in our province, between the Catholic Church and the State."[2] This congress confirmed the strength of the Catholic Church in Quebec. Nevertheless, a controversy emerged during the Congress when Mgr Francis Bourne, archbishop of Westminster, said that "if the mighty nation that Canada is destined to become in the future is to be won for and held to the Catholic Church, this can only be done by making known to a great part of the Canadian people in succeeding generations, the mysteries of our faith through the medium of our English speech."[3] Bourassa responded strongly at Notre-Dame Basilica, saying that "among three million Catholics, descendants of the first apostles of Christianity in America, the best safeguard of the Faith is the conservation of the language in which, during three hundred years, they have adored Christ."[4] This speech clearly expressed the sense of "religious advocacy" that marked French Canadian nationalism, for in the minds of many clerico-nationalists, language and faith were intertwined.

Not everyone shared this point of view in Quebec. But even French Canadians who opposed nationalists in the French-speaking province came to feel marginalized during the First World War. The Dominion of Canada, being an integral part of the British Empire, was automatically involved in the world conflict as a result of Britain's declaration of war. The likes of Henri Bourassa were not pleased by that situation of political subordination. The Conscription crisis, which began three years later, then really pitted Quebec against the rest of the country, and sharply divided Canada along ethnic lines as prominent French Canadian politicians – like the previous Prime Minister of Canada, Sir Wilfred Laurier – refused to participate in the new Union government led by Sir Robert Borden who was perceived as being anti-Francophone. Tensions reached new levels at the beginning of 1918 when a riot in the streets of Quebec City was repressed by imposing martial law and firing on the crowd, killing five people.[5]

The tense context of the First World War prompted a re-evaluation of French Canada's situation. Henri Bourassa encouraged his compatriots to imagine what an independent Canadian foreign policy would be like. Bourassa wrote that "without leaving America, it is good to remember that south of the Rio Grande, fifteen Latin nations are developing, some of which are destined for great things. In their conceited and great ignorance, most Anglo-Canadians think that the South American republics are populated by semi-barbarians who only come out of a revolution to enter another. They completely ignore the fact that many of these countries have already reached a level of civilization far superior to ours; [they also ignore] that Argentine commerce and agriculture already represent a formidable competition in the British market."[6] For Bourassa, pursuing an independent foreign policy in the Americas became a necessity: "Whatever we do, we cannot escape the inevitable laws of nature. Being an American people, our interests are in the Americas."[7] Besides, he claimed, the establishment of autonomous relations with countries beyond the confines of the British Empire could help to improve ethnic relations in Canada, as French was an important language for international diplomacy. This was especially the case for Latin America, where the elite of many countries learned French.[8]

However, the positive comments written by Bourassa about Latin American republics did not explicitly include Mexico. Jacobin anti-clericalism in this country certainly preoccupied a fervent Catholic like Bourassa. The tense situation prevailing in the Mexican republic between Catholics and the revolutionary State actually convinced Quebec clerics to write books and articles about this country in the late 1920s. Mexico, as a country, came out as a bad example to follow; Mexican Catholics, on the other hand, were represented as brethren suffering the imposition of harsh socio-cultural changes by the central government.

Much like French Canadian nationalists during the interwar period, Mexican Catholics used foreign inspiration to defend their religion. Early on, militants in that country sought to forge alliances with foreign sympathizers to safeguard them from radical reformist agendas. The Revolution and its aftermaths explain this hasty resolve. The 1917 Constitution not only irritated foreign capitalists, but it put the Catholic Church on a direct collision course with the revolutionary State. This document reaffirmed many anti-clerical provisions of the 1857 Constitution and pushed certain reforms even further. As I explained in the introduction, some of the most contentious articles concerned the secularization of education, the prohibition of religious processions, the curtailment of religious organizations' ownership rights, and the deprivation of the clergy's political liberties. Enforcing the most controversial aspects of the 1917 Constitution was difficult in the years following its ratification; thus, devout Catholics hoped they would be overturned. Since many of the Revolution's victorious generals were vociferous anti-clericals, the thoughts of reversing these laws without the Catholic Church making substantial concessions proved to be wishful thinking. The multiple attempts to implement constitutional reform – and Catholic militants' reactions to these attempts – ultimately resulted in open warfare after the application of article 130 of the Constitution, which enabled the government to intervene directly in the internal affairs of the Church. Actually, when the Catholic hierarchy decided to suspend religious services – noting that the petitions and the economic boycott organized by lay Catholics were not working – tensions quickly escalated. Reacting to brutal interventions by government forces against Catholics, believers took up arms in Western Mexico (mostly in Jalisco, Colima, and Nayarit) and launched what became the Cristero Rebellion, a civil war that opposed Catholic militants to the revolutionary government from 1926 to 1929.[9] The violence of this conflict – which left more than 100,000 people dead – grabbed the attention of Catholics around the world.

THE CRISTIADA SEEN FROM CANADA

There is no greater glory than to give your life for Christ.

Father Christopher, *For Greater Glory* (2012)

This line from the movie *For Greater Glory* could have been written by a cleric from Quebec in the first half of the twentieth century. The books of the Quebec Jesuit Antonio Dragon on the religious situation in Mexico after the Revolution, for example, convey the same dramatic effect this quote intends: Mexican believers were justified to risk it all for defending the Catholic Church and for preserving their religious freedom. The Revolution, the 1917 Constitution, and the role of the Mexican government in the Cristiada were judged very severely by Catholics from Canada, who could not understand the attitude of the Mexican government. Their assessment of the situation was uncompromising. The State was at fault.

It is true that the nation-building projects launched by the generals who governed Mexico from the mid-1910s onward often resulted in conflict with the Catholic Church, as various presidents tried to limit the social influence of the Church and reduce the political weight of Catholic activists. Thus, the Mexican Revolution and the Cristiada proved to be momentous challenges to the Catholic Church. Yet at the beginning of the Revolution, the formation of the Partido Católico Nacional, right after Porfirio Díaz's downfall in 1911, signified that many Catholics welcomed the change of government and even wanted to have a direct influence on the political process. Francisco I. Madero's administration was generally well received by Catholic stakeholders, but some of his policies were also opposed by the hierarchy.[10] At the same time, many revolutionaries grew increasingly uncomfortable with Catholics meddling into politics during these turbulent times.[11] As a result, when Victoriano Huerta overthrew Madero's government in 1913, some Catholics applauded the coup. The revolutionary leaders that regained power the following year did not forget these counter-revolutionary tendencies and harshly punished Catholics who became political dissidents. Several members of the clergy decided to flee the country and organize their resistance from the United States.[12] Opposition to Venustiano Carranza's presidency helped to launch a transnational dynamic that was strengthened in the following decade when Catholic groups took up arms to oppose the

Revolutionary government and the enforcement of the anticlerical provisions of the 1917 Constitution.

Catholic militants rebelled against the Mexican government during the administration of Plutarco Elías Calles (1924–28). His presidency has been judged very harshly by Catholics. Historian John Lynch explains this is not surprising considering that Calles "was determined to 'defanaticize the masses,' and to exterminate religion in the interests of state power and national progress."[13] Jürgen Buchenau adds that Calles's "detractors recall the Cristeros, the bloody suppression of the railroad strike, and the bodies of Father Pro, Gómez, and Serrano rather than the creation of the Banco de México, his early stand on oil, and his ambitious project to bring education and infrastructure to rural areas. Criticized by Catholics for his persecution of the church, by democrats for his authoritarian leadership style and repressive methods, and by socialists for making labor into a pliant instrument of the state, *el señor presidente* Calles does not enjoy the historiographical cachet of revolutionary icons such as Madero, Zapata, and Villa, or fellow Latin American populists such as Brazil's Getúlio Vargas or Argentina's Juan and Evita Perón."[14] While Latin American populist leaders enjoyed good press in French Canada, President Calles was demonized. This is a result of the Catholic Church's transnational strategy to denounce his actions during the Cristiada.

During the Cristero civil war, supporters of the Catholic Church sought international assistance and protection. Catholic nations like Italy, France, and Spain provided some form of support during the conflict, but as tensions increased, Catholics sought help closer to home, north of the Rio Grande, where members of the clergy took refuge (mostly in San Antonio).[15] Others were simply forced to leave by the Calles administration during the conflict.[16] Catholics living in exile then helped to forge alliances with US Catholics to put pressure on the revolutionary government. But the Calles administration also had a transnational strategy of its own. Julia G. Young explains: "In deporting its enemies and using blacklists and border control to keep them from returning to Mexico during the Cristero War years, the Confidential Department, working in conjunction with the Migration Service and the consulates, ensured that hundreds of troublesome citizens would remain outside Mexico's national territory. Taken together, these activities demonstrate that the Calles government deployed these repressive techniques in a methodical, institutionalized, and systematic way that was unprecedented in previous regimes. Furthermore, these techniques were inherently transnational: they relocated undesirable dissident populations outside of Mexican territory."[17] So, if the US represented a land offering protection for militant Catholics, it also represented a safety valve for the State who could exile dissidents –"up to 2,500 Mexican religious, including priests, nuns, monks, seminarians, bishops, and archbishops" from 1926 to 1929 – and monitor counterrevolutionary plots from afar.[18]

If Mexican Catholics faced opposition in the US, they were nonetheless able to rally to their cause influential co-religionists from that country.[19] Some Catholics from the US were already convinced, as this collaboration began years before during the Revolution. The proximity of the Mexican and US Catholic hierarchies continued throughout the 1920s with US Catholics influencing the Mexican clergy significantly, introducing them to new forms of militancy and lay associations (e.g. the Knights of Columbus). Contrary to Quebec – where the French Canadian hierarchy resisted the inroads made by groups like the Knights of Columbus until the Second World War – Mexicans saw collaboration with associations from the US as positive. In their struggle against the revolutionary State, many actually perceived this collaboration as a complement to Catholic Action, which was a group of laypeople whose mission was to bring a Christian influence on their society or, as Pope Pius XI defined in 1927, "the participation of the laity in the apostolate of the hierarchy."[20] They also collaborated with other powerful groups from the US like the National Catholic Welfare Council and used the American government and business interests to successfully put pressure on the administration of Plutarco Elías Calles in order to reach an agreement.[21] So the Cristiada did bring Mexican Catholics closer to North American Catholicism; the same cannot be said about Canada, but the writings of Dragon came to play a very important role in bringing international attention to the plight of Catholics in Mexico.

Antonio Dragon, Father Pro and the Fear of "Red Mexico" in French Canada

The Church-State tensions resulting from the Mexican Revolution, the Cristeros War, and the virulent opposition of Catholics to the policies of the revolutionary State (1930s) created a stir in Quebec, where important figures of the Catholic resistance, such as Father

Miguel Pro and María de la Luz Camacho, were acclaimed in hagiographic publications. Mexico, as depicted in the Catholic publications of Quebec, served to herald the dangers of a new world order moving away from the principle of subsidiarity defended in the social encyclicals. This perspective was reinforced by Pope Pius XI's encyclicals on the persecution of the Catholic Church in Mexico: *Iniquis afflictisque* (1926), *Acerba animi* (1932), and *Firmissimam constantiam* (1937). As a result, the French Canadian viewpoint on the Mexican situation was initially one of intransigence, demonizing the government of Mexico (although becoming more nuanced at the beginning of the Second World War).

French Canadians really became aware of the situation in Mexico during the interwar period. The Cristiada fostered sympathies (and a wide network of support) for Mexican Catholics in North America. Jean Meyer has exhaustively studied the importance of networking in the North American Church to gauge the influence US Catholics had during the conflict.[22] One of his most recent publications includes a chapter by Marie Lapointe and Catherine Vézina addressing the perception of the Cristiada in Quebec newspapers. The authors explain that the media coverage in Quebec raised public awareness to the point that "municipalities and associations from Quebec and other provinces adopted resolutions exhorting Ottawa to put pressure on Mexican authorities" in order to stop the religious persecution there.[23] The French Canadian population, according to the authors, was then massively mobilized in favour of this cause. But this conflict really piqued the imagination in Quebec following the execution of the Jesuit Miguel Agustín Pro, the most famous of the Cristero martyrs, who had been accused of plotting to assassinate former President Álvaro Obregón. John Lynch explains that the accusation constituted "a false charge never put to the test; there was to be no process, no trial, no judge, simply a peremptory order by Calles on 13 November to shoot them."[24] The injustice of the case and the violent and premature death of the Jesuit at the hands of Mexican security forces galvanized the solidarity of Catholics around the world, who mobilized to combat this type of religious persecution. Yet, no one has provided an in depth analysis of the work that was the most widely circulated at the time and which substantially contributed to the mass mobilization against religious persecution in Mexico of Catholics around the World: the biography of Father Miguel Pro written by his former classmate, the Quebec Jesuit Antonio Dragon.

José Ramón Miguel Agustín Pro Juárez was a Mexican Jesuit deeply involved in the resistance against the revolutionary government in Mexico City during the Cristiada.[25] His arbitrary execution in 1927 shocked Catholics throughout the world. Dragon reacted rapidly to the situation and went to Mexico to gather information for the book he planned to write on his former classmate. The success his publication ultimately had can be surprising considering that the Church in Quebec was not as directly involved in the Cristiada as the US clergy. Few writers from Montreal and Quebec City developed close relationships with the leaders of the Catholic resistance in Mexico during the interwar period. Nevertheless, the publications of Antonio Dragon made an international impact, as those of fellow Jesuit Joseph Ledit would make later on. According to the Mexican Jesuits' official publication, Dragon's book *Pour le Christ-Roi* – which was first published in Montreal in 1928 – rapidly became the most important biography of the Mexican martyr. After only ten years it had been translated into sixteen languages and hundreds of thousands of copies were distributed in its different versions around the world.[26] The writings of Dragon were even more important given that he knew the famous Mexican martyr from his stay in Belgium. The Archbishop of Mexico, Luis María Martínez, explains in the foreword of the Spanish translation of Dragon's biography of Father Pro that the author had revealed the "objective truth" about the soul of the Mexican martyr.[27] The archbishop considered Dragon's acquaintances with Father Pro gave him special insights. Antonio Dragon continued to write about religious persecution in Mexico after this first publication. In fact, to promote the dissemination of the contemporary history of Mexico to different audiences, the Quebec Jesuit published biographies and history books on the subject and even adapted the life of the Mexican martyr into a play.[28]

This presentation of the recent history of conflicts in Mexico was meant to mobilize Catholics in Quebec and around the world. As a result, the biography of Father Pro takes on a hagiographic resonance under the pen of Dragon. The stories of violence Dragon is describing in dreadful detail in his publications were meant to shock international public opinion in order to generate a wave of sympathy for the persecuted Catholics in Mexico while uplifting the image of Miguel Pro. It is within this vein that his works were aimed; a nuanced depiction of the Cristiada would not elicit the desired reaction. He leaves out information that may create confusion, such as the Cristero attack on a train in April 1927 (a deadly attack that was used by the Calles administration as an excuse to exile the bishops from Mexico),[29] and he makes no mention of General Enrique Gorostieta, the Cristeros' most successful military leader (known in governmental circles as a liberal and a Freemason).[30] In order to contextualize the life of Father Pro, Dragon presents his interpretation of the history of the country in very black-and-white terms. For example, he begins his book *Au Mexique rouge* saying: "Two things make the beauty of Mexico: what God has done, what Catholics have built."[31] The State that emerges from the Mexican Revolution is condemned by him as immoral; the Constitution of 1917, which reaffirmed the Separation of Church and State, is described as "a series of insults to any law, human or divine."[32] Although representatives of organized labour, Freemasons, and feminists like Éva Circé-Côté still spread anticlerical ideas in Quebec during the interwar period, such a law would have been unthinkable in the French-speaking province at the time.[33] Nevertheless, the image of Mexico is not completely negative in Dragon's writings, because the resistance of Catholics against the revolutionary State shows that this is a place full of heroism. The celebration of its martyrs had a particular resonance in French Canada.

If Dragon's books about "Red Mexico" were meant to generate support for the Catholic cause (and perhaps frighten French Canadians in favour of the laicization of society), the portrayal of the heroic and brave resistance of Mexican Catholics (ready to die defending their faith) against the revolutionary "brutes," as he describes them, could also be seen as echoing some aspects of French Canada's past.[34] At the time of the publication of Dragon's writings, French Canada celebrated the Canadian Jesuit missionaries martyred in the seventeenth century and canonized by Pius XI at the commencement of the 1930s. Dragon explains at the beginning of Miguel Pro's biography that this type of martyr was still present in Mexico. He claims that the reader should feel proud to belong to the same Catholic family as Father Pro, because it "still produces saints."[35] The comparisons between French and Spanish colonization of the New World (and of the societies that emerged from that colonization) also meant to reinforce the sentiment in the readers that they shared cultural connections with Father Pro. As French Canada inherited its most important cultural characteristic from France, Dragon maintains, "Spain [imposing its authority] was able to gather the different ethnic elements of this country and form Mexico."[36] Both Catholic societies could therefore claim a similar Greco-Roman heritage favouring spiritual values over materialism, a position defended at that time by many Latin American intellectuals influenced by Hispanism. This intellectual posture was used to establish clear distinctions between Catholic Latin America and Anglo-Protestant America. For example, José Enrique Rodó claimed that "the descendants of Greece and Rome, whom Rodó calls the Latin race [that includes Latin Americans], already possess a spiritual and aesthetic superiority over the *yanquis*."[37] Dragon certainly agreed with that intellectual position. All things considered, at a time when French Canada discovered its Latin roots, the French-Canadian reader could perceive a cultural affinity with Father Pro, for he too was part of the same Catholic and Latin "civilization."

Catholic attempts to restore the culture inherited from Spain's colonial past constitute a noble objective, according to Dragon. This is the solution to counter what he considered to be the harmful influence of the ideas coming from the French Revolution and British and American Freemasonry. Dragon favorably compares this colonial heritage to that of the French or the English: "Whatever the faults of the Spanish, their system of colonization gave the best results. For the three great nations who colonized the New World, the same problem occurred. The French, arriving in Quebec, found some twenty thousand natives; they wanted to make them French and they failed. In approaching the coast of New England, the English met many Indians, they resolved to get rid of them and they succeeded. The Spanish kept and Christianized the Indians of Mexico. The civil authority, despite consistently maintaining a lower status, despite the hard life that the large landowners (*encomenderos*) imposed on the natives, firmly established a new race."[38] Dragon supports perhaps the most reactionary politicians in Mexico, offering an uncompromising vision of the recent history of this country; but his favorable interpretation of the interracial progeny of the colonial period opened the way for a more positive assessment of Hispanic and Latin American cultures in Canada (in direct opposition to the racial theories dominant at the time in the Western world).[39] Religious bigotry, rather than racial prejudices, explains his support of counterrevolutionary leaders.

This is why, at the turn of the 1930s, Mexico definitively looked like a place of perdition for a conservative French Canadian audience who could not understand and accept the reformist agenda of the revolutionary government. To make the situation familiar for Quebecers trained in the classical colleges, Dragon cultivates simplistic contextual comparisons between Mexico's important political figures and humanist references. Politicians who have marked the history of Mexico are judged according to their frame of mind. Considering French Canada's Catholic and conservative outlook, it is not surprising that Dragon's judgment of Mexico's recent history is deeply uncompromising. After all, no president had declared his belief in God in this country since the Liberal Reforms in 1855–57 until Manuel Ávila Camacho's presidency at the beginning of World War II. Thus, much like Faucher de Saint-Maurice's account half a century before, Dragon's story is explained as a struggle between the forces of "good" and those of "evil." According to Dragon (who was rector at the College Jean-de-Brébeuf in Montreal), the public school system was responsible for this development. He wrote about the influence of Catholic and liberal schools: "Mexico has been wrought of these two influences which have developed side by side. Impious schools have created the clan of the ambitious or villains who kill out of hatred or ignorance. This has produced a generation of heroes that die martyrs for their faith."[40] As a consequence of this simplistic and biased reading of history, few political leaders find themselves on the side of "good" in Mexico's postcolonial history.

The dictator Porfirio Díaz (1876–1910) is one of them. In fact, he is the only politician to attract praise from Dragon: "The Mexican Catholics maintain positive memories of this 'good tyrant.' This fist of iron, like Mussolini, reorganized the country. He purged the 'undesirables,' surrounded himself with competent men, and multiplied the most useful reforms... If he seemed to forget the religious question, the Church could at least breathe."[41] With this type of comment, Dragon reveals that he could support the most reactionary political options in order to safeguard law and order. Therefore, many important political figures are on the side of "evil" in his books such as President Venustiano Carranza (1914– 20) – main architect of the 1917 Constitution – who he compares to Pontius Pilate. But President Plutarco Elías Calles – whose policies provoked the Cristada – gets the harshest criticism: "This all-powerful fool started well, like Nero... Nero had the nobility of blood to betray; this is the only crime that Calles was unable to commit."[42]

The way in which the audience was presented the heroic resistance of the Catholics tells us about the scale of values accepted in the French-Canadian society back then. The character and commitment of Father Pro in the resistance was demonstrated by a series of contradictions and oppositions that referred to the rightness of his cause and the strength of his morality. Pro is first and foremost a joyful person leaving no one indifferent; but late at night "we would hear him flagellate himself energetically," Dragon recalls.[43] He also highlights that Father Pro was "deeply involved in the affairs of the National League for the Defense of Religious Liberty" (Liga Nacional Defensora de la Libertad Religiosa (LNDLR)) who was helping the Cristeros.[44] But when members of the League were accused of trying to assassinate former President Álvaro Obregón – an action Dragon qualifies as "bold" – there is no doubt that the charges against Miguel Pro and his brothers were false.[45] Finally, the biography makes several references to the desire of the Mexican Jesuit to die a martyr. Dragon cites from a letter written by Miguel Pro his fear "of not being killed in these actions, which would be a disaster for me."[46]

Since Dragon says that the blood of martyrs strengthens the Catholic cause, it is not surprising that the summary execution of Father Pro, which was compared to the Passion, is the culmination of this biography.[47] This comparison to the Passion is consistent with the symbolic meaning of martyrdom. As Jean-Pierre Albert explains, "the martyr imitates Christ's redemptive death and is therefore an instrument of salvation."[48] It is the sense that the Quebec Jesuit gives the "sacrifice" of Miguel Pro, that is, to save the Catholic community from the damnation of "Red Mexico." Dragon described the killing in detail: "He extends his left hand embracing the rosary, and, his arms outstretched, he repeated the words of the Savior dying: 'With all my heart I forgive my enemies!' When martyrs die in Mexico, they loudly shout their favourite invocation: *Viva Cristo-Rey!*"[49] And that was what Father Pro was doing at the moment the firing squad commenced.

Although the security authorities wanted this execution to be a warning to Catholic militants, Father Pro's death backfired. Lynch mentions: "The execution of Father Pro was deliberately recorded by official photographers, but as Graham Greene wrote, 'the photographs had an effect which Calles had not foreseen.' The Cristeros were encouraged, and Catholic Mexico was inspired."[50] This is certainly the reason why Dragon decided to reproduce the photographs

LA DERNIÈRE PRIÈRE DU P. PRO

—

CALLES — OBREGON

—

Les spectateurs; au centre, le général Cruz,
le cigare à la main.

2.1 Father Pro and the individuals responsible for his death. The photographs displayed in the Quebec Jesuit's book illustrate Miguel Pro's final hours and the individuals Dragon considered to be responsible for his execution. This image includes Father Pro's last prayer, the pictures of President Calles and President Obregón, and the spectators present at the execution (including General Cruz). (The image was scanned from Dragon s j, *Vie intime du père Pro*, 313)

VIVE LE CHRIST-ROI !

—

FEU !

—

PÈLERINS AU TOMBEAU DU P. PRO

2.2 Father Pro facing the firing squad. This second image shows two photographs of how Miguel Pro died, and a picture of mourners at the cemetery where he was later buried. Photographs of Father Pro's execution were widely circulated at the time and were included in each version of the biographies of Farther Pro written by Antonio Dragon. (This image was scanned from Dragon sj, *Vie intime du père Pro*, 337)

in his books. The biography of Father Pro explains how the execution galvanized Catholic opposition; in Mexico, thousands of people accompanied the remains of Father Pro to their final resting place, forcing President Calles to see "these heroic Christians singing the triumphal hymn to Christ the King... Thus, nineteen centuries ago, Nero saw the first Christians who just had seen their brothers die passing before him."[51] The parallel with the persecution of early Christians undoubtedly gave legitimacy to the cause of Mexican Catholics in their battle with the revolutionary State.

This is the type of endorsement Catholic militants in Mexico were seeking.[52] The comparison to the persecution of early Christians seemed to justify the violent resistance of the Cristeros – men, women, and children – against government forces. In fact, Dragon directly justifies this violent resistance by including in his biography a call to the youth. He relates in his book that at Miguel Pro's funeral, a mother brought her child to tell him, "My child... look at those martyrs; that's why I brought you here... When you grow up, you'll know how one gives his life to defend the faith of Christ; you will know how to die as they died, innocent and with great courage."[53] This characterization reinforced the impression that Catholic Mexico "still produces saints." From the point of view of a French Canadian reading audience, the mobilizing capacity of the story of Father Pro also strengthened the feeling that French Canadians belonged to a Catholic community at risk, a denominational identity threatened by the atheistic tendencies of liberal modernization and secularization.

This message is also present in another work of Father Dragon, *Au Mexique rouge*, dedicated to the second phase of religious persecution in the 1930s. The title of this work, *In Red Mexico*, has a clear anti-communist overtone. Anti-communist ideas were widely spread in Quebec by members of the clergy, the Société Saint-Jean Baptiste (a French Canadian nationalist association), and other Catholic groups in the interwar period.[54] The economic crisis increased those tensions with the radical left. The infamous Padlock Law against communistic propaganda, promulgated by Maurice Duplessis' administration in March 1937, enforced anti-communist ideas by closing properties where communist thinking (or even only progressive thoughts) were discussed and spread.[55] Pierre Beaudet mentions that at that time, "Duplessis' government virtually outlawed left-wing movements, with the help of the Catholic Church."[56]

CARTE DU MEXIQUE

Les parties en noir indiquent les États d'où tous les prêtres ont été expulsés. Ailleurs le nombre des prêtres est très réduit, comme on peut le voir par les chiffres inscrits près du nom de chacun des États, par exemple, un prêtre pour l'État d'Oaxaca, cinq pour celui de Coahuila, etc. Ces chiffres sont de 1935; le nombre des prêtres autorisés est encore moindre aujourd'hui.

2.3 Map of Catholic persecution in Mexico published by Antonio Dragon. This map was included in the book *Au Mexique Rouge* to illustrate the extent of persecution in Mexico. We can read in French that the blackened states indicate the regions where all the Catholic priests were expelled. Dragon adds that "elsewhere the number of priests is very low... for example, one for the State of Oaxaca, five for Coahuila, etc. These numbers are for the year 1935; the number of authorised priests is even lower nowadays." (Dragon, *Au Mexique rouge*, 20)

Of course, the story of María de la Luz Camacho, the first martyr of Catholic Action shot by the "Reds" in Mexico could be understood by Dragon's readers as an example of the dangers of communistic ideas and practice. Perhaps this is the reason why the image adorning the cover of this book even made the front page of the popular newspaper *L'Action Catholique* in Quebec City on 27 November 1935, to recall the plight of Mexican Catholics. This story, which had anti-communist overtones, was also an opportunity for the author to return to the sufferings of Catholics in Mexico and to legitimize their use of violence to combat the government.

In the chapter "the bloody epic," detailed descriptions of the persecutions arouse horror at the barbarity of the "atheist" government in Mexico: "Riddled with bullets, the corpse of the Father was still standing. A soldier, curious of this fact which seems extraordinary, pulls him by the hair and drags the cleric on the track."[57] In this context, Dragon explains that Catholics had no choice but to respond with violence and to offer their lives in sacrifice. Therefore, the continuation of the undeclared war pursued by the Cristeros after the agreements signed between the Vatican and Mexico City in 1929 perpetuated the Quebec Jesuit's admiration: "Heroic women, children even risked their lives for the sacred cause."[58] Dragon even describes José de León Toral, the Catholic who eventually assassinated President Obregón, as the "most famous liberator!"[59] The uncompromising vision of the Church-State conflict in Mexico produced by Dragon and reproduced in Catholic publications in the 1920s and 1930s raised awareness in Quebec. The statements made about the Mexican government by a Canadian bishop and by Mexico's Consul in Toronto during the Cristiada threatened to provoke an important crisis in Canada at the time, pitting Catholics against Protestants once again.

The Controversy around Sir Henry Thornton's Visit to Mexico

The Cristiada had repercussions in Canada that reduced the prospect of a concrete cultural rapprochement, especially one that presupposed collaboration between French Canadian nationalists and Mexican diplomats. French Canadian empathy for Catholics south of the Rio Grande made relations with Mexico controversial during the conflict. In *Gringos from the Far North*, John Ogelsby recounts how Sir Henry Thornton's visit to Mexico – as president of the Canadian National Railways – sparked a dispute in Canada that threatened to re-open the wounds left by the First World War's ethnic schism. Thornton went there at the turn of 1928 to assess the state of Mexico's railway system. In doing so, he was directly collaborating with the Calles administration, something the Catholic hierarchy disapproved of. Surprisingly, the objections to this came from anglophone Ontario.

On 15 December 1927, the Catholic bishop of London, Michael Francis Fallon, stated his opposition to this collaboration in an open letter published in the pages of Toronto's *The Globe*:

> I notice with some interest that Sir Henry Thornton... after a
> sojourn of some weeks in the society of robbers and murderers
> who now form the Government of Mexico, has returned to

Canada. In this achievement Sir Henry has been much more for-
tunate than the thousands of innocent Mexicans who have been
ruthlessly butchered by the gang of venal ruffians and treacher-
ous assassins who have displaced civilization by savagery, and
have destroyed the last vestige of civil and religious liberty in the
Republic of Mexico... As a Canadian, jealous of the honor of my
country, and as a Catholic Bishop, sensible to the insults and out-
rages inflicted on my fellow-Catholics of both Canada and
Mexico, I protest with all the energy of which I am capable
against your conduct in loaning paid public services of the people of this country to a Government that has been described by
the Father of Christendom in the terms I have quoted above.[60]

The Canadian federal government was not moved by these admoni-
tions and decided to keep a low profile, hoping this controversy
would rapidly die down. The Mexican consul general in Toronto
thought otherwise. Understandably irritated by the cleric's comments, Medina Barron defended the revolutionary government and
tried to gain support from Protestants by expressing anti-Catholic
sentiments. He responded to Fallon the following day in the pages of
The Globe stating that the Catholic Church favoured obscurantism
and that the religion "is the same which established the Inquisition
in Mexico at the time of the Spanish conquest to torture and murder
Protestants. [The Church] has been for many centuries a handicap
for the development and progress of Latin-American countries."[61]
The last thing Prime Minister William Lyon Mackenzie King's
administration wanted was that an affront like this would revive
religious tensions in Canada.

His government succeeded in defusing the controversy in a series
of backroom deals before it could reach the House of Commons.
Despite Barron and Fallon's initial uncompromising attitude, neither Mexico City nor Rome wanted a proxy confrontation in
Canada while it was trying to settle the Cristero War. Ogelsby
writes that the disagreement was rapidly cleared up without much
drama. In the end, the insults exchanged between the consul and
the cleric resulted in an ironic trade-off: Calles called back Barron
to Mexico, but the trade representative left his children in Canada,
in a Catholic school![62]

Canada avoided a crisis that had the potential of pitting Catholics against Protestants. Still, Henri Bourassa – English-Canada's

anti-imperialist bugbear – used the occasion to attack the British
Empire. It may seem contradictory to use Barron's offensive comments to call on Ottawa's political class to loosen the country's ties
with Great Britain and assume an independent posture regarding
pan-American affairs, but that is exactly what the old nationalist
did. His call was heard, but in the province of Quebec rather than
Canada's capital. Barely a decade after this imbroglio, French
Canadian nationalists decided to collaborate with Mexican diplomats to lobby for a diplomatic rapprochement between the two
countries. After the well-publicized violence of the Cristiada, how
could French Canadian nationalists claim – alongside diplomats
from this anticlerical country – that they had "natural" affinities
with Mexicans? To answer this question, we have to look at the
emergence of a new discourse of identity in Quebec during the
interwar period: French Canadian *latinité*.

LATINITÉ AND FRENCH CANADIAN NATIONALISM

Latinité and *latinidad* were understood quite differently in Quebec
and Mexico throughout the nineteenth and twentieth centuries. In
its largest sense, being culturally Latin meant speaking a Latin language, coming from a nation whose roots went back to a
Mediterranean European culture, and being Roman Catholic. In this
sense, French Canada has always been Latin. In addition, the influence of ultramontane ideology on society and the transmission of a
humanist tradition that glorified Greco-Latin civilization – common
in Quebec's academic life before the 1960s – strengthened these
Latin foundations. Those cultural markers provided the underpinnings of an identity differentiating French Canadian from Anglo-
Protestant culture. Yet, the conscious articulation of an explicit
discourse of Latin identity did not emerge before the interwar period,
when French Canadian nationalists started looking toward Latin
societies for inspiration to uphold an independent national culture
in North America.

It also took a while for Latin Americans to become conscious of
their own *Latinness*.[63] Independence leaders rather used the term
Americanos to refer to their continental identity. The concept of
Latin America was not used in the 1826 Congress of Panama, organized by Simón Bolívar to coordinate the defense and facilitate the
interactions between the newly independent republics. If a concept

was used in the first half of the nineteenth century to differentiate the Spanish-speaking republics from the United States of America, it was the term *Hispanoamérica*. Actually, the idea of grouping together Ibero-American nations under the umbrella name of Latin America did not originate in the New World, but in France. During the Second French Empire, two South American intellectuals living in Paris, Francisco Bilbao and José María Torres Caicedo, separately coined the term *América latina*. But the popularization of the concept is attributed to Emmanuel Domenech, press secretary of Emperor Napoleon III, who used it to distinguish *Amérique latine* from Anglo-Saxon America.[64] The logic behind this was the legitimization of French imperialism in the region whereby Napoleon III was placed at the head of Latin nations.

Despite the conservative press's approval of the French intervention in Mexico, French Canadian intellectuals did not apply the concept of Latin identity to their situation in Canada. It took over half a century for these thinkers to start discussing their own *latinité*. In the meantime, French Canada suffered important setbacks. A series of crises between Canada's two main ethnic groups re-ignited nationalism in the province of Quebec and led many to express their discontent toward the British Dominion.[65] By the end of the First World War, many nationalists asserted that the spirit of the 1867 federative pact had been betrayed by Ottawa's political class at the expense of francophones. Like Lionel Groulx, some of them began to visualize an autonomous French State on the banks of the St Laurent River. After seeing roughly a third of the French Canadian population leaving for the factories of New England and witnessing US capitalists monopolize large-scale industry in Quebec, nationalists thought it was time to act to counter the Americanization of the French Canadian population.

Henri Bourassa chose to confront the problem posed by continentalism head-on with an audacious suggestion. He argued in the House of Commons, in 1935, that the best way to safeguard French Canada's unique cultural arrangement was to join the US-sponsored Pan American Union: "Why not join the Pan American union, in which we would be far more at home than we are in the League of Nations? There we would meet the representatives of all those states of South America which, in some respects, are in close understanding with the United States, but in others have the same feelings of diffidence that we have and which are natural in small or weak

nations toward a very large one, dominating the continent."[66] For
Bourassa, Latin America was a natural ally. He had exposed his
thoughts on this in different books and some articles published in *Le
Devoir* at the end of the 1910s.[67] The periodical *L'Action française*,
with Lionel Groulx as editor, reflected on Bourassa's proposal in a
series of articles concerning Latin America at the beginning of the
1920s – the first series to seriously reflect on the benefits of Canadian-
Latin American relations. It is in this publication that French
Canada's *latinité* was first discussed in Quebec. But it is in Europe
that French Canadian writers were first introduced to this discourse
of identity.

Michel Lacroix has written on Quebec's original "Latin network"
in France, where the discourse on *latinité* was first applied to French
Canada.[68] He explains the convergence of interests in 1920s Paris
between a group of artists, diplomats, and intellectuals coming from
France, French Canada, and Latin America. These people were associated with some small publications but principally gravitated
around the magazine *La Revue de l'Amérique latine*. At the time,
France was re-discovering its old colonial territory through *Maria
Chapdelaine*, the literary blockbuster of the interwar period within
which the French Canadians' Latin identity was initially discussed.[69]
From those socialites in Paris, ideas concerning a shared Latin identity in the Americas filtered out to *L'Action française* in Montreal.
The Chilean poet Gabriela Mistral, who mingled with the group in
France, discussed *latinidad* in her own works. Her *Oda a la raza
latina* indirectly influenced nationalist groups in Quebec, which
were all ears for such rhetoric in the 1930s.

Actually, one of their French mentors, Charles Maurras, was
enthused by Mistral's ode to the Latin race and tried to define the
meaning of Latin identity, moving away from a simple cultural
awareness to advocate a more militant ideal of civilization. Lacroix
explains Maurras' contribution to this polymorphous discourse of
identity: "For the founder of *L'Action française*, people loyal to their
Latin heritage can only be on the side of order and Catholicism, sid-
ing against parliamentarism and liberalism. In his case, promoting
latinity goes beyond promoting common cultural traits or favouring
transatlantic intellectual exchanges, to take a clear ideological coloration: the colour of integral nationalism."[70] Throughout the 1930s,
Maurras' thoughts on latinity – close to Mussolini's – had a greater
impact in Quebec and sustained a network of young radicals. During

the Great Depression, a plethora of nationalist groups appeared to challenge capitalism and parliamentary democracy. These small factions, influenced by Lionel Groulx's writings on French Canadian history, campaigned for a stronger State, one that would be led by a charismatic leader who could command respect in Ottawa. Influenced by European fascists and the social doctrine of the Catholic Church, these young reformers campaigned for a corporatist organization of society.[71] Most were hopeful that Maurice Duplessis' Union nationale could accomplish this goal, but they rapidly became disillusioned by his first administration.[72]

By the end of the 1930s, nationalist groups like the Jeunesses patriotes (JP), who began supporting Duplessis, distanced themselves from the populist premier.[73] His government remained too close to Saint-James Street's financial interests, they argued, missing the opportunity to organize a truly autonomous French Canadian community. The JP's leader, Dostaler O'Leary, wanted more than Duplessis' rhetorical nationalism, and even went beyond his intellectual mentor, Canon Lionel Groulx, to promote Quebec's separation.[74] He declared during a gathering in 1937: "Separation is the solution. But first we need to set up corporatism... Our politicians (of all stripes) drop everything once they are in office, and once they have their personal rewards. But the generation under thirty will head in a different direction... Our first goal is to seize power in Quebec, and apply *Rerum Novarum* and *Quadragesimo Anno*, which are impossible to apply in a Confederation based on liberal and Protestant principles... Now it is time to stand up and tell Ottawa: we made a pact 70 years ago that you have betrayed; we want to tear it to pieces and establish an autonomous French dominion in Quebec."[75] As long as this rebelliousness made small waves, such statements were tolerated. But with the Second World War looming, the Canadian State became more preoccupied by the international impact of subversive rhetoric. It objected to the JP's enthusiastic appropriation of latinity as a discourse of identity, as they thought ideological foes might try to take advantage of this. New members of the JP had to swear allegiance to defending at all costs the "ongoing revolution to liberate our people, and spread the influence of our Latin civilization."[76] Youth movements like the JP threatened to occupy an important symbolic space in the Americas with this rhetoric, one that impinged on Ottawa's nation-building ideas and international character. As mentioned above, many Latin

Americans influenced by Hispanism were sympathetic to that kind of rhetoric. After all, the ideas of the famous Uruguyan author José Enrique Rodó were in line with this, as he defended "latinidad" and denounced "liberal democracy as seen in the United States," stating that "US cultural hegemony [was becoming] Hispanism's chief enemy."[77] This antipathy toward Anglo-Protestant cultural hegemony also characterized Dostaler O'Leary's ideas.

O'Leary's J P was not the only nationalist group trying to occupy this symbolic space. For example, Paul Bouchard's Faisceaux d'action séparatiste in Quebec City, also used this discourse of identity to discuss separatism, albeit with a more overtly fascist-leaning tone. Many articles published in Bouchard's publication La Nation, dealt with the "national revolutions of Franco, Salazar, and Mussolini."[78] Robert Comeau mentions that this "enthusiasm for the Latin world enticed Quebec separatists to argue in favour of replacing the Commonwealth by a closer union with Latin America."[79] Whether their inspiration came from Mussolini's totalitarian corporatism or from the corporatist model outlined in the social encyclicals, they used Latin identity to legitimize their political agenda. At the end of the 1930s, the prospect for the survival of a francophone people in North America looked bleaker than ever. Young nationalists like Bouchard and the O'Leary brothers claimed that the nation was "searching for its soul."[80] Since the Patriotes' defeat in the 1830s, these identity crises were solved symbolically by focusing on French Canada's "providential mission" and going back to the roots of this ethnic identity. The Vatican and Catholic France could be of assistance for spiritual guidance and cultural influence. But the Second World War abruptly isolated Quebec from the cultural centres of the Latin world, Paris and Rome. From then on, it became clear that pan-continental relations were inevitable. New cultural models were needed.

When Canada began its war effort in 1939, a few political activists (like Paul Bouchard and Walter O'Leary) left the country to escape potential military recruitment or internment. A number of French Canadian radicals spent years discovering the charms and many advantages of Latin American nations. Mexico was their first and most important stop. They discovered there that Mexico's president, Lázaro Cárdenas, had nationalized oil, put in place a corporatist regime, and opened the door to a lasting peace with the Catholic Church. Suddenly, the revolutionary zeal of this Latin American country acquired a new significance for Quebec's nationalists. They were not so keen on socialist education and active support for Spanish Republicans, of course, but they held Mexico's rebuff of British and US imperialism in high regard and were enthused by its audacious economic nationalism.

THE UNIÓN CULTURAL MÉXICO-CANADÁ FRANCÉS

Quebec's nationalist groups still staunchly supported the social role of the Catholic Church by the end of the 1930s. The leader of the Jeunesses patriotes (J P), Dostaler O'Leary, even criticized Mussolini for his deteriorating relations with the Church.[81] Therefore, the Mexican connection he would ultimately lobby for seems paradoxical, especially since, by the time the Second World War began in 1939, the anti-Catholicism of the Mexican Revolution had achieved international notoriety thanks to Antonio Dragon's biographies of Father Miguel Pro, the press coverage of the Cristero War, and Graham Greene's novel *The Power and the Glory*. I described above how this Mexican conflict had direct repercussions in Canada, when the Mexican consul-general in Toronto attempted to exploit anti-Catholic sentiments in the 1920s. All the same, people previously associated with French Canada's radical Catholic fringe sought to set up contacts with Mexico. But they first established concrete links with conservative groups in that country – and with people previously associated with the religious conflicts of the 1920s and 1930s. Mexican diplomats nonetheless lent them a hand after the Second World War began. How could this have happened? The consequences of Canada's early involvement in the world conflict along with Mexico's political shift under the administration of Manuel Ávila Camacho, help to explain how French Canadian-Mexican relations took form.

Spring 1939, Walter O'Leary Moves to Mexico City

Canada got involved in the European military conflict before any other country in the Americas. As the war loomed, subversive groups came under tighter scrutiny. Without a doubt, the public declarations of associations like the J P had greater resonance and their actions would have been reason for attention. The brother of the J P's leader, Walter O'Leary, left Canada in this context to become a student in Mexico in late spring 1939. Did Walter O'Leary flee to Latin America (in the same way as his fascist-leaning friend Paul Bouchard) to escape being taken into custody like Montreal's populist mayor Camillien Houde?[82] O'Leary's legal situation in Mexico did worry O.D. Skelton, the Canadian under-secretary of state for External Affairs, who asked his staff to keep track of his whereabouts in Mexico at the time.[83] Yet, it seems it was only toward the end of the war, during the summer of 1944, that a representative from the Canadian government asked him to reassess his military exemption.[84] O'Leary had left behind his radical activities and tried not to attract too much attention in Mexico. He followed Bouchard's counsel to "stay in Mexico [during the war] and leave it under no circumstances." Not completely forgetting his antipathy toward the Canadian government, he also followed Bouchard's second suggestion: to write letters in Spanish as much as possible "to give a hard time to those vice-ridden bastards from the censorship office."[85]

Walter O'Leary kept following Paul Bouchard throughout the war by maintaining a correspondence with him and seeing him during his visits to Mexico. Yet, his acquaintances in that country went beyond his Québécois far-right acolytes. His friendship with Montreal-born painter Stanley Cosgrove, for example, introduced him to new ideological horizons. Like O'Leary, this artist spent most of the war in Mexico.[86] Cosgrove had won an important prize to study in France, the Athanase-David bursary. When the war broke out he was forced to go elsewhere. He chose Mexico where he first studied at the San Carlos Academy of Fine Arts.[87] The painter, who had a French Canadian mother like O'Leary, later worked as an assistant to José Clemente Orozco.[88] O'Leary got to know the artists of the muralist movement after meeting his friend at work and going to exhibits and Mexico City's Nouvelle Librairie française.[89] If O'Leary was not sympathetic to the communist tendencies of the movement, he nonetheless rhapsodized about their paintings and celebrated the resolutely sovereign attitude of Mexican arts.[90] Their works certainly exposed him to a left-wing combination of nationalism and anti-imperialism he was not used to in Canada.

The Founding Members of the Unión Cultural México-Canadá Francés

Nevertheless, the first connections Walter O'Leary made in Mexico were mostly with conservative students and professors. Soon after his arrival at the Faculty of Letters and Philosophy of the Universidad

Nacional Autónoma de México (UNAM), a professor of that institution and director of its Summer School, Pablo Martínez del Río, suggested to O'Leary that an association bringing together French Canadians and Mexicans would be a welcome addition to the University's effort to diversify its foreign relations.[91] With the help of influential individuals of that institution, the Unión cultural México-Canadá francés (UCMCF) was consequently formed in September 1939.[92] The founding members of the association in Mexico were: professors Pablo Martínez del Río, Manuel González Montesinos, Manuel Alcalá, and José Rojas Gacidueñas; and students Alicia Aldave, Antonio Gómez Robledo, Carlos Septién García, and Walter O'Leary. José Luis Martínez, who soon became part of the secretarial staff of Jaime Torres Bodet (Secretary of Public Education in Camacho's government), and Alexis Loustau, a member of the French legation in Mexico, were also affiliated with the association.[93] The ex-rector of UNAM, Fernando Ocaranza, and the archbishop of Mexico, Mgr José Luis Martínez, were named honorary presidents of the UCMCF.[94] The intended goal of the Union was to "develop the profound national affinities existing between the French and Spanish cultures in North America, more specifically, between Mexicans and French Canadians." Their motto had religious overtones and called for "continental rapprochement between Latin and Anglo-Saxon America through the providential intermediary of the French Canadians."[95] During the war, other members of UNAM, officials of the Mexican government, francophones residing in Mexico, and people associated with the religious right collaborated with the association's fundamental mission to organize exchanges of students between Quebec and Mexico.[96]

The founding members of the UCMCF shared a francophilia as well as a particular appreciation of culture in the humanist tradition.[97] They emphasized that French Canada and Mexico had a unique Latin heritage that was worth defending in the homogenizing context of Second World War North America. Politically, they also had conservative affinities. At least two of the founding members of the UCMCF were overtly associated with the Mexican right: Antonio Gómez Robledo, an ex-Cristero who escaped execution during the military conflict only because his uncle, a respected revolutionary from Jalisco, intervened to save his life; and Gómez Robledo, also a well-known militant of the Asociación Católica de la Juventud Mexicana (ACJM).[98]

2.4 Emblem of the *Unión cultural México-Canadá francés*. This hybrid emblem combines the national symbols of Mexico (eagle and serpent fighting on a nopal) with Quebec's (its motto *Je me souviens* and the *fleur-de-lys* coat of arms). From a French Canadian perspective during the Second World War, it figuratively linked Quebec's hushed and unofficial symbols to Mexico's thundering nationalism. The UCMCF's official correspondence with university administrators, government officials, and fellow members usually included this emblem, and various examples can be found in archives in Quebec and Mexico.

Carlos Septién García, for his part, at the time of the foundation of the UCMCF, was director of *PROA*, the publication of the Unión Nacional de Estudiantes Católicos (UNEC).[99] He became renowned for *La Nación*, the periodical he launched in 1941 as the organ of the Partido Acción Nacional (PAN), one of the only tolerated opposition parties in corporatist Mexico, along with the informal power of the Catholic Church.[100] Jesús Guisa y Azevedo – who joined the association soon after its formation – was a well-known *maurrassien* who distanced himself from the PAN because it did not align itself closely enough with the precepts of the Catholic Church.[101]

During the *sexenio* of Manuel Ávila Camacho, the UCMCF established ties between people associated with the Mexican right, respected institutions of the *Distrito Federal*, and the revolutionary government. It also linked Catholics in Mexico to sympathizers in French Canada, providing an indirect international counterweight to the precarious position of the Church in the country. In the year before formal ambassadorial linkages were established, when rumors about the imminence of the formalization of Canadian-Mexican relations emerged in the newspapers, Walter O'Leary lobbied Mexican officials explaining they should name as ambassador to Canada a Mexican diplomat who could speak French fluently, as "the French Canadians have been working actively during the last five years in favour of a rapprochement between Canada and Latin American countries."[102] Can the latitude granted to the UCMCF be considered a symbolic concession to the right, which would have been in line with President Camacho's strategy to guarantee national reconciliation? Did the association play a role comparable to the censorship agencies described by Anne Rubenstein, censorship agencies which were used by the State to co-opt conservative political views through symbolic cultural endeavours deflecting middle-class discontent?[103]

Unfortunately, the documentation on the UCMCF in Mexico is insufficient to fully assess its intent beyond the association's direct function of organizing academic interactions with Quebec.[104] Unlike the fervour generated in Montreal in the 1940s by this rapprochement between French Canada and Mexico, it is unclear whether the UCMCF was successful or not in organizing events to stimulate popular interest in this transnational relation.[105] There is no indication the Union attracted a substantial following beyond the strict inner circles of the institution which hosted it and the *niñas bien* who travelled to Quebec for short student trips thanks to their effort at the beginning of the 1940s.[106] Therefore, it is impossible at this point to gauge the association's impact on national politics. What can be said, however, is that the formation of this association in Mexico, involving respected individuals of a renowned institution, gave crucial legitimacy to the sister organization in Montreal. In turn, the UCMCF in Montreal definitively made waves in Canadian politics. In the tense context of the war, when French Canadian nationalism was monitored by the federal government, this association attracted attention by linking together radical French Canadian nationalists, respected political figures from Quebec, and Latin American diplomats in Montreal. This all happened at a time when Mexico City tried to convince Ottawa to establish official diplomatic relations.

CONCLUSION

In light of these developments, the time was ripe for the political interests of certain groups in French Canada and Mexico to converge. Mexican diplomacy was swift to take advantage of this transnational collaboration. The political upheavals in the first half of the century deepened the alienation felt by devout Catholics in Mexico and patriotic francophones in Canada, prompting them to make new alliances with foreign sympathizers and even reconsider the parameters of their national identity.

These factors came together at the turn of the 1940s, when the context of heightened tensions gave a certain political colour to the first cultural interactions between Mexican and Québécois civil society. The following chapters examine this politicization by exploring the content and consequences of cultural encounters, taking into consideration the diplomatic misunderstandings and controversies they caused. While this collaboration influenced Canadian-Mexican relations, it did not change the world in itself. In hindsight, Quebec nationalists' collaboration with Mexican representatives might have forced Canadian foreign policy-makers to have a hurried change of heart toward Mexico, and Catholic militants might have helped to strengthen the practical compromise between the revolutionary State and the Mexican Catholic Church by inviting influential French Canadian dignitaries to make public speeches and appearances in Mexico. But those are still minor accomplishments. It is revealing to note, however, that at the precise moment when the future world order hung in the balance, French Canadian nationalists and Mexican Catholic militants tried to reinvent their transnational relations with foreign groups by sketching the possibilities of an alternative pan-Americanism. French Canadians realized they had more in common with people south of the Rio Grande than previously thought; fervent Mexican Catholics found religious inspiration in the society that developed on the banks of the St Lawrence River and sought its support. The cultural ties they established did influence the governing authorities in Ottawa and Mexico City, who tried to reclaim the symbolic space crafted by co-opting these

Catholics' transnational projects. But beside the impact on formal diplomatic dealings, what is more significant is the fact that these episodes of collaboration constitute a unique and invaluable window on the process of building transnational cultural linkages in times of crisis. This is revealing of the necessity for marginalized groups to craft a meaningful and authoritative imagined community with an international reach to counter the geopolitics imposed by central governing authorities.

3

The Union des Latins d'Amérique:
Re-inventing French Canada's
Transnational Relations

The spring of 1940 brought bad news for the Allies. After months of standoff, the Nazi blitzkrieg succeeded in defeating the French military in a matter of weeks. The news of France's capitulation in June sent shockwaves throughout the world. This rout particularly affected French Canada, which observed with dismay the most important French-speaking nation engulfed by the enemy and lamented the consequent dissolution of cultural connections with the old mother country. Considering the central importance French culture had in the curriculum of Quebec's *collèges classiques*, it is not surprising that the petite-bourgeoisie of the province felt stranded in North America without this transatlantic connection. Would this cultural confinement cause the assimilation of French Canadians? Would the growing influence of the United States alter Canadian foreign policy and force Quebec into an even larger anglophone polity? How could the weight of Anglo-Protestant culture be countered in the French-speaking province? Various political groups and cultural associations proposed solutions to these quandaries. Perhaps none were as original as the Union des Latins' transnational project for French Canada. According to the leadership of the association, there was only one way out to guarantee the survival of the French Canadian nation in this time of crisis: Latin America.

This proposal became the association's mantra during the Second World War. In 1942, during the Union des Latins d'Amérique's (ULA) first annual congress, the president of the association explained that "French Canada, withdrawn into itself since the fall of France, cannot survive unless its elite take the lead and forge connections with a group of nations that share its ideal of civilization."[1]

Dostaler O'Leary put in plain words French Canada's urgent need to establish connections with Latin America. According to him and other U LA spokespersons, these links were the only "natural" ones that could make up for the lost French influence: "Culture is the principal force capable of uniting mankind beyond its economic, political and national rivalries. Therefore, we naturally thought to look toward peoples coming from the same civilization as ours. We have discovered the well-groomed, civilized, and cultured Spanish and Portuguese America. These nations can provide everything we lack on a cultural and philosophical level. Two concepts of civilization exist in the Americas that balance each other out: the Latin concept and the Anglo-Saxon concept. As French Canadians, we belong to the Latin side."[2] This was music to the ears of Latin American diplomats. Bearing in mind Canada's lukewarm attitude to the establishment of formal relations with their countries, this is understandable. They lent credence to this kind of rhetoric by participating in U LA events. Like Carlos Calderón, Mexico's consul-general in Montreal, many Latin American diplomats argued that French Canada ought to be a crucial player in the establishment of diplomatic linkages with the region. U LA organizers and French Canadian politicians believed this international role could constitute an important step in breaking the cultural confinement imposed by the war. Latin affinities were proclaimed to be the cornerstone of any long-lasting rapprochement between Canada and Latin America.

WHY STUDYING THE ULA MATTERS

But was this language of Latin affinities really meaningful after all? Should we simply understand it as another example of diplomatic small talk? In spite of the U L A's membership approaching two thousand by the end of the war, and even though a large contingent of public personalities and politicians participated in their activities, it would be false to claim the association was very important in itself.[3] Even as lobbyists, the members of the U LA achieved little. However, studying the way U LA members mobilized an original identity discourse in a time of crisis for the purpose of influencing Canadian politics and considering how Ottawa reacted to the U LA in relation to foreign diplomats is informative on many levels. In hindsight, the U LA might not have been a significant political player, but their exponential growth and their ability to associate themselves with influential

political figures seriously preoccupied the Canadian Ministry of
External Affairs during the war. Ottawa's nervous reaction to ULA
activities is revealing of a new dynamic emerging in the relationship
between French Canadian nationalism and federal authorities. By
making demands as an ethnic minority, the people who used the concept of Latin identity positioned French Canada as one of the largest
cultural groups of the Americas – a group that theoretically com-
manded some respect at a time when the Good Neighbor Policy
became a war imperative. Therefore, the act of (re)naming – in this
case by asserting the *latinité* of French Canada and later on by emphasizing a distinct Québécois identity – meant a strategic positioning
that many perceived as disrupting the balance of power. Latinity was
an intersubjective construct that French Canadians and Latin
Americans used to legitimate a rapprochement between their countries. But this discourse of identity in Montreal was not used so much
to establish a profound transnational dialogue between these groups,
but rather as a way to negotiate with Ottawa: for the O'Leary brothers and the ULA founding members it was a method of challenging
minority-majority relations in Canada; and for Carlos Calderón and
other Latin American diplomats it was a tactic used to call Ottawa's
attention to their presence. In this way, studying the ULA and the
foreign connections they established constitutes a revealing example
of how civil society can influence international relations. Conversely,
it is an excellent case study of how the symbolism associated with
foreign political actors can be used for local purposes.

As a consequence, I emphasize here the symbolic importance language had in ULA activities and the concrete role it played in the
establishment of connections between Canada and Latin America
during the Second World War. Following Pierre Bourdieu's insights,
I evaluate the symbolic importance of language not so much because this forgotten facet of Canadian diplomatic history needs to be
recovered, but because it is informative of a universal process of
using discursive constructs that facilitate alliances with influential foreign actors in order to legitimize a counter-hegemonic stance at home.
Discursive agency was one of the many strategies used in French
Canada to counter assimilationist policies. Speaking out to assert and
defend a distinct national identity within the British Dominion was a
sine qua non to taking the floor in the House of Commons and
influencing Canadian politics. If control over education and the public sphere were the main sticking points between the revolutionary

government and Catholics in Mexico, the symbolism associated with Quebec's distinct identity in Canada was (and still is) involved in a dialectical process of affirmation and co-optation. Analyzing this process is the preoccupation of this chapter. But to have a meaningful political resonance in Canada, Latin identity needed to be tied to specific international actors. In the 1920s and 1930s, when the concept was first introduced in the country, fascist Italy played this part. By the end of the decade, when Mussolini stopped being the sort of political figure people wanted to be associated with, a new model emerged to sustain this discourse of identity. Mexico filled that void.

THE CONTROVERSIAL BEGINNINGS OF THE MONTREAL BRANCH: FRENCH CANADIAN NATIONALISM AND OTTAWA'S SURVEILLANCE

Since establishing the U C M C F in Mexico in September 1939, Walter O'Leary tried to convince his contacts back home to establish the same in Montreal. The purpose of this collaboration was unclear at first. The initial letters concerning the establishment of connections between French Canada and Mexico involved plans as diverse as importing oil (this right after the British Empire had cut relations because of nationalization), setting up a tourist agency after the war, and founding a magazine dedicated to Latin American culture.[4] These ventures failed to materialize. However, the association established at the Université de Montréal in January 1940 – the first in Canada entirely devoted to relations with Latin America – recovered some of the original ideas expressed. From the beginning, special committees of the Union des Latins d'Amérique (U L A) were formed to reflect on such issues as studying potential economic relations between Quebec and Mexico, facilitating student exchanges between both states, and reflecting on the Latin identity shared by French Canadians and Latin Americans. The direction this reflection could take made some people quite nervous in the Ministry of External Affairs in Ottawa.

Dostaler O'Leary and the Union Culturelle Mexique-Canada Français

Soon after the U C M C F was created in Mexico City, Dostaler O'Leary answered his brother's call and took the initiative to found the Montreal branch of the association.[5] He waited to receive the blessing of Olivier Maurault, rector of Université de Montréal, to host the association in this respected academic institution, just like the U C M C F in Mexico. The founding members were mostly intellectuals or students, either graduates or direct affiliates of the university and its École des hautes études commerciales (H E C). The constitution informs us that the first members were Dostaler O'Leary (then journalist at *La Patrie*) as president, Marcel Thérien (a graduate of H E C and lieutenant in the Canadian Army) as vice-president, Jean-Marie Parent (of Université de Montréal) as secretary, Gilles Sicotte (a language professor at H E C who soon became secretary of the Canadian legation in Argentina) as Spanish instructor, and Daniel Johnson (Canadian delegate to Pax Romana[6] and soon to be Union nationale premier of Quebec) as legal consultant. Sitting members of the founding committee were Jean Drapeau (a law student who became candidate for the Bloc populaire in the 1944 provincial election[7]), Benoît Baril (one of the national leaders of the Jeunesse étudiante catholique (J E C)), and Reynald Pelletier (from Université de Montréal).[8]

These individuals had many points in common with the founding members in Mexico. The first was their conservative affinities. The second was their excellent educational credentials and political connections.[9] People gravitating around the Bloc populaire, the Union nationale, the Jeunesses patriotes, and a federal institution like the Canadian Army worked together to form the U C M C F in Montreal. We can presume as well that Gilles Sicotte had close connections to the Liberal Party of Canada since he obtained an important position in Argentina soon after. Liberals from Quebec soon collaborated with this group and individuals directly involved with Catholic associations also joined the U C M C F, making it a group whose participants came from a broad ideological perspective.

Still, the U C M C F in Mexico and Montreal were different in some respects. To start with, this diversified grouping of individuals was of little consequence for Quebec's Church-State relations, as the clergy already played a decisive role in the province's social sphere. Another noticeable difference was the swift involvement of women in the leadership of the Quebec association.[10] The first committee was rapidly reorganized in the months following its creation to include Yvette Baulu-Germain, who became general secretary of the Union. The next year, she was followed in her role by another woman, Pierrette Girardin. 1943 then saw the first women acceding to the vice-presidency, Manolita del Vayo de Gallagher (the ULA's Spanish teacher following Sicotte's departure for Argentina).[11] Overall, women played an important role in the association in Montreal. Finally, the sheer scale of the group in Quebec seems to have been the most significant difference.

The Association Changes Its Name

The leadership of the Montreal section of the UCMCF changed the name of the association soon after its foundation to be more inclusive after other Latin American consuls in the metropolis showed interest in the group. The association came to be known as the Union culturelle des Latins d'Amérique in 1941, but dropped the term *culturelle* a few years later. The president of the Union des Latins d'Amérique, Dostaler O'Leary, explained this choice by stating that the term "culture" was implied in the word latin; mentioning both in the title of the association was redundant. Other documents in the ULA's correspondence gave a different reason: Maurault seemed to have been uncomfortable with the name because he found it had communistic overtones.[12] Translating a name into French from Spanish could be considered hazardous in Second World War Quebec. The hermeneutics associated with this act of naming proved to be even more contentious for Ottawa officials.

Nevertheless, the *raison-d'être* of the ULA was not significantly different from what was envisioned for the UCMCF in Mexico. The organization's constitution said: "The principal objective of the Union culturelle des Latins d'Amérique is to develop the natural affinities shared by American people of Latin culture. This section intends to: (a) publicize Latin America in Canada, and Canada in Latin America; (b) promote cultural, economic, and political relations between Canada and the Iberian nations of the Americas."[13] Much like in Mexico, academic collaboration was supposed to facilitate this endeavour. We can read in a draft of the constitution: "In the near future, the Cultural Union hopes to forge academic linkages and encourage professor and student exchanges between French-speaking universities and their Ibero-American counterparts. It hopes to create a chair in Ibero-American history in a French-Canadian university, and an equivalent chair in the history of the French penetration in North America in Spanish-speaking and Portuguese-speaking universities."[14] The only thing distinguishing the founding documents of both organizations is the tone. The constitution for the Mexican branch stated more clearly that this association was attempting to facilitate a rapprochement between French Canadians and Mexicans in order to improve relations with Anglo-America – in other words, smooth the progress of North American integration for this Spanish-speaking country.[15] Conversely, the emphasis in Montreal was clearly on the Latin bonds. From the beginning, a transnational discourse of identity stimulated discussions in ULA gatherings. Nurturing Quebec's *latinité* was an end in itself. Yet this rhetoric was couched in the reasonable language of continental collaboration and kindred interests. Members of the ULA constantly justified their action to federal authorities by stating that Quebec, with its Latin culture, was the perfect ambassador to Latin America for Canada's anglophone majority.

This discourse of Latin affinities was nonthreatening to the authorities in Mexico. After all, having a minority group in an industrialized country identifying with Latin American culture comprised potential advantages for Mexican diplomacy. By contrast, the discourse of Latin identity was controversial in Canada. The president of the association had used the concept of *latinité* a few years before to attack the Canadian federation. Indeed, in his essay "Séparatisme, doctrine constructive" (published in 1937) Dostaler O'Leary argued that Quebec needed to break its links with the Canadian federation in order to preserve the essence of its Latin identity.[16] Therefore, civil servants in Ottawa had very good reasons to doubt the ULA's sincerity and suspect its intentions as subversive. The context of the war, in general, and the controversy over conscription, in particular, radically increased these apprehensions and the Royal Canadian Mounted Police (RCMP) was asked to monitor the activities of the association in Montreal.[17]

The Union des Latins d'Amérique under Surveillance

If the meetings of the ULA were controversial for representatives of the Ministry of External Affairs in Ottawa, it is because they became popular in a very specific political context. In early spring 1942, the Canadian government organized a plebiscite to release Prime Minister Mackenzie King from his promise not to impose conscription during the Second World War.[18] The results illustrated the "two solitudes" comprising the country: 64 per cent voted yes in

English Canada, but only 15 per cent of Quebec's francophones did.[19] The ensuing political controversy had the potential of breaking the country apart. The creation of opposition parties like the Bloc populaire was a cause for concern in Ottawa. Parallel to the referendum campaign and the creation of the Bloc populaire, the Liberal government of Adélard Godbout in Quebec gave its full support to the U L A's organization of the first congress on the future of French Canada's relations with Latin America.[20] The meetings of the U L A soon became very popular; a newspaper from Ottawa even reported that this association in Montreal "has been so successful that meetings there are jammed."[21] A few months after the referendum, the U L A further improved its political backing by adding an honorary committee to its formal structure made up of prominent French Canadians. The general-secretary of the association, Pierrette Girardin, proudly announced the composition of this new committee at the 1942–43 annual meeting. The honorary president was, of course, Mgr Olivier Maurault, rector of the Université de Montréal, but the whole committee was under the patronage of the Premier of Quebec, Adélard Godbout. Many important political personalities were part of this committee: the consuls-generals and consuls of Latin America in Montreal, T.D. Bouchard (Quebec minister of public works), Oscar Drouin (minister of commerce), Adhémar Raynault (Mayor of Montreal), Édouard Montpetit (Université de Montréal's executive secretary), Senator Léon Mercier-Gouin, and Paul-Émile Poirier (president of Quebec's federation of Chambers of Commerce).[22]

The support the government of Quebec granted to the U L A at a time of heightened tensions between the province and the rest of the country might not have been directly related, but the coincidence was troubling enough for the RCMP to collaborate with members of the Ministry of External Affairs in gathering intelligence on the association. One secret report stated: "I do not think the O'Leary brothers are up to much good. From sample Censorship intercepts of their correspondence, I should think they were rather unbalanced visionaries."[23] Another report mentioned that the U L A "maintains active relations with the nationalist movements of Mexico and South America."[24] But the participation of Latin American consuls in U L A activities really turned the worries into important concerns, since this collaboration put the federal government in an uneasy position vis-à-vis their requests for formal

diplomatic relations. For example, the RCMP was aware that
Carlos Calderón, the Mexican consul general in Montreal, was
received as a guest of honour in a ULA meeting in 1942 – and given
a seat beside Lionel Groulx – well before Canada accepted to for-
malize its diplomatic relations with Mexico.[25] All things considered, the controversy behind Quebec's support of ULA gatherings
illustrates the beginning of a new dialectical relationship between
the French-speaking province and Ottawa; the protection of specific fields of constitutional jurisdiction characterizes the conflictual
nature of federal-provincial relations in the post-war era. As a result
of this mutual mistrust, the cultural and social spheres became bitterly contested terrain where new programs introduced by one level
of government were challenged by the other. This extended to the
rhetorical devices used to define national identity.[26] The growing
tensions with federal authorities over Quebec's international *prise
de parole* can be observed in Ottawa's oversight of French Canadian
relations with Latin America.[27]

One of Canada's foremost civil servants, Norman A. Robertson,
who was under-secretary of state for External Affairs from 1941 to
1946, mandated his francophone staff to keep an eye on the ULA.[28]
Before the second ULA congress, he asked W.F.A. Turgeon his opinion on the danger such an association represented for Canada.[29] He
also questioned him on the appropriateness of sending representatives of the federal government with direct ties to External Affairs to
the 1943 Journées d'Amérique latine. Turgeon answered:

> You asked me to comment on the proposal that Chaput should
> attend the "Journées Pan-Latines" of the "Union Culturelle des
> Latins d'Amerique." I have had a talk with Cadieux about the
> Union. His feeling is that the danger in any organization like this
> is that extremist members of the Bloc Populaire and semi-Fascists
> may find it a useful instrument for their purposes, that because of
> the Defence Regulations these people have to cover up their real
> ideas and that they are using this Pan-Latinism as an instrument
> of separatism. His argument is that they want to build up in
> Latin America an idea of Quebec as an independent entity in the
> hope that this will make it easier for them to secure support later
> on when they demand international recognition of the separate
> existence of French Canada. As you will have seen from the pro-
> gram of the Journées Pan-Latines, it is supported by a number of

respectable and eminent people, including Senator Gouin, Premier Godbout, the Lieutenant-Governor of the Province, and the Mayor of Montreal.[30]

This affiliation of eminent French Canadians with notorious radical nationalists was worrisome for Ottawa. Would they use this platform to promote their subversive agenda?

Political life was closely monitored in Quebec during the war. Real seditious elements were easily neutralized, but larger dissatisfaction was harder to deal with. Resentment against Mackenzie King's about-face concerning his promise not to impose conscription mobilized nationalist sentiment in the province. In their undercover surveillance of U L A meetings, agents of the R C M P noted: "Though it is customary to close such meetings with the National Anthem, this was not done. [This incident] leads us to believe that this association is inclined towards Separatism. In view of the above and the close connection between the O'Learys and Paul Bouchard, the activities of this society will be kept under observation and periodical reports will be submitted."[31] For some, the language of Latin affinities was problematic in itself. Robertson considered the U L A's Latin connection as nominally excluding Anglo-Saxons and playing on this nationalist dissatisfaction. He was preoccupied by the U L A's leadership and the role such a group could play in this tense context. Robertson summoned Olivier Maurault and Dostaler O'Leary and told them that this group "is not made to allow any foolish demonstrations of ultra Nationalist or Separatist movements, and if some of its members cannot be properly controlled in that respect they should be invited to leave the Association."[32] More importantly, he questioned the very affirmation of a distinct French Canadian identity in the context of the war and warned them to "bear in mind that Canada vis-à-vis the foreign world is a whole, a united nation, and that especially in our dealings with South America there should be no hyphen after the word Canada." [33] According to some civil servants in Ottawa, defending *la nation canadienne-française* was not a suitable stance.

The very act of expressing discontent proved to be controversial during the war. According to staff members of the Canadian diplomatic corps, emphasizing the social inequalities between French and English Canadians during U L A gatherings represented a threat to the British Empire because the association had a transnational character. Turgeon confided to Robertson that separatism was not the most preoccupying aspect of the association; broadcasting French Canadian alienation to territories in the neo-colonial sphere of influence had the department much more preoccupied:

> The leaders of this movement have a political object in view, probably the securing of the political independence of the province of Quebec by the assistance of these Spanish and Portuguese nations with whom the French-Canadians have "affinities." Such an idea, if it really exists, is of course nonsensical. I need not dwell upon it in writing to you… There is something else to be noted. It may well be that, by the manner in which associations of this kind present themselves to the people of other American countries, they give the impression that the French-Canadians are an ill-treated, dissatisfied race, unhappy by reason of their association with Anglo-Saxons in a British Dominion, and longing to set up another Latin State in America. Besides showing a false picture of French Canada, this attitude on the part of propagandists might do us all a certain degree of harm, especially in these times.[34]

The harm consisted of tarnishing the reputation of the British Empire in Latin America. The rhetoric of social justice for francophones highlighted the intrinsic inequalities of British rule, directly contradicting the imperial claims to fairness.[35] Concerned with this point, Robertson added: "If we have any 'dirty linen to wash,' we should do it 'en famille' and refrain from inviting our friends from the South to attend to this 'washing' or to help in this job."[36] Yet, the ULA's leadership in Montreal constantly denied these allegations of seditious intent. They kept claiming that French Canada's interest was not inimical to the larger good of the federation.

Actually, members of the association were generally cautious when publicly expressing their affinities with Latin Americans. They kept legitimizing this rhetoric by using the language of the Good Neighbor Policy. From the beginning, they had stressed that using latinity as a discourse of identity for French Canada was only for the greater good of the country in its dealings with Latin American countries.[37] As Maurault later expressed to a representative of the Canadian government: "When we began this movement to support a rapprochement between the Latin republics and

Canada at Université de Montréal, we positioned ourselves from a Catholic and French point of view because we knew this would be the most effective way to call the attention of our southern cousins. Personally, I am still convinced this was the right approach, and I would add that everything we do in favour of this rapprochement, we do not only in the name of the province of Quebec, but also in the name of Canada, which Quebec is an integral part of."[38] Dostaler O'Leary also mentioned that French Canadians could serve as the first Canadian emissaries in this region. He argued that their "natural" interest in Latin American culture facilitated diplomatic connections, ultimately benefiting the Anglo-Saxons themselves.[39] This logic might sound awry in the mouth of the ULA's president, but influential individuals became convinced of the opportunity of using French Canadians as this British Dominion's public face in Latin America.

If eminent French Canadians were already convinced of this, it is the voice of a British diplomat that gave legitimacy to the idea in Ottawa. Turgeon confided to Robertson in 1943 that while he was in Argentina, the British ambassador had revealed the special role French Canadians could play for the greater benefit of the Empire in Latin America:

Sir David [Kelly] said that he had given much thought to Canada, and its "vocation" in America and in the Empire. He thinks that the great value of Canada's position lies in the fact that she is qualified for a dual role: (1) that of intermediary between the British Empire and the United States, and (2) that of intermediary between the British Empire and Latin America, (which is all of America south of the United States), by reason of the existence of 3 1/2 million French Canadians of Catholic and Latin culture, recognized as an entity by the fact that their language is an official language, and who, by their survival and the conditions of their present-day life, are a proof of the Empire's spirit of tolerance and fair-play, and a proof also of the more general proposition that Latins need not fear the strangling of their own culture by too close association with Anglo-Saxons, (a fear which exists here in respect of the Americans).[40]

Nationalists in Quebec might disagree, saying that French Canadian culture "survived" in spite of the British Empire and that socio-economic conditions were far from equal. All in all, French Canada

survived despite a dependent economy in a country it did not politically control.[41] In this context, members of Canada's External Affairs
were understandably concerned that the U L A would present French
Canadians as "an ill-treated, dissatisfied race, unhappy by reason of
their association with Anglo-Saxons" to their Latin American contacts.[42] Turgeon clearly specified that "Healthy French Canadian
propaganda in Latin America should be along the lines of Sir David
Kelly's thoughts. The French Canadians should approach the Spanish
or Portuguese Americans on the basis of French Canada being a part
of Canada as it is and as it intends to remain."[43]

The U L A leadership agreed to play the role of informal representatives of their country in Latin America, but not at the expense of
negating their French Canadian identity and Latin roots. They also
wanted to maintain their freedom of movement, not limiting themselves to cultural and educational projects, but taking on economic
and political ones as well. The president of the association, Dostaler
O'Leary, said in the closing speech of the 1943 congress: "*Primum
vivere, deinde philosophari.* We want to live in North America as a
French and Catholic people and we want to use all the space that
falls to us. We are well-disposed to help everybody, English Canadians
as much as French Canadians. For the latter, to help them establish
contacts in Latin America; to the former, to serve them as ambassador. But nobody should take offence to our affirmations and positions. Latin and Catholic, we want to develop, extend, and bring
ourselves closer to the other Latins of the Americas. We want to keep
and improve the cordiality of our relations with Anglo-Saxons, while
asserting loud and clear our Latin character."[44] In the end, Dostaler
O'Leary realized that French Canadians could not impose their
views on federal authorities, and had to cooperate with them in
order for the U L A to survive as a strong association. At the same
time, governmental representatives recognized the U L A was there to
stay, considering the association had already positioned itself favourably in the field of informal relations with Latin America, especially
with Mexico. From 1944 on, Canada supported U L A's activities
such as their congresses and student excursions. Still, as long as the
group was headed by the former leader of the Jeunesses patriotes,
the discomfort remained obvious.[45] This is why the Canadian government tried to favour the emergence of other associations to organize linkages with countries with which they were establishing
diplomatic relations.

Other Canadian Associations
Favouring Relations with Latin America

The ULA was the first Canadian association completely dedicated to relations with Latin America. During the war, other societies devoted to this endeavour surfaced in Montreal, Ottawa, Quebec City, and Toronto. The groups Cercle Cervantes and Canada-Amérique latine were university associations in Quebec City and Ottawa dedicated to Hispanic culture and promoting continental relations. The Canadian Inter-American Association (CIAA) and the Panamerican League were professional societies – respectively from Montreal and Toronto, but with branches throughout the country – who were also promoting closer relations between Canada and Latin America, although with a clearer business focus. The Ministry of External Affairs in Ottawa very clearly expressed its preference for these two latter groups.[46] Did the ULA feel threatened by this favouritism?

Some members of the ULA reacted ambiguously to the creation of the CIAA by the Mexican consul-general in Montreal, Carlos Calderón, in 1941. At first, they saw collaboration with this association as inimical to their underlying principle. If the goal of the ULA was what members of External Affairs suspected – planting the seeds for recognition of an independent Quebec – any collaboration with this association would have been, indeed, strictly impossible. Armour Landry, a member of the ULA and organizer of the Trois-Rivières branch, confided in a series of letters to Walter O'Leary that he was shocked to see his brother Dostaler collaborate with a "rival" group. Was Dostaler selling out to this "anglophone" association, they wondered?[47] Bitter letters were exchanged between the brothers. In the end, the controversy was resolved with Landry explaining to Walter in Mexico: "Our friends from the Union slowly infiltrate the association and they just seized the office of secretary for this society."[48] The language of covert-operation coloured these epistolary exchanges. The tone of these letters certainly expressed the uneasiness certain members of the ULA felt in collaborating with other groups. On the ground, however, that collaboration was given a different spin by the president, Dostaler O'Leary.

Dostaler might have been the main problem the Ministry of External Affairs had with the ULA, but the correspondence between the original organizers of the association show him to be a voice of reason compared with some radical elements. This radicalism never found public expression with the U L A. The author of *Séparatisme, doctrine constructive* seems to have seen the writing on the wall at the beginning of the war. His actions portray him as a pragmatic actor. Latin Americans were sympathetic to French Canadian nationalism, he realized, but this would not help the independence of Quebec. His close partnership with Carlos Calderón illustrates this point. From the beginning, Dostaler collaborated with the Mexican consul-general's group because Calderón valued Canada as a *bicultural* country. The consul-general represented the nationalists' best ally because he supported basic French Canadian objectives in the federation: their recognition as equals with English Canada.

The goals of the Canadian Inter-American Association supported French Canadian nationalists' understanding of Canada as a binational State. The association was formed by the Mexican consul-general in collaboration with influential members of Montreal's financial community and representatives of the federal authorities to facilitate contact between the Canadian government and representatives of Latin American administrations in the country. In setting up the group, Calderón himself was not shunning the U L A (quite the contrary), but he apparently realized Ottawa's aversion for this group and that another venue would therefore be more conducive to accomplishing Mexican objectives in Canada. Still, Calderón made sure that Canadian duality would be represented in the C I A A. Their "Outline for Activities" states:

> We must first of all have a friendly basis for our relations so that when we resume normal trade we will already have that essential of intercourse: mutual confidence. Canada can accomplish this easily if she shows herself as she is; a nation with strong Anglo-Saxon traditions of which she is proud and also a strong Latin dimension rooted in her French population. The latter cannot be too firmly emphasized, because for that reason she will be better understood to the south. However, she must not create the impression that either of these elements [English or French] is dominant in her national life, but that they both are present and live in harmony. In that way she will prove by her tolerance at home that she is capable of understanding and getting along with the rest of the Americas. To most of Latin America, Canada is merely an English colony to the north of the United States, and therefore not an important factor in international relations.[49]

This last point went along the lines of the British ambassador's comments. French Canadians could show a different image of the Dominion.[50] The picture of a harmonious bicultural country (Anglo-Saxon/French) was appealing to Latin American republics. But Calderón held Canada to its words on this bicultural representation and lent support to demands for bilingualism during the war. The sympathy for the French Canadian cause made Calderón very popular among Quebec's political class. For the consul-general, French Canada was a precious asset in securing sympathy for Canadian-Mexican relations in the Dominion. Moreover, whether he acted consciously or not, Calderón identified a vulnerability in Canadian politics. By cozying up to nationalists in Quebec, he pressured Ottawa to position itself in relation to Mexico's request (considering that the government in Ottawa was not willing to let the ULA occupy that very symbolic space in Canadian foreign affairs). In the end, the CIAA might not have been controlled by the ULA's leadership, but as long as Carlos Calderón was its president, the goals of the association were not inimical to those of Dostaler O'Leary's group.

As for the other professional association, the Panamerican League's ties to the ULA were more overt during the war. This group was organized in 1943 in Toronto, but the association was soon extended to Montreal. Much like the CIAA, English Canadian entrepreneurs and politicians seem to have been the main coordinators of this group, although a French Canadian presence was noticeable in Montreal. Influential members of the ULA collaborated with this group, and Hector Boulay, who was the ULA's vice-president at the time and main organizer of student exchanges with Mexico, became national director in 1944.[51] At this point, I cannot assess Boulay's long-term influence over the association, but since the president and honorary president of the ULA also collaborated with the League's events, it is safe to assume they did not perceive this group as a direct threat. Finally, at the university level, both the Cercle Cervantes and Canada-Amérique latine had an overwhelming French Canadian membership with a leadership that enthusiastically collaborated with ULA activities.[52] Representatives of both associations were present at the 1943 Journées d'Amérique latine organized by the ULA.[53]

To a large extent, ULA members were able to join other associations because they had a very basic knowledge of Latin America that

members in English Canada lacked. The need for trustworthy qualified personnel was a major obstacle for Canada in the establishment
of formal diplomatic relations with Latin America. For example, it is
mentioned in a memorandum to the Prime Minister of Canada entitled "Diplomatic Relations with Mexico," that this country had difficulty establishing diplomatic relations with Mexico in 1941: "The
main difficulty in acceding to Mexico's request is, as you have always
emphasized in matters of this kind, that of getting the right man for
the job. The minister to Mexico could scarcely be French Canadian
in view of the appointments of Turgeon and Desy."[54] So, federal
authorities could not ignore the input of groups in Quebec who
rushed to occupy this space. The government of Canada tried to resist
these pressures by attempting to co-opt Quebec's nationalists' transnational project. This was done primarily to limit the potential dam-
age the unbounded expression of Latin affinities could have on the
reputation of the Dominion; at the same time, it was done to gain
some benefit out of these kindred interests. In the end, both positions
were transformed by this process. A middle ground emerged at the
end of the war, somewhat diverging from the initial schemes.

THE UNION DES LATINS D'AMÉRIQUE

At the outset, the O'Leary brothers dreamed of an aggressively self-
assertive association of Latins assisting French Canada in command-
ing respect in Ottawa, but the contingencies of the world conflict
rapidly intervened. When the ULA surfaced in Montreal in 1940, the
association was not framed as a venue to allow "demonstrations of
ultra Nationalist or Separatist" sentiments.[55] Instead, a new geopolitical reality directly influenced the burgeoning of this association and
its popularity among Montreal's "*gente decente*."[56] The fall of France
changed the outlook of Quebec's cultural relations. At the time,
francophones still relied greatly on the aura of France's cultural
and intellectual production to defend themselves against Lord
Durham's modern disciples.[57] While the future strength of the British
Commonwealth remained uncertain during the war, the province's
connections with France were definitively put on hold. The 1940
Ogdensburg Agreement (a bilateral military accord that established
the Permanent Joint Board of Defence) and the 1941 Hyde Park declaration (an economic agreement between Canada and the US designed
to facilitate wartime production) unequivocally demonstrated that US

influence would not go away. Canada could no longer avoid recognizing its American identity, and because of this, many French Canadians felt trapped in an Anglo-Protestant straitjacket.

Establishing new cultural alliances beyond the confines of Anglo-America became a concern in Quebec. Hundreds of students, academics, clergy, politicians, and professionals soon joined the ULA, and used it as a platform to discuss the consequences of this turning point. The president of the association remarked in 1942: "We are isolated; if we don't want to perish from exhaustion and inertia in the midst of a civilization that is not our own – as beautiful as it might be – we need to open the windows and seek new places where we can find a rejuvenating breeze." It is clear that French Canadians' first motive for supporting continentalism was to compensate the loss of French influence. They found their "rejuvenating breeze" with Latin America and its francophile *bonne société*. "Since France is bent under the yoke of Teutonic barbarism, the only obvious place we should look to – and I really don't see any other – is Latin America, which is so beautiful, so great, so civilized," O'Leary concluded.[58] Discussing with Latin America's upper classes was like seeing an improved reflection of oneself in a mirror. Learning about their culture and politics therefore inspired many French Canadian political stakeholders and drove them into the ranks of the ULA.

The interest in Latin America was not only motivated by political concerns. Much like the 1920s tango craze in Paris or the "vogue for all things Mexican" New York experienced in the interwar period, Latin America also became popular in Montreal at the turn of the 1940s.[59] Montreal followed the cultural trends of the French and American metropolises and was introduced to Latino music roughly at the same time.[60] During the Second World War, the popularity of Latin American culture became undeniable with the emergence of a home-grown talent, Alys Robi, who sang Latino serenades in French. This chanteuse made an international career out of her performances. She apparently became a member of the association and participated in their gatherings where she could improve her knowledge of the culture she embodied on worldwide stages.[61]

The cultural curiosity of the French Canadian petite-bourgeoisie in Montreal provided a critical mass for the ULA. The attendance of the 1943 Journées d'Amérique latine proves this point, with more than three hundred people participating.[62] In the end, it was the unique intersection of cultural and political motives that made the U L A's message significant during the war. Socializing at their events not only provided a pleasant relief from the dire events of the war, it offered new ways to think about the best approach to reconfigure French Canada's cultural network of support during this time of national crisis. When all is said and done, political opponents *in Quebec* could meet at U L A functions to muse on the future of the French Canadian nation without the usual politicking associated with this intellectual exercise. That was achieved by couching this reflection on the language of the transnational discourse of *latinité* used at U L A events.

National Impulses for Transnational Encounters: the 1943 Journées d'Amérique Latine

The published report of the 1943 Journées d'Amérique latine, the U L A's yearly congress, illustrates how French Canadians used the polymorphous concept known as *latinité* to imagine the future of their nation more than to establish tangible and long-lasting connections with Latin American administrations.[63] At a time when Ottawa worried about what they were discussing (and sent representatives to report on U L A events), the association became a forum for questioning the orientation of Canadian foreign policy and its consequences for the French Canadian people.[64] The speeches made at the congress illustrated the fact that French Canada's new imagined transnational community sprung out of national anxieties since they connected two main themes: the precarious position of the French Canadian nation in cultural isolation, and the strength of Latin civilization in the Americas.

Nationalist sentiments were expressed at the congress held at the Cercle Universitaire de Montréal, but not along the lines of Dostaler O'Leary's pre-war point of view. The French Canadian nation's survival within the federation was the central concern of participants at the Journées d'Amérique latine. To sustain an autonomous existence on this continent, invited speakers explained that French Canada had to embrace its own *américanité* and break its cultural confinement by establishing links south of the Rio Grande. The Jesuit François Hertel, who used to work with Dostaler in the J P, said during the congress: "The upcoming generations want more and they want something better, let's give them what they are expecting from us... French by history, we are also American by geography; let's not forget this fundamental aspect of the nature of our nation. Born in the Americas, raised in a century of material and intellectual progress, we live in a historical moment in which audacity and adventure have the place of honour; our youth will only devote itself to dynamic values."[65] But how could *American* dynamism be integrated into French Canadian identity without discarding traditional values? For so long it had been argued that French Canada could only survive by barricading itself within its ethnic identity, with language and faith acting as ramparts against assimilation. Members of the ULA made peace with the notion long rejected by French Canada's social elites that its *américanité* was an essential component of national identity. In order to do so, they first had to establish that French Canadians were part of the same cultural family as Latinos; second, they had to demonstrate that Latin America was a model of civilization worthy of inspiration (against the grain of dominant studies on the region in anglophone academia).

Part of the language used to discuss the concepts of nation and civilization (blood and race) made discussion about Latin identity complicated and controversial. Senator Léon Mercier-Gouin's explanation on the uses of French Canada's "natural" connection with Latin America is a good example: "We belong to the great Latin family: the one with ties to the Spanish and Portuguese cultures... In this rapprochement, we must act as a link between our English-speaking compatriots and the parts of the Americas that we share religious, cultural, and blood ties with."[66] Claiming blood ties with Latin America was not a threatening nationalist affirmation. Blood was understood in its spiritual dimension, much like race was used to refer to ethnic groups. Nevertheless, ULA detractors attacked the association by emphasizing that it was nonsensical to speak of French Canada's natural affinities with Latin America since there was no racial bond to start with in this Latin "family."

When N.A. Robertson met Mgr Maurault and Dostaler O'Leary to tell them that he disapproved of the ULA's make-up, he mentioned that *latinité* was discriminatory not only for Anglo-Saxons but for French Canadians as well. He added in all seriousness that the association excluded "French Canadians who are not Latin by origin, but Norman, Briton, Picard, etc." – an observation the *French Canadian* Dostaler O'Leary must have found amusing, considering his Irish ancestry.[67] The lack of physical resemblance between French Canadians and Latin Americans was a second point that detractors of the ULA exploited to undermine their venture. Jean-Charles Harvey – a vocal opponent of nationalists in Quebec and especially of the O'Leary brothers' radicalism – ridiculed the concept of Latin identity used by the ULA.[68] In her 1948 review of French Canadian sentiments over pan-Americanism, the American scholar Iris S. Podea noted Harvey's arguments against *latinité*: "Are the Laurentians Latins? Is their language Latin? Where is the physical resemblance between French Canadians and Mexicans and Cubans? One thing is certain, there is more resemblance between the 'Pea Soups' of Laurentia and the 'accursed English' (*maudits Anglâs*) of Ontario than between the Trifluvians and a Haitian... English would be far more useful for French Canadians than Spanish, and it would be as well to forget the expulsion of the Acadians as we have the Spanish assassination of Montezuma and the massacre of the natives of Mexico."[69] Imagining transnational affinities or criticising them amounted to expressing the same position stakeholders had in national politics, but with an exotic colour palette. When adversaries had completely different conceptions of the country – its future as well as its past – no common ground could be found in this transnational construction.

In general, however, the concept of Latin identity was vague enough to allow its usage by political opponents in Quebec. For example, T.D. Bouchard – an unambiguous opponent of nationalists in Quebec – defended Dostaler O'Leary's right to use latinity as a discourse of identity and embraced the ULA's purpose saying: "the good old French-speaking Canadians wholeheartedly approve of your venture and wish you all the best."[70] It is worth mentioning that "in creating the *Institut démocratique canadien* around 1940, Bouchard renewed with the *Institut canadien de Montréal* of 1844," the very institution, Yvan Lamonde explains, that "evoked forms of nineteenth-century liberal contestation and anticlericalism."[71] Bouchard had more ideological affinities with Harvey than with O'Leary. It goes on to show that latinity in itself was not divisive or exclusively associated with nationalists. Actually, Bouchard even became part of the ULA's honorary committee and gave a speech in Spanish at the Journées d'Amérique latine.[72] Bouchard's presence favoured a constructive exchange of ideas at ULA venues using this deflecting language of transnational affinities.

Employing the concepts of race and blood did not raise eyebrows at ULA meetings since their usage to mean culture and civilization was common at the time. When the adjective *culturelle* was taken out of the association's name, Dostaler explained that *latinité* could not refer to anything else but culture: "As I have explained in an informal talk on the radio and in press declarations, the word *latin* implies culture; clearly, we cannot seriously speak of Latin race or Latin blood. We are obviously talking about culture. When we talk about Latin people it implies people that share a Latin culture and that they are the tributary of Latin civilization. I think that's clear enough."[73] Most people in Quebec, whether strict federalists or autonomists, agreed with the basic tenets of this explanation; French Canadians were *latins* because they were part of a French-speaking nation rooted in an idea of Western Civilization that put Catholicism as its crowning achievement. Respectful cohabitation with Protestants was either desired or a reality to come to terms with, but complete amalgamation into a single mould was over-whelmingly rejected in Quebec. The crux of the federative pact relied on the maintenance for both cultural groups of a lively public sphere with international ties to a broader intellectual and spiritual family that could nurture their national distinctiveness. Latin America, and especially Mexico, could provide that for Quebec.

Throughout the congress, the presentations discussing Mexican national life shared a similar point of view: its cultural and intellectual achievements were undeniably admirable and represented an inspiration for French Canada. Maurault opened this discussion by noting that Mexico paved the way for Catholicism on the continent with the foundation of its first dioceses and university. Manolita del Vayo de Gallagher, for her part, made an enthusiastic presentation on the vitality of Hispano-American literature. She stated that the enlightening influence of France was preserved in this production and even enriched by authors such as Rubén Darío and Amado Nervo.[74] Finally, Lucille Lévesque-O'Leary – Dostaler's wife – read a paper written by Walter O'Leary on Mexican painting. She mentioned that the muralists "emancipated themselves from European and US influences to paint typically Mexican masterpieces."[75] These accomplishments were proof that another pathway to modernize French Canadian culture existed beyond the Anglo-Protestant model. Moreover, the Latin American example did not clash as much with traditional culture since it was rooted in the same Latin civilization that constituted the basis of French Canadian culture. Latin Americans were perhaps threatened as much by US hegemony as

francophones, but at least the strongest nations of the region pos-
sessed a sufficient degree of economic and political autonomy to
ensure their cultural and intellectual independence.[76] Various speakers argued that their national survival was secure despite these
troubled times, unlike the uncertain fate of French Canada.

Breaking the Glass Ceiling of Foreign Relations?

At the end of the congress, the U L A boasted a series of accomplishments and future projects that set the association apart in Canada in
terms of acquaintance with Latin America. Coverage of the event by
the French and English-speaking press conveyed this point.[77] It illustrated the enthusiasm for nurturing Latin affinities in Quebec and
the support in the province for closer links between Canada and the
Latin American republics.[78] The relative popularity of the U L A
strengthened their position; the membership had increased twofold
in the aftermath of the 1943 congress to over one thousand.[79] These
numbers made the U L A the largest of its kind in the country. The
Montreal francophone elite's penchant for the U L A's endeavours
gave a relative political weight to the association, enough to secure
its right to speak out and organize the first large scale exchange of
students between Canada and Mexico.

The popularity of Spanish and Portuguese classes offered by the
U L A attests to the desire among Montreal's petite-bourgeoisie to
learn more about Latin America.[80] But that was not the only
accomplishment the association took pride in. By 1943, the U L A
could claim they had arranged the distribution of publications
between Quebec and Latin America, put together art exhibits and
public lectures to broadcast their aspirations, and created welcoming committees to receive foreign diplomats in Montreal. Each of
these activities were covered by the media. The successful organization of two congresses attended by Quebec's foremost policy-
makers further gave legitimacy to the role played by the U L A. With
these achievements, the leaders of the association openly expressed
their intention to get the U L A involved in all fields of foreign relations: cultural, economic, and of course, political. But in the end,
despite the political coloration of many activities, the exciting
social life offered by U L A activities seemed to have been the most
important attraction for new members.

The glamour associated with U L A gatherings explained the success of many of their events. The organization of the first Latin American exhibit in Montreal in 1942 is a case in point. The display, put together by the U L A, consisted essentially of memorabilia coming from various Latin American countries presented along with basic facts, flags, and maps. By the organizers' own admission, this exhibit was modest at best. The annual report made clear that difficulties caused by the war regulations prevented the organization of a larger artistic display. Yet, the event was covered by Quebec's newspapers as the first of its kind in Canada and was officially inaugurated by the mayor of Montreal himself, Adhémar Raynault.[81] Descriptions of the U L A's balls support this point as well; this annual event attracted more systematic attention from the media. The Journées d'Amérique latine's report boasted that this event, inaugurated in 1942, brought "the French Canadian elite" together with "most members of Latin America's diplomatic corps."[82] A quick glance at the list of personalities attending published by a newspaper confirms this affirmation.[83] U L A events were generally well covered by the Montreal press because famous people occupied the centre stage. Dostaler O'Leary's connections with Quebec media certainly helped as well. Some members indeed thanked him for his public relations flair.[84] Still, the founding members of the U L A had larger aspirations than simply raising their glasses to Latin America once in a while. However, as many explained, not much more than these symbolic gestures could be accomplished in the context of the war. Once the conflict came to an end, many hoped, the U L A could then act on a series of projects.

During the closing meeting of the 1943 congress, presided by senator Mercier-Gouin, Yvette Baulu-Germain read a series of projects the U L A wanted to put in place "as soon as the war was over."[85] Topping this list was the organization of exchange programs for students and professors, as well as the creation of a university chair of Latin American studies in Montreal. In his presentation at the Journées d'Amérique latine, Daniel Johnson explained the crucial role students must play in this rapprochement. The future premier of Quebec stated that "students must carry the responsibility of creating for the French Canadian people relations beyond those imposed by geography and politics. A cultural union with Latin people will help French Canada to survive."[86] To provide logistical support, the

ULA also planned to organize excursions to Latin America. Baulu-Germain said: "The Canadian section intends to organize low-price trips to Latin America as soon as possible. It will also arrange official missions to meet with sister sections abroad and establish contact with officials from the political, economic, and intellectual world."[87] To publicize this endeavour and "create a current of sympathy," the ULA also proposed publishing a bulletin to keep members informed of the evolution of these projects.

The final scheme mentioned by Baulu-Germain concerned the creation of commercial delegations in Latin American countries to work with those supposedly envisioned by the province of Quebec. This last point concerning the international affirmation of the State of Quebec was a potentially contentious precedent for federal-provincial relations in Canada. The minister of Commerce in Adélard Godbout's government, Oscar Drouin, said in a speech during the congress that Quebec was planning to open commercial delegations in Latin America to give a new voice to the French Canadian nation: "The province of Quebec has distinctive national characteristics that need to be represented abroad. It is the Quebec government's duty to promote cultural and commercial linkages with Ibero-American countries. It is our intention to establish agencies in most South American countries after the end of the war. Funds will be allocated in the following budget towards relations with South America. We will establish agencies there like we did in New York, because we are convinced this is in the country's own interests."[88] To a large extent, this proposal was a blueprint for the 1960s Gérin-Lajoie doctrine.[89] During the Quiet Revolution, the Liberal government of Jean Lesage used this doctrine to act on demands made by the province to assert an independent voice internationally in its fields of constitutional jurisdiction. Judging from William Coleman's description of the emergence of this doctrine, Drouin's project constituted the earliest set of guidelines – a precedent not taken into consideration by the historiography.[90]

Oscar Drouin's speech at the Journées d'Amérique latine touched an emotional chord in Quebec. Discussions ensued on this subject in Quebec's public sphere. A journalist at Le Devoir, Roger Duhamel, commented on Drouin's "important speech" and wrote that a more comprehensive policy to frame French Canada's interactions with other nations was imperative: "Would it be the outline of a true prestigious policy that we always lacked? We hope so. For that to be the case, it would be important to consider the larger implications of this project, and that adequate and complete solutions must be provided. Therefore, why not consider an Office of National Propaganda in Quebec City?"[91] Could the government of Quebec take concrete action to foster French Canada's independent cultural voice on the world stage? Could the Québécois really stand for French culture in the Americas? To rally the francophone population behind the war effort (and compensate for the conscription crisis), Mackenzie King asked French Canadians to stand for their motherland, France, much like English Canada was acting for the British Empire in this time of crisis. However, it was clear from an Ottawa perspective that this substitution did not give Quebec an independent voice. In his article, Duhamel wrote that it was necessary for the province to design a plan of action: "*Je me souviens*, we read on our province's coat of arms. Well, memory is meaningless unless it becomes a motive for action, unless it triggers sweeping decisions."[92] Formal international representation could certainly not sidestep Canada's ambassadorial arrangements without giving more weight to the state of Quebec. To do this, the province needed to be ready to confront Ottawa on that matter.

CONCLUSION

Canada emerged from the Second World War with a new international personality.[93] From then on, diplomats presented the country as a middle power, a force that could be used to the advantage of international peace and stability. They argued that Canada, a country used to cultural compromise, could play a conciliatory role on the world scene. Interestingly enough, when the ULA leadership used similar language to express the purpose of their association, it provoked uneasiness at first. According to the ULA's logic, Quebec was supposed to be Canada's intermediary in Latin America, capitalizing on Latin affinities to establish cultural ties with the region. The ULA acted as a precursor in this scheme. I explained above why this logic proved to be paradoxical at times. The following chapter sheds light on this paradox using the case of the 1944 student exchange to show how the ULA's transnational project conflicted with Canada's ambiguous image abroad.

What can be said for now is that the Godbout government's project to enlarge the influence of the State of Quebec never directly materialized. Indeed, the Quebec Liberal Party lost the election in 1944 and did not return to power until 1960. The second Duplessis administration might have been ready to confront Ottawa on issues relating to provincial rights, but it refused to indebt Quebec's tax-payers by expanding the role of the state to foster a truly autono-mous foreign policy. Quebec's civil society remained the only sector representing French Canada in Latin America. Missionaries, clerics, and students acted as the first unofficial ambassadors of the French-speaking province, without comprehensive governmental support. This representation remained essentially symbolic. But even then, the symbolism associated with speaking out abroad as French Canadians stirred potential controversy in Canada. The ULA found this out rather quickly as their transnational project was neutralized in the direct aftermath of the war due to political controversy over national representation.

Michel de Certeau writes that there can be no long-lasting *prise de parole* without an effective *prise de pouvoir*. French Canadians were certainly not powerless in the 1940s, but the state in Quebec had not yet become the effective counter-weight to federal power it would turn into during the Quiet Revolution. Mobilizing latinity to support the international assertion of French Canadian identity could only produce limited results without an alteration in the bal-ance of power in the country. Yet, this chapter illustrates how the discourse articulated at ULA events crafted a safe space in Quebec to express independent views on Canada's foreign policy orienta-tions at a time when the war circumscribed this freedom. It also demonstrated how prominent French Canadians' interest in Latino culture enabled many of them to access diplomatic careers in Latin America, since a similar familiarity with the region's culture was lacking in English Canada. In retrospect, the direct political return for these actions remained meagre. For example, diplomatic appointments in Latin America were not the most prestigious, as the region remained a low priority for subsequent Canadian gov-ernments. In addition, the expression of Latin affinities lost part of its subversive resonance after the defeat of fascist Italy and the removal of Dostaler O'Leary from the ULA's presidency. Quebec nationalists could not expect to make significant symbolic gains using this structure of feeling without their province's strong back-ing. But it would be wrong to conclude that the struggle over Canada's foreign policy in Latin America was meaningless. On the contrary, the way federal authorities neutralized the U L A's transnational project for French Canada is instructive of the discomfort demands emanating from Quebec produced in Ottawa. This is revealing of a new dynamic emerging in the relations between French Canadian nationalism and federal authorities.

As a final point, the way the O'Leary brothers and their supporters worked in favour of links with Latin America and how Latin American diplomats wilfully embraced this scheme demonstrates how the affirmation of foreign affinities originated from very local concerns. How this connection was conceptualized as being "natural" further highlights how French Canadian identity was malleable enough to be symbolically redefined in a time of crisis. U L A spokespersons asserted that it was essential to recast French Canadian identity into a wider cultural space – *latinité* – to support its survival, isolated as it was in the midst of English-speaking North America. Reaching out to a larger transnational community promised to break this geopolitical isolation. The result offered an alternative to forced *américanisation*. For the U L A's leadership, Latin America represented the ideal complement to their national solitude; its bold cultural and political self-affirmation constituted a rejuvenating influence for French Canada. Ties with the region could perhaps support and legitimize the existence of this distinct North American society. The 1944 student exchange trip organized by the association – which sent 125 people to Mexico – constituted its proudest achievement toward fulfilling this rationale. At the same time, the controversy it generated represented the swan song of the politicization of Latin affinities. At least, until the Parti Québécois came to power in the 1970s.

The Poetics of Student Exchanges: Fighting the War's Homogenizing Consequences

In a defining scene of *Amar te duele* – a Mexican movie released in 2002 – an inflexible father threatens his daughter with a peculiar punishment in order to put an end to her relationship with a young man from a lower social class: if his daughter Renata refuses to break up with her boyfriend Ulises, she will be sent off to a private school in Canada![1] Renata refuses to comply, which sends the couple on the run in an attempt to escape their fate. Their love story meets its destiny when Renata's family and friends catch up with the pair before their departure from Mexico City. At the bus station, Renata's sister tries to convince her to stick to people of her social class, while her friend confronts Ulises. The altercation escalates and Renata's friend fires a shot at Ulises, accidentally killing her instead. The Mexican Juliet breathes her last breath in the arms of her boyfriend saying "I love you." The finale implies that risking death for love and ideals – by discarding paternal dictates and overstepping class confines – is preferable to being secluded in a foreign institution.

How did Canada enter Mexicans' imaginations as a kind of colonial-era cloister? No direct answer is to be found here. It is not the purpose of this chapter to deconstruct Canada as a lovers' Gulag, nor to scrutinize transnational love stories. This chapter rather tells the story of the symbolic role student exchanges acquired in Canada and Mexico when they were created in the 1940s. French Canadians used these exchanges to justify the affirmation of their national identity on the American political stage and to fight the war's homogenizing consequences. In Mexico, Catholic traditionalists (or militants) used academic linkages with Quebec as political capital in the symbolic struggle against secular modernizers. The image of Canada conveyed in *Amar te Duele* is a consequence of that political struggle sixty years earlier.

THE INTERSTICES OF POWER:
STUDENT EXCHANGES AS A METAPHOR

Contrary to what is depicted in the movie, the first student exchanges between Canada and Mexico were not merely private interactions; they were given national importance by their organizers.[2] The Canadian and Mexican media even described them as diplomatic accomplishments. Nevertheless, the decorum, fond memories, and enthusiasm accompanying the first exchanges of students are generally left out of diplomatic accounts of Canadian-Mexican relations. The stories about violent clashes at UNAM witnessed by Canadian students and the ensuing controversy are ignored as well. One reason for overlooking this may be that neither Canada nor Mexico had a long-lasting impact on the other's educational system. The symbolic importance of these academic encounters might be confined to the context of the war, but the dynamics of power relations they reveal are part of a wider process.

On the one hand, being located at the moment when Canadian-Mexican relations were made official, student exchanges represented gestures of goodwill between both countries. On the other, under this diplomatic façade these Second World War meetings meant something more important to the organizers of the travels. We can read into their aspirations an example of how foreign relations have a direct national impact on actors from civil society and vice-versa. More than a story of a short-lived project, this chapter clarifies the role played by actors from civil society in diplomatic undertakings. It also illustrates why governments either hesitated or were in fact interested in using these connections. To start with, this series of events is revealing of how the limits of the *modus vivendi* between the revolutionary State and the Catholic Church were tested in Mexico. It illustrates how Catholic and conservative groups stabilized their relationship with the revolutionary government. At the same time, it shows Ottawa's discomfort with the emerging French Canadian voice in international relations and the attempts by nationalist leaders to delineate French Canadian distinctiveness in North America by broadening the scope of foreign identity markers.

In this analysis (or poetics) of student exchanges between Canada
and Mexico, I am arguing that the main actors organizing academic
encounters attempted to use these events as a metaphor to articulate
their particular vision of national politics. By describing these episodes of collaboration as a metaphor, I am granting more weight to
the symbolic significance of the encounters than to their tangible
results. These transnational meetings served first and foremost a discursive purpose in themselves. They constituted an attempt to strike
a figurative balance of power between the groups organizing them
and the State, one they hoped would ultimately be reflected on the
political stage. The lack of official channels to organize contacts
between both countries enabled them to use those established by the
UCMCF/ULA between French Canadian nationalists and Mexican
conservative groups from UNAM. In this way, they could shape the
exchanges in their own image. But the political colouration given to
the exchanges by the organizers was disputed by their detractors.
The new language of pan-American collaboration was re-written
at the time to include Canada, and controlling its content became a
contested terrain for all stakeholders.

Consequently, this chapter traces the genealogy of academic connections between Canada and Mexico. These Second World War
encounters can be categorized as accidental in nature, and studying
them through this Foucauldian perspective will help us appreciate
the meanings embedded in them. The fact that academic linkages
came to have such an importance for French Canadian nationalists
and Mexican Catholic militants is surprising since both certainly
would have looked somewhere else for academic solidarity and support before the war. The war induced them, in some ways, to look at
each other. A collateral consequence of this accident was to force
these groups to respect war imperatives. This helped them dilute the
most controversial aspects of initial schemes of pan-Latin collaboration. In the end, it better legitimized attempts by French Canadian
nationalists and Mexican Catholic activists to craft an autonomous
space to voice their concerns in the public sphere.

Yet, the symbolic politics for which student exchanges stood
would have been impossible in Mexico before a tangible concilia-
tion had been drafted in the conflict opposing the revolutionary
State to Catholic groups. The Cristero War has been covered in previous chapters; there is no need to dwell on this episode at this
point. But it is necessary to review the ideological defence of traditionalist groups' right to speak out, since this part was mainly

articulated and violently fought for at UNAM, and it is vital to contextualize the intricate relation linking the Mexican State to UNAM before analyzing the exchanges as a metaphor.[3] This will explain why some conservative scholars who resolutely opposed socialist education in the 1930s had become founding members of the Unión Cultural México-Canadá Francés (UCMCF) by 1939 and came to promote academic links with Canada during the presidency of Manuel Ávila Camacho.

UNAM AS A BATTLEGROUND: FIGHTING TO PRESERVE CATHOLIC HUMANIST EDUCATION IN A POST-REVOLUTIONARY COUNTRY

The modern National University of Mexico (UNAM) was created as the Porfirian regime which supported its conception was about to crumble.[4] From its inception, the current secular version of the Catholic university founded in 1551 saw its fate intertwined with the Revolution.[5] Justo Sierra, the Secretary of Public Education during the last days of the Díaz dictatorship, let the institution be organized as a haven for independent thinking. A new generation of scholars used this latitude to favour teaching in the Catholic humanist tradition. This course of action was taken in order to counterbalance the excesses of austere Porfirian positivism; in turn, this had a huge impact on UNAM's evolution.[6]

The generation of scholars known as the Ateneo had a penchant for high culture that came to dominate UNAM when one of its members, José Vasconcelos, became rector of the University in 1920. The author of the *La raza cósmica* decidedly influenced the iconography of the Revolution when he was later named Secretary of Public Education under President Álvaro Obregón.[7] His patronage of the muralist movement was in accordance with the Ateneo's beliefs that Mexican culture should be celebrated like classical masterpieces. Still, his standing could not prevent secular reformers from challenging the intrinsic worth of the humanistic tradition's speculative nature and opposing its ascendancy over university education.[8] Strikes and protests soon rocked the institution and launched a pattern of student mobilization against the ideological tendencies of UNAM's administrators. Vasconcelos ultimately resigned from the rectorship and was also forced out of his post of Secretary of Public Education in 1924 as a result of his hostile relations with Mexico's new president, Plutarco Elías Calles.

Vasconcelos's ousting – and that of subsequent humanist adminis-trators – represented the first steps in U N A M 's decades-long standoff between secular reformers willing to impose the dogmas of revolu-tionary orthodoxy and traditionalists ready to die for academic free-dom and the right to educate pupils according to the Catholic humanist tradition. But before academic dissension could ignite a deeper crisis, the country was engulfed in a civil war. President Calles provoked the hostilities in 1926 by enacting the most anticlerical provisions of the 1917 Constitution in an attempt to eliminate the Catholic Church's sway over civil society. The Cristero War had a deep impact on schooling. On the one hand, the prohibition of Catholic elementary education mobilized peasants in Western Mexico in a bloody uprising against the State.[9] On the other hand, the gov-ernment recruited lay teachers as political organizers.[10] Educators became essential in mobilizing the population against the Cristeros and in inculcating the new revolutionary ethos to the masses.[11] Student activism was radically transformed by the conflict.

Producing Identities: Clashes over Mandatory Socialist Education

The main impact the Cristiada had on U N A M was the mobilization of Catholic and conservative students. At the outset of the civil war, these traditionalists formed the National Catholic Student Union (U N E C) with the help of the Society of Jesus.[12] U N E C provided logistical support to the counterrevolutionary struggle, and many of its members died during the conflict. Yet tensions only reached their apex on the grounds of the university at the end of the civil war when traditionalists supported Vasconcelos's 1929 presidential cam-paign. From then on, right-wing student activism was considered a thorn in the Revolution's side, a direct threat to the regime. When it became clear Vasconcelos lost because of blatant fraud, the "genera-tion of 1929" decided to preserve their right to speak out about their ideological leanings at all costs.

A short time after this political defeat, minor disagreements over administrative reforms had the university erupting in violent clashes. The first major strike in U N A M 's history was organized by U N E C, leading to deadly confrontations with Marxists.[13] To prevent desta-bilizing consequences for the government, the new president of Mexico, Emilio Portes Gil, decided to make a concession to the striking students. He decreed a limited autonomous status for

U N A M, loosening up state control over the university.[14] 1929 therefore saw two major decisions cooling down the stand-off: U N A M's semi-autonomous status and the agreement between the State and the Catholic Church to officially end the Cristiada. Yet the conflict over education lingered.

Barely two years after these agreements were signed, tensions arose once again when Narciso Bassols became Secretary of Public Education. The agenda adopted by the Secretaría de Educación Pública (S E P) became sharply radicalized. Conflicts over the nature of education instantly re-emerged on the national scene.[15] Calles's political party moved in the same direction shortly after and asserted that "scientific rational education based on the postulates of 'Mexican socialism' would be instituted" and should form the guiding principal of educational reform.[16] For Bassols and his colleagues, religion definitively constituted an "opiate" that needed to be purged from the educational system.

U N A M's limited autonomy did not shield the institution from the implications of this statement. Marxist students and scholars used Bassols's language to request a closer alignment of the university curriculum with revolutionary goals. This was especially true of the Confederación Nacional de Estudiantes (C N E) – U N A M's other major student union. The director of the Graduate Normal School, Vincente Lombardo Toledano, used the platform that the 1933 C N E congress provided to make an attack on non-conformist intellectuals rejecting revolutionary dogmas. The congress's closing statement was unequivocal: professors had a "historical responsibility" to work in favour of the advent of a "socialist society" in Mexico, starting with their classrooms at the university.[17] The intellectual defence of academic neutrality – and Catholic humanists' elitist conception of education – was articulated more eloquently by an original member of the Ateneo, Antonio Caso. The historian Enrique Krauze described this debate, which lasted for weeks in the country's newspapers, as the most important polemic in twentieth-century Mexico.[18] But it is the battle against leftists on campus that determined U N A M's orientation, and a sturdier conservative scholar, Rodulfo Brito Foucher, led the fight.[19]

When the conflict between pro and anti-Toledano supporters exploded, Brito Foucher – a descendant of French Canadians who migrated to Louisiana and then Mexico – was the outspokenly anti-Marxist director of U N A M's Law School at that time.[20] Brito

Foucher's ideas and positions followed a particular ideological and political trajectory in the first half of the twentieth century, one that was far from simplistic.[21] Yet, his actions in the 1930s against the governor of Tabasco, Tomás Garrido Canabal, and the positions he held as director of UNAM's Law School and later rector of the whole university identified him as a counterrevolutionary political actor. From the beginning, the positions he took at UNAM identified him as a reactionary. On 10 October 1933, right-wing students violently purged the Law School of radical leftists. Brito Foucher agreed with the traditionalist students' aggressive attack on CNE offices that day. In response, UNAM's administration relieved him of his duties. UNEC organized massive student demonstrations in his support and in reaction to socialist principles. The disturbances forced Toledano and the rector to resign. President Abelardo Rodríguez then declared UNAM's complete autonomy from the State for the same reason the limited status was granted four years earlier.[22] CNE's leftist radicalism was also neutralized for a time since UNEC imposed its control over student activism. Yet, despite these achievements by traditionalists, national politics continued to destabilize UNAM.

In July 1934, *Jefe Máximo* Calles poured oil on the fire when he called for renewed cultural hostilities.[23] He said in his famous *Grito de Guadalajara* that the Revolution was not over yet: "We cannot surrender the future of the Patria and the Revolution to the enemy. With what treachery the reactionaries and the clergy claim the children for the home and youth for the family. This is an egotistical doctrine, since children and youth belong to the community, the collectivity and the Revolution has the essential duty to attack this sector, appropriate consciences, destroy all those prejudices and form a new national soul."[24] Violence erupted throughout the country in what many historians have called the second wave of the Cristiada. At the end of 1934, Article 3 of the 1917 Constitution was reformed to establish that "education... will be socialist and in addition to excluding any religious doctrine, will combat fanaticism and prejudices, for which the school will... create in youth a rational and exact concept of the Universe and social life."[25] The aggressive defense of higher education's autonomy the previous year ensured that this constitutional amendment did not directly apply to UNAM. But the conflict still made the institution ungovernable.

The two rectors who governed UNAM following the 1933 crisis (Manuel Gómez Morín and Fernando Ocaranza) were conservatives who enjoyed substantial support in Catholic circles. They protected the status quo at UNAM, including the recognition of high school degrees from Catholic institutions, even though secular reformers tried to do away with such recognition. But soon after UNAM was granted full autonomy, traditionalists realized that it was a bittersweet achievement – autonomy guaranteed academic freedom, but not financial solvency. UNAM's budget was reduced by 75 per cent following the new status. Moreover, student mobilization remained at its peak during the period. This was the result of the unions' make-up. David Espinosa explains: "Claiming a national membership of 110,000 secondary, preparatory, and university students throughout Mexico, the CNE under UNEC's tutelage waged a countrywide campaign against... socialist education."[26] With pro and anti-Callista forces clashing in the streets of Mexico, UNAM remained unmanageable. In 1935, the assassination of Rodulfo Brito Foucher's brother, and the incarceration of Archbishop Pascual Díaz after he said religious persecution was worse than ever, provoked student activists. Violence resumed.[27] Before long UNAM's leadership, the Catholic hierarchy, and the new president of Mexico, Lázaro Cárdenas, all realized they had nothing to gain from a new war on religion. They worked together to find a solution that would enable them to save face while making the necessary concessions to achieve lasting peace.

Toward National Reconciliation: the Difficult Equilibrium between Appeasing Local Tensions and Upholding Pan-American Concord

The stand-off between UNAM and the revolutionary government was mainly resolved through highly symbolic cultural concessions on both sides. This paralleled the rapprochement made between the Cárdenas regime and the Catholic Church. Yet, violence was still employed to break up sporadic scuffles. For example, UNAM's administrators felt compelled to use force to distance the institution from the radical elements in its midst. Rector Luis Chico Goerne, a moderate Catholic, used the persistent fighting on campus to aggressively crack down on student rebelliousness by using shock troops known as *porras*.[28] Yet, overall, it was symbolic politics that helped to settle the dispute and stabilize relations with the revolutionary government.

To prevent a coup by far-right groups and the destabilizing consequences from radical anticlericalism, President Lázaro Cárdenas offered an olive branch to moderately dissenting groups.[29] Since Goerne showed goodwill by cracking down on extremists, Cárdenas reinstated the governmental stipend to UNAM in 1937. The following year, Goerne and traditionalists publicly backed Cárdenas's project to nationalize foreign oil companies. This essentially symbolic gesture sealed the reconciliation of UNAM with the State. The endorsement of the government's controversial move by the academic world and the Catholic hierarchy helped it re-establish crucial linkages with countries affected by the nationalization. It showed a US administration which had been critical of religious persecution that this bold economic move – albeit detrimental to their direct interests – nonetheless opened the way for peaceful social relations in Mexico at a crucial moment in history. As for UNAM intellectuals, the benefits were unequivocal. Peace had been achieved with the revolutionary State without sacrificing academic freedom. UNAM was confirmed as a haven for "free-thinkers" and remained one of the only "oppositionist centers to the national government."[30]

Mexican academia's foreign connections were essential to counterbalance secular reformers' influence on the revolutionary government. At the onset of the 1920s, humanist scholars under the impulse of rectors José Vasconcelos and Ezequiel Chávez had launched UNAM's Summer School. State-sponsored US-Mexican academic relations generally favoured the applied sciences, but the *Escuela de verano* had as a central project the establishment of better cultural understanding between nations.[31] The goal of the Summer School was to act as the principal intermediary linking Mexico to important social and political stakeholders from Europe, the US, and Canada. Their enterprise might have been affected at the height of the standoff between the State and traditionalist groups between 1926 and 1938, but UNAM's intellectuals nonetheless built a crucial network of support with North American institutions in the meantime.[32]

Public opinion in industrialized countries was principally antagonistic to the second wave of the Cristiada. We have seen above that French Canada was rather unanimous in condemning the attacks against Catholics at the time.[33] UNAM scholars and the

Mexican Catholic clergy's networks of support north of the border were authoritative, and this proved to be a decisive factor in their resistance to revolutionary orthodoxy and hegemony over the public sphere.[34] The Cárdenas government wanted to maintain ties with imperialist nations despite its readiness to confront them on critical issues. The government had always walked a fine line in its relation with neo-colonial powers.[35] Academic and cultural relations helped to diffuse tensions and maintain the precarious equilibrium between institutionalizing the Revolution and avoiding excessive antagonism.

The rebuff suffered by US oilmen in 1938 did not prevent a renewed emphasis on pan-American collaboration. Washington rapidly consented to the nationalization of petroleum since maintaining its access to Mexican reserves of crude became a crucial geopolitical concern after Hitler's invasion of Poland.[36] Good cultural relations became a critical wartime priority after Pearl Harbor.[37] Mexican scholars generally welcomed US initiatives, but right-wing traditionalists were sometimes uncomfortable, fearing their foreign connections could be unfavourably interpreted in the Mexican context. On the one hand, if their links with US institutions were valued by the State, their loyalty to the country could be publicly questioned in light of a Mexican nationalism that was staunchly anti-imperialist. On the other hand, the support of many Catholic militants and conservative scholars for Franco's troops during the Civil War in Spain simultaneously exposed them to accusations of fascist affinities.[38] The Second World War provided an opportunity to counter these perceptions.

Manuel Ávila Camacho's presidential campaign focused on national unity. To support this political direction he accelerated the gestures broadening the base of government to conservative and Catholic groups begun at the end of Cárdenas's rule. This tendency became a top priority of his administration. The first signal he sent to traditionalists was his public declaration of faith during the campaign, which drew approbation from the archbishop of Mexico City. Another unmistakable sign of opening was the appointment of Jaime Torres Bodet to the post of Secretary of Public Education. Torres Bodet was a well-respected conservative among the "generation of 1929" since he had acted as Vasconcelos's Under-Secretary during his tenure at SEP in the early 1920s.[39] The government's consensus politics even included collaboration with UNAM's new rector,

Rodulfo Brito Foucher. This political figure associated with the far-right took over the rectorship of the institution thanks to the backing of the clerical faction during the 1942 election. Gabriela Contreras mentions that right after his election, the new rector made a speech in which he celebrated Mexico's Hispanic heritage and underlined the affinities of Latin American countries, which are united by the "same races, the same language, and the same religion."[40] Brito Foucher even dared to say at his inaugural speech that "the most important post in Mexico after the Presidency of the Republic is the rectory of the University."[41] This political pronouncement was tempered by an opportune usage of the rhetoric of national unity and pan-American concord. The entry of the US and Mexico into the World conflict did indeed provide traditionalists with a perfect opportunity to re-position themselves on the scene of Mexican and inter-American affairs.

The 1943 Los Angeles zoot suit riots – which sparked denunciations of North American racism against Latinos throughout the continent – provides a good example of how traditionalists like Brito Foucher attempted to use the controversy to boost their political standing as mediators of pan-American concord.[42] At the time, Marxist students demonstrated in the streets of the capital to condemn collaboration with Uncle Sam. The new rector confronted the students and supported cooperation with the US, describing it as a moral duty. But while defending Roosevelt, Brito Foucher added: "the North-American public [must] realize that the people of Mexico, mostly of mixed Indian and Spanish blood, cannot fight in this war with enthusiasm on the same side as a country that harbors racial prejudice."[43] Traditionalists were quick to point out that in this fight against the evils of Nazism, the US had no monopoly on racial progressivism, quite the contrary. And if this war was a clash of civilizations, neither the US nor the Soviet Union had jumped into the fray at the outset. In fact, they could think of another example of an American country accomplishing its moral duty, a modern country where the Catholic faith still played a momentous role in society: Canada.

SECOND WORLD WAR CANADIAN-MEXICAN ACADEMIC RELATIONS

Leading traditionalist professors laid the foundations of an alternative model of north-south cooperation at UNAM, one that could diffuse some accusations of fascist leanings or imperialist bias. Early on, conservative scholars like Rodulfo Brito Foucher, Pablo Martínez del Río, and Fernando Ocaranza encouraged new connections with Canada. The francophone (and Catholic) part of the country was especially of interest to them since intellectual connections with its institutions of higher learning could nurture their humanist academic curriculum while proving the point that the Catholic Church could play a progressive role in society. Moreover, this country was undeniably modern.

As I have mentioned above, the association they helped to create for the organization of Canadian-Mexican academic relations saw the light of day in Mexico City in this particular context. The UCMCF positioned itself very clearly on the side of traditionalists at UNAM. After all, founding members listed in the previous chapter unmistakably exposed the right-wing affiliation of these individuals. The official letterhead of the association also made clear the humanist inclination of the group, since it incorporated "For the development of Greco-Latin culture in the Americas" as a motto.[44] As a sign of a new era of conciliatory politics between Mexican conservatives and the revolutionary State, this association did not draw much controversy. The UCMCF in Mexico City and the ULA, its sister organization in Montreal, played a crucial logistical role in setting up the first academic connections between the two countries.

The founding members of the UCMCF did not have to justify their connections with Canada the way ULA's leadership had to legitimize theirs with Mexico. This can be explained in part as a consequence of the meaning that relations with Canada acquired. On the one hand, the strength of the country's Catholic institutions provided an interesting alternative for Catholics in Mexico to compensate for the loss of similar connections with European establishments. On the other hand, Mexican officials saw diplomatic connections with Canada as an opportunity to repair the country's broken links with the British Empire and improve relations with Anglo North America in general. Finally, the province of Quebec became interesting for all francophiles in Mexico after the fall of France – conservatives and revolutionaries alike – since it became the only point of (re)production and distribution of French publications in the Americas.[45]

Canada was presented in Mexican media as the product of a unique dialectic between *North American* modernity and *European* traditionalism. This relationship encompassed intersecting and sometime contradictory undercurrents of identity (French, British,

North American, Catholic, and Protestant). In this manner, Canada could be presented as an example supporting the causes of various ideological groups, from capitalist liberalism to corporatist Catholicism. One cannot ascribe a unique meaning to how Mexicans understood Canadianess in the 1940s. This was meaningful in a country which was coming to terms with tolerating the coexistence of various political currents. In this context, relations with Canada could serve a symbolic function, one that assisted national reconciliation by letting dissenting actors from civil society organize Mexico's cultural underpinnings.

Furthermore, Canada was characterized as a model of peaceful social relations by various stakeholders. A newspaper from the capital presented this North American neighbour in these terms:

> The absence of civil wars has given rise among Canadians to a spirit of noble tolerance, under which two different civilizations live in harmony: the French and the English civilizations. This may seem illogical to such peoples that are suffering from intolerance and hatred and who will not understand that culture always reconciles all that uncultivated spirits consider antagonic [sic] and irreconcilable. In Spanish America it is thought that in order to be liberal it is necessary to be inimical to the Church; but Canada is showing us by her luminous example that it is possible to respect traditions and at the same time love Right and Liberty. Canadians are believers as far as religion is concerned, and advanced as regards institutions. The country is full of convents and churches; but its regime is [not] ecclesiastic.[46]

Some people would have begged to differ in Quebec at that time. Claude Racine explains that a growing number of Quebec novels expressed anticlerical ideas from the 1940s onward.[47] But Mexico was not the place to address this issue, especially considering that the strongest connections in the country were with Catholic groups. At the end of the day, the only transnational group lobbying for closer relations, the UCMCF/ULA, accepted this representation of French Canadian culture and presented, in turn, a Canadian appraisal of Mexican culture contrasting with some racist tones coming from the US. Thus, connections with Canadian institutions of higher learning were encouraged by the Mexican State, despite the fact that some people organizing them were considered disruptive.

The First Academic Connections during the Second World War

The organization of academic relations mirrored the various moti-vations behind the larger diplomatic rapprochement. To be sure, links with Canada were desirable for the humanistic orientation of its French-speaking institutions, but English-Canadian universities were interesting as well for their expertise in cutting-edge scientific fields.[48] Some officials in the capitals of both countries favoured these connections over the cultural ties organized by francophone Catholic universities and traditionalist scholars in Mexico.[49] Steps were indeed taken by civil servants to prioritize this propensity.[50] Nevertheless, the project of humanist scholars took precedence over this tendency during the war. With the help of the UCMCF, the ULA, and the Cercle Cervantes at Université Laval, Mexican institutions invited academics from Quebec Catholic universities to come to Mexico and vice versa. Rodulfo Brito Foucher and Richard Pattee exchanged letters in the early 1940s on the advantages of collaborat-ing with Université Laval after Pattee gave a talk in Quebec City in 1942. Pattee explained he was invited to Laval while he was teach-ing in Middlebury, Vermont. Visiting Quebec City and Université Laval "roused a particular sympathy" for the French Canadian cause, he explained.[51] He then petitioned Brito Foucher to send books to Quebec City to facilitate the teaching of Hispanic studies and Mexican history in that province. These are the individuals and the groups which, in the end, provided the logistics for arranging the first student missions.[52]

The idea to send students from Quebec to study in Mexico was facilitated by the new positive image the revolutionary country enjoyed in the French-speaking province. From the inception of the ULA in Montreal, Catholic intellectuals gave presentations at their gatherings on the state of affairs in Mexico. For example, the Jesuit Antonio Dragon – author of a popular biography of father Miguel Agustín Pro – gave a lecture on the evolution of the relations between the Catholic Church and the revolutionary state in Montreal in March 1941.[53] These talks helped to improve Mexico's image in Quebec. ULA events had repercussions even in rural Quebec since the press covered them. For instance, Georges Villeneuve, a pupil at a collège classique from the Saguenay Lac-St-Jean region who had read Father Pro's biography, wrote to Walter O'Leary three months after Dragon's presentation in Montreal. He shared with him his joy at hearing that "thanks to President Camacho, persecution draws to a close... We are interested in what is happening to our Catholic brothers in Mexico, and the fondness for this country is great in French Canada."[54]

Talks given at the 1943 Journées d'Amérique latine made it clear that student contacts between both countries would be mutually beneficial. In his presentation entitled "Collaboration entre étudiants latins dans Pax Romana," Daniel Johnson made a plea to promote these encounters to "create a favourable geopolitics for French Canada."[55] His call was first answered in Quebec City. The Cercle Cervantes at Université Laval, along with the UCMCF at UNAM, drew up the blueprint of the December 1943 trip of 25 students.[56] The students were formally invited by the rector of UNAM, Rodulfo Brito Foucher, and the director of the Summer School, Pablo Martínez del Río. This exchange also received crucial governmental support from Quebec and Mexico City. *Excelsior*, a prominent conservative newspaper from Mexico's capital, reported that: "It is the first time that the Tourism Office of the Government of French Canada [sic], in Quebec City, officially organized a mission of cultural rapprochement between the Latins of the North and the South. Thanks to the chief executives of tourism in Mexico, in collaboration with Mexico's Consul in Quebec City, *señor* Turcot, and the director of Quebec's Tourism Office, *monsieur* Hebert, this excursion was made possible."[57] Other high-profile personalities endorsed this trip: Mexico's consul-general in Montreal, Carlos Calderón, and the archbishops of Quebec and Mexico City, Jean-Marie Rodrigue Cardinal Villeneuve and Luis María Martínez y Rodriguez.[58]

This first academic exchange was apparently a success. Students perfected their Spanish, took history classes and also heard lectures on the social organization of Mexico.[59] Reactions in the newspapers were positive. The rectors of the universities seemed satisfied. The Mexican government also expressed its desire to continue down this road when the director of the Department of Social Affairs, Arturo Gacía Formentí, declared in Montreal a few weeks after the exchange that more substantial contingents of students would come both from Quebec and Mexico shortly.[60] The ULA used this example of a productive encounter to justify its academic enterprise to federal authorities in Canada. Reports coming from Mexico supported their point.

French Canadian associations like the Cercle Cervantes and the ULA achieved another important political objective with this trip:

publicizing their distinctive national character in Mexico. Crafting a space on the international political scene for French Canadians to speak out as French Canadians was certainly an objective of the O'Leary brothers when they founded their transnational association. The Université Laval students' trip provided them with a first opportunity to broadcast these goals to a national audience in Mexico. The article published in *Excelsior* on the Canadian students arriving in the country used this occasion to present the bicultural nature of Mexico's new diplomatic partner. Readers of the newspaper could learn in the article that "French is an official language all over Canada, along with English. The French Canadians form a nation of five million inhabitants. They are loyal to the king of England, because the monarchy protects their rights, guaranteeing the equal treatment of Canada's two great races."[61] Underlining abroad the existence and contribution of Canada's two main ethno-cultural groups and stating that French Canadians formed a nation was in line with Quebec nationalist discourse. International representation of Canada's bi-national character was an objective of the ULA that the UCMCF accomplished in Mexico. And they were especially skillful at doing so by using the media and the network of support provided by traditionalist scholars.[62]

The 1943 trip represents a good first example of the symbolic value academic relations could have. French Canadians and their Mexican sympathizers used these tangible academic connections to legitimize future projects. They helped each other achieve their particular national objectives along the way. Sometimes, perplexing depictions of identity resulted from the way they broadcast their agendas. This became clear during the 1944 mission of 125 Canadian students to Mexico. The diplomatic faux pas that were made then during the celebrations were in line with the pre-war subversive politics of their organizers. These misunderstandings helped them to test the limits of tolerance in Mexico City and Ottawa.

Organizing the 1944 Trip: A Concession to Political Outsiders?

The 1944 student trip was different from the one organized by Université Laval. In some ways, this trip constituted a sort of compromise between the "dissenting" actors who originally conceived the plan (French Canadian nationalists like the O'Leary brothers) and the federal government officials who gave their crucial blessing

to this more substantial project. The U L A was not officially regis-
tered as one of the direct organizers. Instead, a new group was
formed in Montreal, the Comité Canada-Mexico (C C M), to handle
the project. This was due to the make-up of the group going to
Mexico; students and dignitaries came from both Université de
Montréal and McGill University. Incorporating anglophones
reflected the demands of Canada's under-secretary of state for
External Affairs. This also seemed to make this project more palat-
able for Ambassador del Río Cañedo, who underlined the strong
presence of students from Montreal's English-speaking university in
Mexico City.[63] At first glance, the U L A's original objectives concerning this mission seemed to have been overtaken by the State. A closer
look suggests otherwise.

The direct connections between U L A's decision-makers and the
Comité Canada-Mexico were obvious. Three out of the six organiz-
ers were members of the U L A executive: Hector Boulay acted as
secretary-treasurer of the C C M, Armour Landry as press agent, and
Dostaler O'Leary as president. The two vice-presidents of the C C M,
Robina Henry and L. Philippe Moquin, represented the two universities involved.[64] The last member of the committee, who acted as
adviser, was Francisco de P. Rivera Torres, a representative of
Mexico's consulate in Montreal. Finally, the C C M also named Carlos
Calderón as its first honorary president. Calderón was replaced by
Ernesto Martínez Trejo when he took over as Mexican consul-general in Montreal.[65] Mixing U L A and non-U L A members, francophones and non-francophones, acted from the beginning as a firewall
against charges of French Canadian nationalist bias and increased
the group's manoeuvrability.

All the same, the C C M kept a safe distance from contentious
political issues. This was similar to the U L A's non-partisan
approach as far as provincial political party affiliation was concerned, accommodating the various ideological strains of its members. This allowed the C C M to receive complete support from
federal authorities. In return, the U L A was even publicly recognized for the crucial role it played in the C C M. The identity-based
language used at U L A events to explain Canada's rapprochement
with Latin America was employed publicly, even by a prominent
federal minister. With the litigious elements of the U L A apparently
neutralized, the participants in the mission could be presented by

Canadian and Mexican officials as informal ambassadors. This assigned role greatly increased the visibility and symbolic importance of the mission.

Media coverage of the group's departure at the train station in Montreal conveyed the symbolic importance given to this mission. An article from *Le Canada*, a Montreal newspaper, offers a good example of this point by naming all the personalities who made official speeches at the delegation's departure: "The Hon. Louis St-Laurent, minister of justice, the Hon. Oscar Drouin, provincial minister of municipal affairs, industry and commerce, Mgr Olivier Maurault, M Francisco del Río Cañedo, Mexican ambassador in Ottawa (who spoke in Spanish), the Hon. Mayor Adhémar Raynault, M Dostaler O'Leary and M Hector Boulay all made speeches broadcast by the C B C. [It was declared] that the authorities of this country are pleased by the Union des Latins d'Amérique's initiative."[66] A newsreel produced in French by the National Film Board of Canada underlined the "impressive ceremonies" surrounding the departure, along with the large number of people present at the station. But their coverage failed to mention the presence of students from McGill University.[67]

Nevertheless, the presence of students from both institutions was important for the diplomatic symbolism associated with the trip. Louis St-Laurent told the students before their departure for Mexico: "You are going on a journey; you are going on a mission... let the Mexicans know – if they are not already acquainted with this fact – that in our country, two races, two cultures and different religions live side by side... Tell them how much we are enthused by the establishment of these linkages... The Canadian government wishes you an excellent and productive trip; we are expecting a lot from your group."[68] Right after St-Laurent's declaration, Dostaler O'Leary used the opportunity to reinstate the "providential" role French Canadians could play in this new diplomatic relationship.[69] While this language would have caused controversy at the beginning of the decade, it appears that it satisfied everyone during the ceremonies. The apparent bridge built between the U L A and the Canadian State mobilized all forces in favour of a rapprochement with Mexico.

Echoes of the importance given to this trip in Canada were heard in the Mexican press.[70] This further encouraged the revolutionary State to collaborate closely with the traditionalists of the U C M C F and UNAM's administration. The 1944 student mission provides a good example of how Camacho's campaign of national unity worked on the ground. Representatives of the State and conservative stakeholders joined in their efforts to welcome with panache the elite of Montreal in Mexico City.

Travelling with Montreal's Elite:
The 1944 Delegation's Social Composition

Coverage of the event usually emphasized the standing of the delegation, mentioning that it was composed of "the cream" of Montreal society. This was also the point made by the Mexican ambassador in Canada in his correspondence with the government. Río Cañedo stated in one letter: "Very important people are coming with this group. Among them you will find the Mayor of Montreal (who is one of the most important labour union leaders in the country), newspapers' directors, the rectors of both universities, and other personalities of great social importance. I hope this excursion turns out as the best publicity in favour of our country in Canada, where there is so much interest in Mexico."[71] A quick glance at the group's social make-up backs up these claims. Indeed, the dignitaries who were part of the group were very influential individuals in Quebec. However, the composition of the student contingent, including its intellectual character, had the potential to stir controversy.

There is no doubt that those who went to Mexico were individuals of appreciable financial means – hence the focus on the "respectability" of the delegation. Each person's trip cost a few hundred dollars for transportation alone.[72] Lodging depended on the type of accommodation preferred, some desiring to reside at the posh Hotel Reforma for the two months of their stay.[73] Like the young Pierre Elliott Trudeau (future Prime Minister of Canada), who went to Mexico with the group, many members of the delegation came from upscale neighbourhoods in Montreal or cities like Outremont and Westmount.[74] Fourteen people were foreign students studying in Montreal.

Women constituted the overwhelming majority of the contingent, reaching up to 70 per cent of the participants.[75] This ratio parallels their participation in the ULA's Spanish classes.[76] This can partially be explained as a consequence of the war, since many men were overseas. It also may well be that Spanish lessons were first and foremost social activities and attracted a significant participation of women of the petite-bourgeoisie. Still, this illustrates how essentially conservative women widened the confines of domesticity to socialize with Montreal's *bonne société* while asserting a growing influence in cultural endeavours.[77]

The actual occupation and average age of members of the delegation might seem somewhat puzzling to outside observers. The average age of the women who went to Mexico was 24.7 years old, not surprising for an excursion of this kind. However, an important number of them did not list "student" as their occupation. Twelve were actually housekeepers (housewives) and nine were either secretaries or stenographers.[78] Of the 118 persons who declared an occupation, only fifty-five were students and six professors.[79] Almost half of the forty-one men were thirty years old or more. Most of them would be considered dignitaries. Only eighteen were students, including five minors, the youngest member of the delegation being fourteen years old.[80]

If these considerations raised eyebrows, it was not reflected in the welcoming ceremonies. As noted earlier, the symbolic weight of the delegation resided in the dignitaries travelling with the students. They were the ones who made public speeches covered by the press. Some festivities might have been organized to honour the *muchachas canadienses*, but it was the dignitaries, once again, who received decorations and official tributes.[81] This was particularly true for the rector of *Université de Montréal*, Olivier Maurault, and the president of the ULA, Dostaler O'Leary. What these two individuals represented seems to have struck a chord with the traditionalists who planned the ceremonies at UNAM.

Hidden Fire: Honouring the French Canadian Organizers in Mexico

The Mexican government collaborated fully with the UCMCF to welcome the Canadian students and dignitaries. Just before the arrival of the delegation, the Secretary of Public Education, Jaime Torres Bodet, wrote to Jesus Gonzales Gallo that the Mexican Commission of Intellectual Cooperation was organizing official activities for the visitors through SEP.[82] Of course, this also meant collaborating with the organizing committee for the festivities, which was composed of the UCMCF's executive. José Luis Martínez, a founding member of the U C M C F and Torres Bodet's Under-Secretary, acted as one of the three vice-presidents of this organizing committee in Mexico, further underlining governmental support and collaboration with the group.

Among the other personalities from U N A M on the committee were three professors: Manuel Alcalá as president and José Fuentes Mares and Jose Rojas Garciadueñas as vice-presidents. Students also participated: Felix Riojas was the secretary and Walter O'Leary, Braulio Peralta, Luis Weckmann Muñoz, and Michelle de Brabant performed various other functions. An honorary committee comprised of Rodulfo Brito Foucher, Pablo Martínez del Río, and Antonio Caso was added to the group for official functions.[83] These events were covered by U N A M's radio thanks to Weckmann Muñoz and by Radio-Canada as a result of de Brabant's work. With this composition, the committee organizing official receptions and activities for the group in Mexico mirrored the importance given to this trip in Montreal. It also shows the extent of the collaboration between governmental representatives and radical conservatives like Brito Foucher.

Mexico City newspapers covered the official program as well as aspects of the trip. The agenda included: official greetings at the Buenavista train station upon their arrival on 22 June; a banquet in Xochimilco offered by Mexico City's mayor, Javier Rojo Gómez, in honour of the mayor of Montreal; an official presentation of the delegation to Manuel Ávila Camacho and Jaime Torres Bodet; a reception at the Canadian embassy; and finally, a reception at the British Society to honour the rector of McGill University and another at the Nouvelle Librairie française of Mexico City for the rector of Université de Montréal.[84] Olivier Maurault also said mass at various churches, including one at the Basilica of Guadalupe.[85]

This enthusiasm surprised the Canadian government. The report on official activities prepared by Ambassador W.F.A. Turgeon mentioned that Mexican officials went to considerable trouble to entertain their French Canadian guests: "Señor Torres Bodet, the Minister of Public Instruction, invited them all to Cuernavaca, where they spent a day; Señor Maximino Ávila Camacho, the Minister of Communications and Public Works, gave them a week-end at Puebla; and Señor Miguel Alemán, the Government Secretary provided thirty of them, selected by themselves, with a visit of several days to Veracruz and to several intervening points. On all these occasions, the expenses were either paid by the Mexican Government or by the Minister who issued the invitation... and the cost to the students was nil."[86] Overall, the lavishness of the receptions dumbfounded the Canadian diplomats who had a hard time explaining to their US counterpart why Canadian students received all this attention, and why French was spoken so much.[87]

Notwithstanding governmental extravagance, the largest ceremonies were the semi-official ones held at UNAM. These celebrations and cultural activities were more meaningful to the original organizers because they enabled them to fully take centre stage. The fact that Mexican conservative leaders like Brito Foucher could rub shoulders with representatives of the Canadian clergy certainly helped them articulate an alternate reading of Canadian-Mexican diplomatic dealings. In these encounters, the French Canadian dignitaries could underline that their ethnocultural group represented Mexico's best ally in Canada, while Mexican conservatives could attempt to draw on the symbolic capital associated with their Catholic counterparts. Putting the French Canadians at the forefront of cultural activities celebrating the new diplomatic partnership enabled conservatives to indirectly identify themselves as the "natural" intermediaries of Canadian-Mexican affairs.

This process was expressed clearly two days after the arrival of the Canadian delegation in Mexico City. The Canadian and Mexican students were invited to UNAM's Bolívar theatre to celebrate St-Jean-Baptiste day.[88] The festivities organized by the Mexican institution to honour French Canada's national holiday deeply touched the francophone organizers of the mission. In his memoirs *Le Mexique de mes souvenirs*, Maurault remembered with nostalgia and deep affection that day: "the celebration of St-Jean-Baptiste Day, which began with a pious mass... ended in grand style at the Bolivar theatre."[89] In this room "overflowing with people," Maurault was glad to see that "much like in Canada, everything begins with speeches and ends with songs."[90] The cleric did not mention personally singing any song, but as the main guest of honour, he certainly gave a speech. In fact, the addresses of the rectors of Université de Montréal and UNAM were designed to be the political highpoint of the St-Jean-Baptist Day celebrations.

Maurault spoke directly after Brito Foucher's intervention on Canada's importance for Mexico. The Sulpician rector of Université de Montréal told his Mexican audience there were many similarities between the history of New France and New Spain. He recounted the difficult struggle French Canadians had to keep their faith and language alive after the conquest of New France by the British Empire. His own presence as guest of honour personified the success of this effort and expressed the strength of Catholic institutions in the province of Quebec. For this reason, Maurault said, although French Canadians are loyal to the king, "Pro-imperialist policies never won them over."[91] He then reiterated that the main architect of the Statute of Westminster – the statute granting Canada's full diplomatic independence – was a French Canadian, Ernest Lapointe.[92] His speech exposed the role played by the French-speaking Catholic minority of Canada in influencing the country to act as an autonomous nation in the Americas and in pulling this newly independent state away from neo-colonial attitudes. The audience was free to draw from Brito Foucher and Maurault's interventions their own parallels with Mexico and the role played there by Catholic militants.

French Canadians received other marks of respect at UNAM beyond the organization of St-Jean-Baptiste Day. A Montreal newspaper reported that the Catholic rector of Université de Montréal was given an official decoration from the Mexican institution, alongside the nationalist Dostaler O'Leary. French Canadians could read in *La Patrie* that they both received UNAM's highest distinction, the order of Aguila y Condor [Eagle and Condor], during a ceremony held at the Faculty of Philosophy and Letters and presided by its director, Julio Jiménez Rueda.[93] Renán Rodríguez Vado, the president of the student association, also directly participated in the academic tribute. Finally, the Society of Jesus celebrated Mgr Maurault at the same faculty.[94] These tributes by members of the Faculty clearly demonstrate how UNAM had become a haven for publicly expressing one's Catholic faith and conservative convictions during the rectorship of Brito Foucher. However, this would not last long.

The activities organized at UNAM were planned to demonstrate the positive role political outsiders could play in national and international affairs. This was apparently the point of the series of lectures on Canada organized by Julio Jiménez Rueda. This academic activity showed deference to the place of French Canada in the new bilateral relationship, since it put the rationale articulated at ULA gatherings centre-stage.[95] Olivier Maurault was supposed to give the first lecture of the series with a presentation entitled "The history of the French regime in Canada." The other five lectures all dealt, more or less, with aspects of the history of French Canada: the cleric Robert Llewellyn on "French survival in Canada"; Dostaler O'Leary on "The present situation of French culture in Canada"; Jean Nolin on the intellectual life and history of francophone Catholic universities in Canada; and Louis-Philippe Moquin and Jean Langlois on the history of Canada and its cultural and economic linkages with Mexico. Armour Landry was to close the series with Canadian movies.[96] The lectures were supposed to be held at the Faculty's Salón de Actos on six different evenings at 7:30 from August 1 to the 11. However, due to the violence at UNAM at the end of July, it remains unclear whether they were cancelled or not. One thing is certain, the commotion at UNAM made waves in Mexico City and Ottawa.

THE LIMITS OF TOLERANCE: REMOVING THE DRAMA FROM CANADIAN-MEXICAN RELATIONS

Although they might not have realized it right away, from the moment brutal force was used on 25 July 1944 and shots were fired against reformist students, the days were numbered not only for Rodulfo Brito Foucher but for Dostaler O'Leary as well. The time when these two individuals could use their positions of leadership (respectively as rector of UNAM and president of the ULA) to broadcast their particular political agendas was fast drawing to a close. They both had successfully pushed for broader federal acceptance of their political stances and imposed the symbolism of pan-Latin friendship on Canadian-Mexican relations, using the opportunities and uncertainties of a time when the new world order was in the balance. They did it by securing a consensus within their constituencies, one that warranted collaboration with governmental authorities. The cultural connections between the northern and southern part of the continent they helped to foster made them valuable people for a time. When all is said and done, the symbolism associated with their actions and militancy positively helped to test the limits of Canadian and Mexican tolerance of conservative and nationalist counter-hegemonic discourses. But by the end of the summer of 1944, their political capital was spent. They both had to step down from their functions, victims of the controversy created by the student revolt. But were they really responsible for the revolt? Did the symbolism associated with the Canadian trip have anything to do

with the fighting? What is certain is that the metaphor of Latin sympathy that had until then brought life to Canadian-Mexican academic
relations lost some of its shine.

Deadly Clashes: The Downfall of Rodulfo Brito Foucher

In all likelihood, the fast downfall of Brito Foucher and the belated
removal of O'Leary do not appear to be directly related. In any case,
no archival or published sources openly indicate that the honours
bestowed on the deeply Catholic and conservative French Canadian
guests played any role in sparking the crisis at UNAM. At most, the
symbolism associated with the decorations given to Maurault and
O'Leary played a supporting role in a drama that was decades in the
making. The left had been opposed to the conservatism Brito Foucher
represented since the early 1930s. Troubles were brewing on campus
since his election as rector in 1942.[97] The unabashed promotion of his
political connections made things worse. Left-wing groups had vowed
to overthrow him as soon as they could, since they feared that this
"devil felt he had the makings of a president."[98] Brito Foucher's relent-
less use of *porras* to curb his opponents' mobilization resulted in
resentment against his dictatorial approach. The July 1944 election of
the various faculty deans represented a perfect opportunity for the left
(and not only the far-left) to finally make a move against him.

Reformist student opposition coalesced in reaction to the election
of the very conservative Antonio Díaz Soto y Gama at the preparatory school, which they claimed Brito Foucher rigged.[99] The rector
offered to hold new elections but to no avail. On 17 July, student
factions clashed in the streets of the capital. The rector was blamed
for the escalation of the conflict. Strikes were then organized at
UNAM throughout the following weeks to denounce Brito Foucher's
domination of the institution. The rector used his customary shock
troops to win back control, which drew negative media attention.
On 25 June, the stand-off degenerated into open conflict. When the
striking students threw incendiary bombs in order to seize the law
school, Brito Foucher sent his "*pistoleros* to try to throw them
out."[100] Shots were fired by Brito Foucher's men, killing one student
and wounding dozens. An important number of UNAM scholars
then resigned in protest and appealed to the president. The rector
had no success trying to explain his position to President Camacho
and had to resign on 27 July to stop the violence.

Brito Foucher's use of excessive force against striking students was the reason for his ouster. Donald J. Mabry nonetheless offers a different reading: "It was Brito Foucher's conservatism and apparent political ambitions that necessitated his removal; his use of porras was a convenient excuse. The state would not allow him to use the university as his personal, conservative power base."[101] According to Mabry, Brito Foucher had become a nuisance to the governing Party of the Mexican Revolution not to mention presidential hopefuls for the upcoming 1946 election such as Maximino Ávila Camacho and Miguel Alemán. After the rector stepped down, in an extraordinary move the president directly intervened in the affairs of UNAM to force a new status on the institution, one which "returned the university to its pre-1929 relationship to the State as an agency of the national government."[102]

The reformed statute of UNAM did not signify the end of symbolic concessions to traditionalist lobbies – actually the reform of article 3 of the constitution the following year (scrapping socialist education) represented one of the most important concessions of his administration to Catholic militants. However, if individuals wanted to claim political capital with these symbolic concessions, the State would intervene. Neither were they supposed to encourage the creation of spaces completely beyond the reach of the State.[103] Many concessions were tentative at first in order to gauge their repercussions. Camacho's administration was lenient with the right during the Second World War, but only as long as traditionalists did not provoke a re-mobilization of Callista-style anticlericalism that would have destabilized the government and threatened its grip on power.

The French Canadian dignitaries who experienced the political upheavals first hand had a completely different understanding of what actually happened at UNAM in July 1944. No mention was made of Brito Foucher's brutal repression of opponents. For Maurault, left-wing subversive forces were behind the shocking attacks on Brito Foucher. The rector of Université de Montréal said that the Canadian delegation became conscious of the genuine threat posed by Communism. He commented: "We were appalled by certain occurrences as much as we were filled with admiration for the celebrations in our honour at the Bolivar theatre on June 24... In the same theatre, a few weeks later, while the Canadian and American students were there, a communist group caused a real panic when

they threw firecrackers in the crowds yelling like madmen. Our students evacuated the room... The same agitators burned cars parked
at the Zocalo (right beside the Plaza of the Constitution), threw
rocks in the crowd, wounded the rector's secretary, and killed a student in veterinary medicine. Gunshots were also heard. The rector
gave his resignation in order to calm the situation."[104] This reading
of the situation mirrors the anti-communist propaganda of the
1930s in Quebec: left-wing forces are the only ones to blame.[105]
Notwithstanding Maurault's obvious bias in favour of Brito Foucher,
it is worth mentioning that his presentation of the situation reflects
an overriding trend in Camacho's Mexico: the Catholic Church and
the revolutionary government used conservative nationalism to
unite the nation. What the Sulpician rector seems to have failed to
understand – or perhaps understood too well – is that the exacerbated anti-communism Brito Foucher embodied could also become
a liability. A new anti-communist nationalist discourse emerged during the war as the ideological upshot of closer pan-American collaboration. But this ideology represented a double-edged sword for
people with counterrevolutionary leanings. Embracing this discourse
to win the governing authorities' favour necessitated cautious symbolic gestures of goodwill, not threatening political statements. Soon
after Brito Foucher stepped down, Maurault also had to defend himself against his protection of people seen as subversives in the
Canadian delegation. However, these accusations did not come from
Mexican authorities, but from the Canadian Department of External
Affairs, which kept a close eye on the group's endeavours.

Mgr Olivier Maurault's "Subversive" Peregrinations

The violence at UNAM in late July sparked frenzy among Canadians
back home interested in knowing what was really happening on the
1944 student trip. The sudden resignation of Rodulfo Brito Foucher,
the person who invited the Canadians to Mexico in the first place,
stirred controversy over the purpose of the mission and its organizers' genuineness. These doubts about the trip had repercussions in
Canada in August. One report noted the Canadian stakeholders'
apprehensions: "there is already a storm brewing as a result of
Dostaler O'Leary's visit to Mexico with a body of Montreal students."[106] The father of one student, Charles-Aimé Kirkland, Liberal
MP at the Quebec Legislature, made "energetic protests" to the

Mexican consul in Montreal and demanded that his daughter be immediately repatriated, threatening to raise the issue at the next parliamentary session.[107] Tensions at UNAM deeply affected the academic outcome of the trip. Maurault said: "One of our students told me that when the riot started disturbing the peace at UNAM, they realised that there are other things to do in Mexico besides attending Spanish classes."[108] Despite all the uncertainty in late July and early August, the courses planned for the Canadian students were not cancelled. The very low turnout at student activities in the aftermath of Brito Foucher's resignation apparently acted as a confirmation in the minds of diplomats of the suspicion they had all along: the "mission" was a foil for covert intentions, subversive goals Dostaler O'Leary (president of the group) embodied. After all, some suggested, the composition of the group gave the impression of a tourist undertaking, while the reaction to the diplomatic faux pas by students close to the O'Learys revealed a French-Canadian nationalist bias that put into question the organizers' good will to represent Canada.[109]

In the weeks leading to the violence, minor diplomatic incidents related to the singing of national anthems prompted this suspicion. In fact, it all started at the St-Jean-Baptiste day ceremonies where the Mexicans played "La Marseillaise" and "Ô Canada," thinking these were the *Canadiens'* national anthems. Reports were made to External Affairs, since this episode received press coverage in Mexico. Ambassador Turgeon wrote to the secretary of External Affairs: "I read a report of the affair in 'Ultimas Noticias' under the heading 'Canadian students weep on hearing their national anthems played in Mexico'; and then the report went on to tell that these 'national anthems' which caused the tears to flow were *Ô Canada* and *La Marseillaise*.[110] The newspaper failed to mention that Canada's official anthem was neither of these, but rather "God Save the King." These incidents kept repeating themselves during the trip to the dismay of Canadian diplomats.

Contrary to External Affairs, Maurault interpreted these incidents light-heartedly. In an ironic twist of history (or simply as a desperate attempt to defend his collaboration with the O'Leary brothers), it was the Sulpician rector of Université de Montréal who defended the singing of "La Marseillaise," an anthem still considered controversial in Catholic Quebec. He commented: "Our group Canada-Mexico was mostly formed of French Canadians. When the Mexicans

heard that we were speaking French, they thought that 'La
Marseillaise was our national anthem; actually, that was convenient
to believe considering that they are not familiar with the hymns 'Ô
Canada' and 'God Save the King.' Now, as a goodwill mission, our
student delegation had a semi-official status; we were always accompanied by two very helpful Mexican consuls, and sometimes by the
Canadian ambassador or our chargé d'affaires (who had to show up
at governmental happenings or public celebrations). Did a malicious
spirit mislead Mexican fanfares and orchestras to play 'La
Marseillaise' when we showed up? Anyway, each time it happened,
the consular and plenipotentiary corps panicked."[111] As far as
Canadian diplomacy was concerned, this mischievous mind had a
name: O'Leary. The two brothers were blamed for acting in concert
in order to mislead Mexican officials.[112] It may well be true that the
O'Leary brothers provided inaccurate information to their Mexican
sympathizers to make sure the diplomatic blunders would be recurring.[113] That would have been in line with their pre-war politicking.
Yet, the president of the ULA was careful to avoid making contentious statements throughout the war, so much so that his public declarations were supported by a wide array of highly regarded
individuals with significant political leverage in French Canada.
Nevertheless, he always found a way to irritate his detractors by his
pronouncements on the place of French Canadians in a country still
frequently called the Dominion of Canada. At the end of the day, it
seems that what was really at stake beyond personal aversion to
O'Leary's politics was the image of Canada conveyed abroad. Many
anglophones were still very uneasy with presenting an image of the
country that contrasted with traditional British symbolism. Suffice it
to say it was only in 1965 that the Canadian flag was adopted, in
1969 that French and English were both formally declared the official languages of the country, and in 1980 that "O Canada" became
the national anthem. The French Canadian organizers of the
exchanges had been pushing all along to have a different image of
the country presented abroad, one that would proudly illustrate
Canada's bicultural nature.

According to Maurault, the legitimate pride felt by the organizers
in their French heritage was unjustly maligned because the Canadian
authorities exaggerated the diplomatic gaffes in light of the chaos
prevailing at UNAM. "From this moment, a deep suspicion surrounded our endeavour: we were, obviously, dangerous nationalists.

They threatened to send reports to Ottawa, etc., etc.... It seems that our Canadian representatives received a specific protocol from Ottawa prescribing them to play 'God Save the King' first, and then, if they really care, *Ô Canada*. That's the way the Statute of Westminster is understood in our chancelleries."[114] As a result of this suspicion, the mission came under tighter scrutiny. State representatives made sure that diplomatic etiquette was respected and that Canada's true national anthem received the respect it deserved. The French Canadian organizers had no objections to respecting this diplomatic protocol but were outraged by restrictions imposed on communications in French and demanded that their language be considered on an equal footing with English.[115] Indeed, international communications in French by phone or telegraph were forbidden after the incidents. And yet the group had received the assurance from federal authorities that such communications would be allowed, thanks to pressures exerted by the Mexican Consul in Montreal, Carlos Calderón.[116]

This acquaintance with Mexican diplomats had previously enabled French Canadian nationalists to organize the first cultural connections between Canada and Mexico. The controversies surrounding the 1944 summer trip destroyed the ULA's political capital. To start with, the federal authorities made clear they would not collaborate with this organization again as long as Dostaler O'Leary remained president. Mgr Maurault's defence of his "subversive" friend was of no avail.[117] As Hector Boulay confided in a secret report to Hugh Keenleyside, O'Leary resigned from the ULA's presidency shortly after "as a consequence of the handling of the trip."[118] The diminished political leverage was also partially attributable to the loss of credibility of their Mexican allies. Indeed, Canadian officials covertly blamed Mexican diplomacy and UNAM's inflammatory political climate for the disillusionment associated with this mission of goodwill. For example, Norman A. Robertson wrote to Louis St-Laurent at the end of August to inform him the "mission" he had bid *bon voyage* to was an utter failure as a result of the O'Leary brothers and their Mexican acolytes: "I should perhaps add that this Department was dubious of the venture, but had no information concerning it until practically all the arrangements had been completed. While it is unfortunate that the Mexican Government should have taken this visit at a high rating and as a consequence extended over-lavish hospitality, I feel that a considerable portion of the blame rests with the Mexican Consul General in Montreal who also made no effort to consult our department about the visit."[119] The metaphorical meaning given to student exchanges by actors from civil society had lost its direct political resonance with the governing authorities.

Interestingly enough, this controversy did not find its way into the media. Press coverage of the trip in Quebec was laudatory and the mission was described as a success. Proposals of marriage were even said to have been made.[120] The organizers gave many interviews, including one by Dostaler O'Leary who told a Radio-Canada host that he was impressed with modern Mexico and that this trip confirmed his belief that French Canadians had found true "spiritual brothers" south of the Rio Grande.[121] The only public glimpse into the underlying conflict came with the publication of *Le Mexique de mes souvenirs* the following year. In the last sentence of his account, Maurault used irony against federal authorities. He stated that he thought the masses gathered at the Montreal train station were there to greet the returning delegation, only to find out that it was "to cheer M Camilien Houde who was coming back from vacation."[122]

Private Catholic Visits: A Depoliticized U L A Receives Mexican Students in Montreal

The reference Maurault made to Montreal's quintessentially populist politician could not hide the fact that U L A endeavours gradually slid down into political irrelevance. To be sure, various cultural activities were still covered in the media. Membership even sharply increased in the aftermath of the trip, reaching close to two thousands members by the end of the decade.[123] But never again would the association organize cultural trips to Mexico that would have the aura of a semi-official diplomatic mission. Never again would their events be used to highlight their stand on the future of the French Canadian nation. To cut the ground from under their feet, Ottawa even ignored work permit requests from Université de Montréal for lecturers invited to Latin American universities.[124] The interest nationalist circles had in promoting Quebec's *latinité* abroad slowly but surely dwindled. Positioning of the French Canadian nation on the scene of pan-American affairs seemed to have lost its use for Quebec's political class altogether until the Gérin-Lajoie doctrine was instated more than two decades later.[125]

In the aftermath of the controversy with Ottawa, the U L A's new president declared that his association would henceforth keep a safe distance from contentious political questions.[126] The weekly *L'Autorité*, a staunch opponent of French-Canadian clerico-nationalism, expressed its satisfaction with O'Leary's departure and was glad to note that the U L A had distanced itself from "all those explosions of sentimentalism so frequent in Quebec."[127] Sentimentalism and *joie de vivre* did not completely fade away from U L A happenings. After all, their opponents continued to dub them the "*Lapins d'Amérique*," a moniker belittling their gatherings as shallow and promiscuous.[128] Yet, the drama generated by letting a controversial political figure give meaning to expressions of Latin affinities was indeed neutralized. The likes of Dostaler O'Leary lost their privileged standing as principal spokespersons of the association. In this sense, the U L A stopped stirring nationalist passions by lobbying for a transnational rapprochement among Latin people. But it would be false to assert that French Canadian-Mexican relations lost all relevance in the aftermath of the 1944 student trip. After all, the student exchanges between Quebec's Catholic institutions and U N A M continued.

Although these connections could no longer be used by French Canadian nationalists or Mexican traditionalists to gain direct political leverage, they still had a real social value – at least from a Mexican viewpoint. Relations between Catholics in Mexico and confessional institutions in French Canada did not decline... on the contrary. Rodulfo Brito Foucher was invited to speak at Université de Montréal barely three months after his ouster from U N A M.[129] He was even given an honorary degree from Université Laval during this trip, although the Mexican ambassador was uncomfortable with this and refused to attend the ceremony.[130] Mgr Cyrille Gagnon, the rector of Université Laval, specifically mentioned during his address honouring Brito Foucher that he played a crucial role in the foundation of the first Catholic Universities in Mexico since 1867.[131] He continued his homage saying: "I want to congratulate him for his noble attitude, in 1924, when he decided to combat the antichristian revolutionary movement that led to the election of the sinister president Calles, the author of the bloody persecution the Mexican Catholic Church endured from 1924 to 1935. [Rodulfo Brito Foucher] also organized a movement [that ultimately] overthrew the dictator from the state of Tabasco, Tomás Garrido Canabal, the most cruel persecutor of the Catholic religion."[132] The ambassador was tipped about the nature of the tribute in advance and decided not to attend because President Calles and Governor Garrido Canabal would be disrespected. He later explained his concerns in a letter to the President: "I discussed over the phone the incident at Laval University with our Consul General in Montreal. [I told him] to refrain from attending an event organized by the Catholic or the separatist element of the Province of Quebec paying any tribute to Mr Brito Foucher while he is visiting Montreal to avoid misinterpretations, as these tributes from members of the Union Nationale or the members of Catholic groups seem to follow a plan, determined in accordance with similar groups in our country."[133] Apart from this comment, the Mexican government did not apparently object to these Catholic encounters in Canada. Mexican officials replied to Canadian diplomats after some of them were blamed in veiled terms for the uneasiness generated by the 1944 mission, saying that they wished they had received a contingent with better academic credentials.[134] Nevertheless, this did not prevent UNAM from welcoming at least three other groups of students from Université de Montréal and Université Laval in the next couple of years with governmental blessing.[135] The Camacho administration also formally invited the Université de Montréal to participate in the 1946 Mexico City Book Exhibit.[136] So despite Ottawa's discomfort with these connections (and the discomfort of Ambassador del Río Cañedo), the Mexican government continued to encourage them.

Mexicans also started to study in Montreal. Two student missions were planned for 1945 to visit Université de Montreal.[137] These trips were sponsored by UNAM and planned by the UCMCF, with Renán Rodríguez Vado as president of the mission. A memorandum from the association also specified that the official committee was formed by "students and young women from the best families of the capital."[138] The Mexican government supported these transnational Catholic encounters because they acted as a safety-valve for middle-class dissatisfaction back home, in this case discontent concerning religious restrictions. In a country where Catholic education was still officially shunned, transnational connections worked, to a large extent, as a symbolic concession to the Catholic right. Moreover, they enabled some politicians of the governing party of this secular nation to covertly give some sort of religious education to their children while preserving their revolutionary credentials. For this reason the U C M C F was quoted in a Mexican newspaper as saying: "French Canadian-Mexican relations... serve pan-American peace and [are] a factor of constitutional harmony."[139] President Miguel Alemán seemingly did not disagree: his daughter Beatriz apparently later studied incognito in a Catholic school in Montreal![140]

The first contingent of Mexican students to visit Montreal during the winter of 1945 provided a good example of the dynamics that came to characterize Canadian-Mexican academic relations. This group – composed mostly of young women – was received with as much excitement as the Canadian students had been in Mexico six months before, without the fanfare associated with diplomatic representation. A variety of courses were planned for them mostly in French, but also in English.[141] Beyond classes dedicated to perfecting their knowledge of these two languages, they also received courses in French, English, and Canadian literature. History was not neglected; the Mexican students were given classes on the history of Canada by Guy Frégault and the history of Catholic missionaries by the cleric Guillaume de Vaumas.[142] These courses were all given in the pious surroundings of Université de Montréal, an institution sharply contrasting with U N A M since religious personnel taught in religious garb.

Cultural activities were planned as well. Students did some sightseeing of the province, visited its important institutions, and, without a doubt, went to its most famous places of worship. They were shown Canadian movies and introduced to French-Canadian folklore. Hockey was not overlooked, and the students were invited to watch Maurice "Rocket" Richard and *Les Canadiens*. Notwithstanding the charm of the old Forum, the high-point of this list of educational undertakings was the ball organized by the U L A.[143] Nearly 300 people from Montreal's *bonne société* participated in the event where the Mexican *niñas bien* were guests of honour.[144] Although the invitation stipulated that the Mexican girls "should not be accompanied" since they would be presented to "young Canadian" partners, we do not know if any romance resulted from these encounters.[145] What is certain is that the assertive political overtones that had accompanied such fashionable gatherings were now absent. French Canadian nationalists and Mexican traditionalists could still use these connections to support each other's culture, but without making waves. Transnational kindred interests had to respect the national status quo.

CONCLUSION

This chapter has explored the use and misuse of symbolic politics in the context of the first Canadian-Mexican diplomatic dealings. With the Second World War raging, cultural activities were used to create better understanding between allied nations and facilitate political ties. Overall, I have shown how transnational academic contacts between Canada and Mexico were given symbolic meaning by their organizers, contacts that helped them negotiate their relationship with the State. At the same time, I provided examples of how federal authorities attempted to capitalize on these transnational relations. The 1944 student mission saw this logic pushed to its limits: the Mexican and Canadian States both intervened – each for different reasons – to remain in control of the situation and avert political outflanking.

I have shown, first, how symbolic political gestures of mutual respect played a crucial role in appeasing the decades-long conflict opposing U N A M's traditionalists to the revolutionary government. This symbolic rapprochement was made possible because U N A M's academics had previously created crucial networks of support north of the border that enabled them to resist the ebbs and flows of religious violence in the late 1920s and 1930s. In turn, when the Second World War imposed pan-American concord, they found themselves in a privileged position to act as go-betweens in the realm of cultural relations, connecting Mexico and its North American diplomatic partners through educational undertakings like the Summer School. This was especially true in the case of early relations with Canada. Various influential traditionalists founded the U F M C F at the beginning of the war. This association provided the logistics on the Mexican side for organizing student exchanges with Canada while infusing meaning into this transnational relationship. The Camacho administration found this undertaking mutually beneficial since it facilitated the establishment of diplomatic contacts with a reluctant diplomatic partner while contributing to the campaign of national unity in Mexico.

French Canadian nationalists jumped at the opportunity to collaborate with the Mexicans. The fall of France had persuaded them to look toward Latin America to defend their precarious political position on a continent at war. They occupied the political terrain of cultural relations, positioning themselves when the time was ripe for

Canada to organize missions of goodwill with Mexico. They tried to use this project to counterbalance the homogenizing consequences of the war effort. They did this by broadcasting their vision of the country abroad, attempting to secure cultural alliances that could be used as political leverage back home.

The image of the country they presented contrasted with traditional representations since it put francophone and anglophone cultures on equal footing, therefore rejecting narrow British symbolism. Canadian diplomats were uncomfortable with this representation, as was the Anglo majority. What made things worse for the French Canadians who wished to promote these ideas in Mexico is that one of their spokespeople, Dostaler O'Leary, was previously associated with Quebec far-right separatist groups. Canadian authorities obviously had very legitimate reasons to be concerned with the influence he exerted over Canadian-Mexican relations. The turmoil caused by Rodulfo Brito Foucher's sudden ouster exaggerated the importance of minor diplomatic problems, and the O'Leary brothers were blamed for these faux pas. In hindsight, the accusations of subversive behaviour concerning the singing of "La Marseillaise" and "Ô Canada" seem farcical, but Canadian authorities nonetheless used them together with the confusion at UNAM to successfully demand O'Leary's resignation from the presidency of the ULA. This course of action prevented the ULA's spokespersons from using transnational relations with Mexico to discuss the French Canadian nation's future.

As long as it benefitted its internal and external objectives, the Mexican government had no such reservations regarding the Quebec-Mexico-Canada triangular relation. The controversy surrounding Rodulfo Brito Foucher's resignation did not directly concern the Canadian group in Mexico, although the way the rector acted with the French Canadian dignitaries might have reinforced the perception among his opponents that he truly felt he had the makings of a presidential candidate. Nevertheless, the Mexican government's continued support of academic relations with French Canada demonstrates that the real problem did not concern the symbolism associated with establishing close cultural ties with this deeply Catholic society. These relations could even be useful to appease some social dissatisfaction in Mexico. The rector's demise, therefore, was the result of his own making. Proclaiming one's conservative convictions – and mildly antagonizing the left along the way – was not so much a problem in Camacho's Mexico as was striving for effective political control and destabilizing the *modus vivendi*. Brito Foucher overstepped the line of "national unity" by acting as a presidential hopeful and provoking a mobilization of secular reformists. With time, the traditionalist forces that supported him at first came to see his rectorship as a failure. His aspirations nonetheless effectively tested the limits of the *modus vivendi* in Mexico – to his personal loss. The Church certainly learned from experiences like these and began to more effectively frame its pressures for a larger presence in Mexico's public sphere. The following chapter on the 1945 public celebrations of the golden jubilee of the Virgin of Guadalupe's crowning sheds light on this process of covert negotiation between Catholic groups and the revolutionary State.

5

The Virgin and the Cardinal: Symbolic Politics in Manuel Ávila Camacho's Mexico

The 1917 Constitution imposed harsh limits on the Catholic Church in Mexico. The purpose was obvious: curbing its social and economic power. The anticlericalism of the Revolution's victorious faction motivated this stance. Catholic support of Victoriano Huerta's counterrevolutionary government in 1914 also prompted this course of action. The anticlerical development of the Mexican Revolution seriously antagonized ecclesiastical authorities. The new political elite wanted to put Mexico's public sphere under hegemonic state control, and this ambition provoked intense resentment in Catholic circles. The anticlerical articles written in the nation's foundational document – and the victor's desire to exert absolute control over the country by restoring the intent of the 1857 Constitution – put the Mexican State on a collision course with the Catholic Church. The dispute over effective control of the political process slowly shifted toward a cultural war over the place of religion in society. Catholic symbolism became a contested terrain since its most potent representation, the Virgin of Guadalupe, was at the junction of religious and nationalist sentiments.

Of course, the place of religion had been a contentious issue in Mexican politics since the middle of the nineteenth century, when liberal decision-makers enacted the first laws to secularize the country. Catholic reaction against these laws caused civil war and foreign intervention. This clash of ideas was amplified during the Revolution and lingered on until the beginning of the Second World War. The hostility was hard to overcome because, "in revolutionary eyes, the Catholic church was an antinational force, in thrall to the Vatican, hostile to the new regime and its reformist program, allied to conservative vested interests, and supportive of superstition and backwardness."[1] For Catholic militants, this hostility reached an emblematic peak on 14 November 1921, the day when the Revolution attempted to "kill" the Virgin of Guadalupe. The explosion of a bomb in the Basilica on Mount Tepeyac was seen as a deliberate attempt to destroy the holy representation of the Virgin displayed there on Juan Diego's mantle; believers reacted with dismay upon learning that the bomb attack was organized by a member of the president's staff.[2] What the Revolution had failed to co-opt, it sought to destroy. Episodes like this gave the impression that no middle ground could be found. On one hand, Catholic militants refused to recognize the legitimacy of the Revolution; on the other, religious activists aggressively objected to revolutionary appropriation of Catholic imagery. Symbolic violence – on both sides – remained a serious motive for bloodshed for years to come.

The conflict opposing anticlerical factions to Catholic counter-revolutionaries left the country in turmoil for the next two decades. This lingering tension constituted the most important factor destabilizing Mexico until the Second World War. Contrary to agrarian revolt, working-class rebellion, or military uprising, religious discontent could not be silenced by the guns of government. The outcomes of the 1926–1929 Cristero War and the anticlerical campaigns of the 1930s demonstrate this point. The Revolution was neither successful in vanquishing Catholic reaction nor in co-opting the symbolism associated with their counter-hegemonic struggle. In this context of acute tension, how could a truce come about? What cultural and geopolitical factors favoured a demobilization of opposing factions? How could the same symbolism that triggered attacks in the 1920s and 1930s be recorded at the turn of the 1940s to signify open-mindedness and tolerance? This chapter answers these questions by deconstructing the most important religious celebration held during Manuel Ávila Camacho's presidency: the 1945 golden jubilee of the Virgin of Guadalupe's crowning as Queen of Mexico.

The golden jubilee was a defining moment in the reconciliation of the Catholic Church with the revolutionary State as it effectively tested the limits of the *modus vivendi* designed in 1938; the public processions held during this event marked the end of a conflictive era in Church-State relations. In this chapter, I will demonstrate this contention by examining the micro-histories of intercultural encounters and the symbolic resonances associated with this event. First is an analysis of how the nationalistic symbolism associated with the Virgin of Guadalupe evolved over time to be used by Catholics as political capital to negotiate their inclusion in the public sphere. And second is an examination of how the clergy used this symbolic capital in Second World War Mexico. It is essential to consider the context of the war and the pan-American state of affairs in any understanding of the closing stages of anticlerical violence in Mexico since both the Catholic Church and the government of Manuel Ávila Camacho tried to use this geopolitical situation to their advantage.

Strategic alliances with North American sympathizers were necessary for the protagonists of this conflict. I am examining this dynamics from the angle of Canadian-Mexican relations, since these links played an important part in the process analyzed in this chapter. There is a reason why the archbishop of Mexico City, Luis María Martínez y Rodríguez, specifically wanted the archbishop of Quebec City, Jean-Marie-Rodrigue Cardinal Villeneuve, to act as papal legate *a latere* for the festivities.[3] Tactics also explain governmental tolerance of unconstitutional acts performed during the cardinal's visit, as it was in line with Manuel Ávila Camacho's national unity campaign to stabilize governmental hold of the country. During the celebrations, Mexican Catholics could publicize their firm ties to Mexico's new diplomatic partner, Canada. Since the Catholic Church played a prominent social role in this country, many argued the State should make the most of religious networking to smooth the process of building an alliance with this modern North American nation. The commemoration had a political colouration highlighting the progressive aspects of pan-American Catholic solidarity. After the success of Ezequiel Padilla, Secretary of Foreign Relations, at the 1945 Inter-American Conference held in Mexico City – which produced the Act of Chapultepec on inter-American security – it was time for the Mexican clergy to display their privileged connections with modern North America during the golden jubilee. This was done to carve out a secure space for Catholics in Mexico's public sphere.

THE VIRGIN OF GUADALUPE'S SYMBOLIC SIGNIFICANCE

As a symbol, the Virgin of Guadalupe had multiple meanings that interfered with certain revolutionary discourses, such as those on indigenismo, femininity, and nationalism. It is important to note that a very important devotion to the Virgin of Guadalupe characterizes popular religiosity in Mexico.[4] This devotion is mostly organized by Guadalupan associations (*sociedades guadalupanas*), but the religious piety associated with Our Lady of Guadalupe is also diversified as it is "profoundly rooted in the country's different ethnicities and social classes."[5] The Catholic Church tried to take advantage of this popular piety by organizing celebrations honouring the Virgin of Guadalupe, promoting along the way "notions of *patria*, faith, and family" consistent with Catholic teachings.[6] In its opposition to the Catholic Church, the revolutionary government attempted to control or neutralize this competing emblem of *mexicanidad*; in the eyes of many revolutionary leaders, too many Mexicans still considered that *she* represented the nation's soul. It is therefore necessary briefly to explore the Virgin of Guadalupe's significance before the Mexican Revolution in order to understand how her image was used later by Catholic groups as symbolic capital to negotiate with the State.[7]

Catholic hagiographies agree on her appearance to the Indian Juan Diego in 1531 on Mount Tepeyac, an earlier site of Aztec devotion. This detail produced a unique syncretism between her representation in Extremadura – where devotion to Our Lady of Guadalupe originated – and the geopolitical landscape of the colony.[8] It took more or less a century for devotions to her image to become widespread in Mexico and for the first imposing sanctuary to be erected atop this hill. On 25 May 1754, Benedict XIV formally proclaimed Our Lady of Guadalupe patron of the kingdom of New Spain. Devotion to the Mexican Virgin replaced the fervour to Our Lady of Los Remedios in creole elite circles, and Guadalupe became a common name for Hispanic and mestizo girls in the colony.[9] Her representation progressively became associated with an emergent nationalism.[10] The War of Independence provides the most compelling example of her image being appropriated as a distinctive symbol of identity. Miguel Hidalgo y Costilla, a priest from central Mexico, called for an uprising against Spanish rule on 15 September 1810. To identify his revolutionary movement, he crafted a distinctive Mexican banner using the Virgin of Guadalupe's classic representation. The Indians and mestizos who supported the pro-independence rebellion launched by Miguel Hidalgo and José María Morelos identified with her image of racial inclusiveness and opposed it to Spanish tyranny. These actions by the first independence leaders represented Guadalupe "as the mother and symbol of an insurgent Mexican nation."[11] This nationalistic representation also enabled the Church to position itself as "a fundamental and inalienable legacy of the Mexican nation in all the principal laws and documents of the early independence period."[12]

This symbolism was contested after Independence as the new country became polarized between liberals and conservatives. The Virgin of Guadalupe was identified with conservative forces: namely, the Catholic Church, Indian communities, and political supporters of Emperor Maximilian I of Mexico. Removing the collective privileges of the Church and Indian communities was an objective of the liberal State. These objectives turned into foundational laws of the modern nation after the failed French invasion, when the liberals triumphed over the conservatives. Religious and racial tensions plagued the first liberal administrations.

The positivism of the Porfiriato (1876–1910) clashed with Catholic doctrine and symbolism. Nevertheless, a rapprochement between Porfirio Díaz's administration and the Catholic Church loomed on the horizon.[13] His authoritarian regime reached a tacit understanding with the archbishop of Mexico City, Pelagio Antonio de Labastida y Dávalos, favouring conciliatory relations with the Church. Although the Reform Laws were not altered, the Catholic Church could rest assured that it would have a wide degree of freedom to re-organize its educational activities and expand its institutional presence in the country. This tacit agreement was first symbolized in 1889 by the attendance of a government insider at the celebrations held to honour Labastida's fiftieth anniversary of priesthood. None other than Díaz's own wife, Carmen Romero Rubio, attended the ceremony.[14] This Porfirian *modus vivendi* with the Catholic Church was internationally publicized in 1895 in a grandiose celebration: the crowning of the Virgin of Guadalupe as Queen of Mexico.

The Crowning of the Virgin of Guadalupe in 1895

The 1895 festivities honouring *la morenita* had clear political overtones in Mexico City. Church-State relations turned a new leaf just in time for Mexican Catholics to adjust to Pope Leo XIII's encyclical *Rerum Novarum*. This document delineated the social doctrine of the Church, proposing Catholic solutions to solve problems affecting the working class, while clearly reiterating the Vatican's condemnation of liberalism and socialism as alternatives. The new freedom,

along with the arrival of the first graduates from the Pontifical
Collegio Pio Latinoamericano, infused new life into Church structures and paved the way for a Catholic revival in Mexico.[15] The
Coronation hinted at the confidence Catholic authorities had in the
future of the Church in this country.

The splendour of the celebration, the magnificence of the crown
created for the Virgin, and the renovations of the sanctuary on
Tepeyac were meant to emphasize this message more than any official declaration. These gestures implied mutually beneficial Church-
State relations that could help create bonds of solidarity in the
Americas. The international attention generated by the event
expressed this point clearly and showed the Church's new position
of strength in Mexico. David A. Brading mentions: "On 12 October,
there assembled at the sanctuary twenty-two Mexican archbishops
and bishops, fourteen prelates from the United States, and another
three from Quebec, Havana, and Panama. The arrival of these foreign bishops created a stir in Mexico City since, rather than being
lodged in hotels, they were welcomed into 'the homes of wealthy
Catholics of our cultured society.'"[16] Of course, the press from the
dioceses of foreign dignitaries reported on the celebrations. This
coverage also made special mention of the numerous pilgrimages
organized throughout the year from the four corners of Mexico.
Some pilgrims came from outside the country, one walking from as
far as Quebec City![17] For a few weeks in October 1895, Mexico
seemed to be the centre of attention of American Catholicism. The
Church took pride in this feat.

This corroborated an important nationalistic argument made by
Catholic authorities in the country: modern Mexico could claim
some form of ascendency over Latin America through the glory of
the Virgin of Guadalupe. The most important religious symbol in the
Americas was Mexican, and the whole country should take pride in
the fact that some people had crossed the whole continent to pay
homage to her. On the significance of the 1895 coronation, Brading
concludes: "Viewed from the immediate perspective, the coronation
expressed the public resurrection of the Mexican Church after the
long-drawn-out agony of the Liberal Reform and the French
Intervention. During the civil war of those years the Mexican bishops had been charged with treason, with being guilty of associating
with a foreign prince and his European forces. But in 1895 the bishops once again claimed to speak and act on behalf of the Mexican

nation when they paid homage to the Virgin of Tepeyac."[18] The Catholic Church's nationalist scheme was given a second chance after the War of the Reforms and Maximilian's execution. The impression of speaking and acting on behalf of the nation enabled the Church to seek the assistance of European Catholic religious orders without being accused of disloyalty. As I mentioned in the previous chapter, this process was crucial to rebuilding the institutional network of Catholic education. Indeed, since the end of the nineteenth century, French religious communities created and directed new schools in Mexico in the wake of the anticlerical laws passed in France.[19] Along with their educational expertise, they brought to the New World the practise of European social Catholicism and their experience of confronting anticlericalism. This international network of support had a significant impact on the rehabilitation of the Catholic Church's social role in Mexico.

Conflicting Appropriation of the Virgin's Symbolism during the 1910s

Religious activity dramatically increased at the turn of the century. By the time Díaz's regime was about to fall, Catholicism had recovered most of its ground in the country. The 100th anniversary celebrations of the 1810 Insurgency exposed this fact. On September 17, a banner representing the Virgin of Guadalupe was at the head of a military march in the streets of the capital. The government organized the parade to escort the relics of José María Morelos, a hero of Mexican Independence whose corpse had been recently repatriated from Spain.[20] It seemed as if the religious nationalism of the early Republic had found its way back into Mexico's public sphere. To make sure this discourse carried more weight in Mexico, Catholic authorities attempted to secure an official declaration from the Vatican to enlarge the Virgin's protectorate – and indeed on 24 August 1910, Pius X proclaimed Our Lady of Guadalupe patron of all Latin America. No other Mexican symbol called the attention of the international community as effectively. But the Revolution that swept away the Porfiriato jeopardized the Virgin of Guadalupe's nationalist appeal.

At first, the Revolution was not inimical to representations of the Virgin as the soul of the nation. A significant number of Catholic politicians were elected during the presidency of Francisco Madero. The formation of the Partido Católico Nacional in 1911 stirred little

controversy; José López Portillo, a staunch defender of the Catholic
Church and author of the *Himno guadalupano*, was elected governor in Jalisco where he smoothly imposed a reformist agenda.[21]
Demands made by Catholic groups for social reforms and inclusion
in the public sphere became more assertive. The government com-
plied with some requests, and the official newspaper of the Catholic
Party responded with reciprocal approval of Madero's policies.[22]
But overall, Catholic stakeholders were divided on the Maderista
presidency, and some even welcomed Victoriano Huerta's counterrevolutionary coup. That support had far-reaching consequences.

This fact alone did not delegitimize using the Virgin of Guadalupe
as a nationalist symbol. After all, Emiliano Zapata fought his revolutionary struggle in the state of Morelos with the image of the Mexican
Virgin prominently displayed on the banner of his troops, a direct
reference to the heroes of the first independence insurrection.
Members of his revolutionary forces even prayed at the basilica on
Mount Tepeyac at a time when Mexico City was controlled by the
conventionalists. But the constitutionalists who finally defeated Villa
and Zapata's troops were hard-nosed anticlericals, as indicated by
the most contentious articles of the constitution they promulgated:
"Article 3 prohibited religious instruction in all schools; article 5
equated religious vows with slavery; article 13 denied legal status to
religious organizations; article 27 nationalized all church property;
and article 130 established the state's right to limit religious worship
and delegated this responsibility to the local congresses."[23] From
then on, Catholic activists objected to any attempt made by the government to appropriate the symbolism associated with Guadalupe.
Her representation stood for an alternative vision of the country, one
that escaped governmental control. The potential uses of the multiple
meanings embedded in her image represented a predicament for early
revolutionary iconography. The visceral anticlericalism of constitu-
tionalist decision-makers prevented a shrewd appropriation of this
powerful figure; the symbolic capital associated with the Virgin of
Guadalupe remained the prerogative of Catholic groups.

Catholic Reaction to Revolutionary Anticlericalism:
Nationalistic Symbolism and Transnational Solidarity
as Leverage for the Church in Mexico

Despite what the 1921 bomb attack at the basilica suggests, Álvaro
Obregón's administration could not afford to intensify actions

against the Church. The country was bankrupt and unity remained the government's priority.[24] Obregón himself was first perceived as a political leader who could bring some form of consensus with dissident groups.[25] Nevertheless, the orientation taken by the Revolution polarized Mexico. Military uprisings soon destabilized the country and the prospect of an alliance between dissatisfied generals and Catholic militants put the revolutionary government at risk. The opposing factions of the Cristiada were gradually taking up their positions.

Catholic associations proliferated during the long period of violence stretching from the fall of the Porfiriato to the end of the Cristiada. The difficulties experienced during the Revolution stimulated the formation of new structures by which to organize the Catholic laity. Grassroots militants and members of the clergy created a strong institutional network of Catholic cooperatives, schools, and unions throughout the country. Newly formed dioceses and parishes assisted in the revitalization of Mexican Catholicism. They provided, among others, an effective structure for the distribution of these associations' numerous publications. Catholic groups were ready to confront the State over its revolutionary principles if they conflicted with their beliefs, and they used this network to publicize their ideas and organize rival social institutions. Considering the difficult consolidation of the Revolution, Catholic structures and social programs became a serious alternative to the Revolution's nation-building project. Obregón's successor, Plutarco Elías Calles, decided to break this momentum once he took office.[26]

Skirmishes and squabbles rapidly intensified during Calles's administration. As stated before, symbolic violence became a motive for bloodshed. The formation of a schismatic Church by the government and the Confederación Regional Obrera Mexicana (CROM) exasperated Catholic militants. The foundation of the Iglesia Católica Apostólica Mexicana directly led to the establishment of a counterpart to fight government initiatives: the Liga Nacional de la Defensa de la Libertad Religiosa (LNDLR).[27] All the major associations created since the Porfiriato – Unión de Damas Católicas Mejicanas (UDCM), Asociación Católica de la Juventud Mexicana (ACJM), the Confederación Nacional Católica del Trabajo (CNCT), the Unión Nacional de Padres de Familia (UNPF), and the Mexican section of the Caballeros de Colón (K of C) – joined forces to form and galvanize the LNDLR.[28] Calles took this development as an act of defiance. State officials reacted, asserting their intention to enforce the anticlerical articles of the Constitution. During the summer of 1926, the government forced priests to register with the State and get its approval before performing their duties. This legislation, known as the Ley Calles, sparked direct confrontation. For the first time since the end of the Revolution, the Church hierarchy officially rebelled against this deliberate attempt to impose governmental ascendency over the spiritual realm. It first adopted the strategy of Anacleto González Flores, a charismatic Catholic militant from Jalisco, and launched a campaign of passive resistance by suspending worship and closing down churches,[29] which seriously antagonized Catholic believers. However, contrary to Gandhi's use of civil disobedience, Catholic authorities did not preemptively ask their followers to restrain from using violence against the government. Civil war became inevitable.

This is not the place to dwell on the course of the Cristiada, nor to reassess the conflict over education in the 1930s. I have already discussed the Cristiada in the introduction and the second chapter and the conflict over education was examined in detail in the forth chapter, "The Poetics of Student Exchanges." However, two points need to be re-emphasized. First, after threatening the very survival of the Catholic Church in Mexico, the civil war ended up strengthening Catholic institutions and helping expand its network of support beyond national borders. Second, the contingencies of the Cristiada and the conflict over education paved the way for the Church's repositioning at the end of the 1930s and made it possible for them to use the Virgin of Guadalupe as symbolic capital, once again, to re-establish the nationalist credentials of Catholic militants.

This civil war galvanized Catholic Mexico. Yet, the Cristeros did not win the military conflict; the Catholic Church ended up settling with the State without getting concrete concessions beyond the end of anticlerical attacks, and they abandoned the Cristeros' cause along the way.[30] Thousands of people died in Mexico, and violence did not solve the fundamental dissension. The Mexican government's imposition of socialist education in the 1930s reignited the conflict as if the *arreglos* of 1929 had never existed. Catholic groups continued to react to anticlerical measures with the same vehemence as before. Their resistance would have been nearly impossible had they not benefitted from the material support of exiled Mexicans in the United States and the moral caution of foreign sympathizers like the Québécois Jesuit Antonio Dragon who publicized Catholic persecution in Mexico. Cristero deaths were presented in the North American Catholic press as martyrdom experienced under a totalitarian state. Governmental expulsion of Mexican prelates backfired, since they helped to establish a privileged network of support north of the border. This became a serious concern for the Revolution as influential Catholic groups had the ear of Franklin Delano Roosevelt. Jean Meyer argues that the Mexican government "realised that the creation of a favourable climate of opinion towards the Mexican Catholic Church in the United States in relation to religious liberty reached the depths of the problem and constituted a threat."[31] The diplomatic price to continuing anticlerical measures was high.

At the national level, Catholicism experienced a fundamental renewal in those years. Mexican Catholic associations coalesced under a new umbrella group in 1929, the Acción Católica Mexicana (ACM).[32] Like the Catholic hierarchy, the ACM distanced itself from the Cristeros and unequivocally rejected violence. The ACM organized a strong intellectual defence of the right to express their faith publicly and fought against the imposition of socialist education.[33] Their purpose was to win "the battle of consciousness."[34] Progressively, the unbridled violence of the Cristeros was marginalized as a strategy used by Catholic groups. Two different political movements emerged out of the 1930s conflict over education directly challenging the governing party's hegemony in Mexican politics: the Partido Acción Nacional (PAN) and the Unión Nacional Sinarquista (UNS).[35] These movements also officially rejected violence, although the "most outstanding characteristic" of synarchists was "their utter and complete willingness to suffer death if need be for the cause."[36] Notwithstanding differences over the use of a military option, Catholic groups had proven their capacity to mobilize the masses for their cause and fight the government. They also had shown their ability to garner crucial international support. It was up to the government to decide whether they wanted to discuss with peaceful groups or to fight an unwinnable war against Catholic fundamentalists.

By the end of the 1930s, the religious conflict entered its final phase. The prospect of a new world war presented both opportunities and constraints. On the one hand, the government of Lázaro Cárdenas acted boldly by nationalizing the oil industry at a time when the world's attention was devoted to European problems. His government was successful in testing international forbearance. On the other hand, on the national scene, the country was on the brink of division at a crucial moment for revolutionary consolidation. Political schisms were perilous at a time when international forces were attempting to pull Mexico into their coalitions.[37] The Mexican right had to be appeased, and symbolic concessions on the religious front became the obvious answer. A new *modus vivendi* was crafted by Mexico's political and religious authorities. Symbolic politics was the mechanism used to achieve and defend this accommodation. The Allies' war effort in the Western Hemisphere ended up strengthening this course of action as well. In this overarching context, the symbolism associated with the Virgin of Guadalupe made an assertive comeback in Mexico's public sphere, representing the soul of the nation and continental concord.

TOWARD A CATHOLIC REVIVAL? THE CHURCH-STATE MODUS VIVENDI AND THE SECOND WORLD WAR

Many scholars have identified the Catholic Church's support for Cárdenas's nationalization of oil companies in 1938 as a turning point in Church-State relations.[38] With this move, Catholic authorities wanted to send a strong message to the revolutionary government telling them they "were in favour of supporting the formation of a patriotic consciousness in Mexico... and that the Church was as nationalist as revolutionary sectors were."[39] The *modus vivendi* was therefore founded on common nationalist grounds. But as Roberto Blancarte mentions, many factors could still undermine a concrete ideological rapprochement and violent actions could overturn the détente.[40] Nevertheless, the bond between the Catholic Church and the revolutionary State was solidified during the *sexenio* of Manuel Ávila Camacho. His mandate, beginning in 1940, established tolerance as the new government's attitude toward the Church and enabled Catholics to carve out a safe space in the public sphere. The 1945 commemoration of the golden jubilee of the Virgin of Guadalupe's crowning was planned as the apotheosis of this arduous process.

"Soy Creyente": Openings and Constraints during the War

Mexico's conservative shift following Cárdenas's rule still puzzles many people who see the general as the incarnation of the Revolution's social ideals. Indeed, the architect of the most comprehensive land redistribution scheme the country ever saw, the staunch defender of workers' interests, and the president who dared to nationalize Mexico's most precious natural resource hand-picked a conservative-leaning candidate to stand for the Partido de la Revolución Mexicana (PRM) in the 1940 election. Right after the election, Manuel Ávila Camacho confessed "I am a believer," thus further indulging Catholic desires. This declaration took everyone by surprise, not least his revolutionary colleagues, since "no Mexican president had gone that far for a century."[41] Some historians maintain that "when the candidate for the Party of the Mexican Revolution... declared himself a believer, the *modus vivendi* really began."[42] Whether the détente started in 1940 rather than 1938 is not the point of this book. What is important to acknowledge, however, is that from Camacho's election onward governmental and ecclesiastical authorities did enforce a truce between revolutionary anticlericals and Catholic militants.

Concessions to the right were inevitable if the Revolution was to maintain its grip on power.[43] The Catholic Church also needed to find a middle ground with the State to prevent being outflanked by ultra-Catholic groups like the UNS. The practical compromise built by them during Camacho's *sexenio* was a constant work-in-progress in need of a symbolic gesture of goodwill to remain sustainable. The previous chapter addressed part of this process by analyzing openings and constraints in the academic world. The ability of scholars to express dissent and push for social alternatives to the State's hegemonic control of Mexican civil society was substantial during Camacho's rule. Many defenders of the Church used it to establish bonds of solidarity with Catholic institutions north of the border and to actively promote the Vatican's social encyclicals as a serious option to consider. But this flexibility came with strict conditions: if scholars took advantage of their position to embarrass the State, governmental authorities retained the sole privilege of acting against them. I demonstrated this point in the previous chapter using the case of UNAM's conservative rector, Rodulfo Brito Foucher, who had to resign in 1944 after left-wing students rebelled against his actions and political ambitions, putting the president of Mexico in a delicate situation. There was a fine line in perception between taking the floor and militating against the government.

President Manuel Ávila Camacho's documents in Mexico City contain a great deal of evidence reflecting the difficulty of appeasing

Mexican conservative sectors without alienating the revolutionary base of the P R M. Catholic groups took advantage of Camacho's apparent expression of Catholic identity to push for better representation in Mexico's public sphere, petitioning the government for the right to organize public acts of faith and display Catholic symbolism outside the confines of religious buildings.[44] One group even sent a notarized petition to name the Virgin of Guadalupe "the Insurgent Army's highest General (giving her the actual rank of Divisional General of Mexico's Constitutional Army), and naming her Honorary President of the Mexican Congress in perpetuity."[45] Many requests remained unanswered. Catholic aspirations were met with multiple denunciations by anticlerical groups who protested their unconstitutional deeds.[46] In some regions of the country ensuing unrest boiled over into violence.[47] In this context, keeping everyone satisfied was a real balancing act. Compromise had to be framed appropriately in order to bear fruit.

Camacho's 1940 confession that he was a believer was motivated by political-interest. Many Catholic activists supported the candidacy of General Juan Andreu Almazán and were disillusioned about the outcome of the vote (especially in Mexico City where support for the P R M was weak). To make matters worse, violence marred the election result.[48] Camacho's national unity crusade was in need of a gesture of goodwill toward these disgruntled voters if social peace was ever to be achieved during his *sexenio*. But his administration went further than simple symbolic politics. Real concessions were made to the religious right: among others, his administration passed a new Law of Nationalizations which subtly re-established part of the Church's juridical personality; it relaxed State oversight over private education without reforming the Constitution too abruptly; and it progressively permitted public acts of faith.[49] Subtleness and progressiveness are key words to understand the success of his balancing act. At the same time as he made concessions to religious groups, Camacho also shrewdly marginalized the P A N and the U N S's social projects, therefore preserving his revolutionary credentials and neutralizing the more perilous forms of Catholic discontent.[50]

The state of affairs resulting from the context of the Second World War facilitated this course of action. Mexico might not have fought a "total war" in the 1940s, but the collaboration with the US had deep cultural and political impact at the national level. Monica Rankin notes concerning changes of attitude in Mexico: "By 1940, new understandings of Nazi aggression and new opportunities for a resolution with the United States brought with them new concerns, demands, and expectations. US officials wanted assurances that Mexico was not becoming a haven for Axis saboteurs. At the same time, Mexico's mainstream press changed its approach to wartime coverage. Periodicals such as *Excelsior* and *El Universal* were still extremely critical of the United States, but they also had become alarmed by the rapidity with which Germany seemed to be overpowering most of Western Europe."[51] The war represented an opportunity for all political stakeholders in Mexico to reposition themselves on the national scene as patriotic social actors. Indeed, Alan Knight mentions that "Mexico's participation [in the Second World War] had been endorsed by the left (CTM, PCM) and, surprisingly and significantly, by the Catholic hierarchy, by most of the right-wing press, by the PAN and other conservative groups."[52] This situation also discredited political extremism and fascist-leaning Catholic reaction as much as socialistic anticlericalism.

A more conservative understanding of Mexican nationalism became a discursive point of convergence between the "revolutionary" government of Manuel Ávila Camacho and the Catholic Church, a point where their institutional interest came together. In this international war effort against fascist totalitarianism, the Mexican State attempted to appear inclusive, while Catholic authorities tried to turn around perceptions of preference for conservative despots. Concessions were not presented as exceptions, but rather as reflecting Mexico's democratic nature, an argument Church publications gradually consented to. Mexican ecclesiastics also attempted to reposition Catholic discourse by framing its fundamental ideas and actions within Mexico's new nationalist framework. The result of this concerted effort was a tacit agreement of mutual respect strong enough to overcome periodic crises, like the governmental prohibition on the wearing of military uniforms at religious ceremonies or the attempt on Camacho's life by a Catholic army officer. These setbacks did not derail the Church and State rapprochement as "both powers still found that preserving the *modus vivendi* was essential to their institutional survival."[53] The increasing public vitality of Mexican Catholicism was undeniable as religious associative life blossomed and religious symbolism gradually made a comeback in the nation's public sphere thanks to its national unity and pan-American appeal.[54] International Catholic authorities noted this positive development with acute interest.

Richard Pattee's Report on a Catholic Revival

Transnational actors concerned with Mexican Church-State relations were generally the ones reporting back to foreign countries
about developments on this matter. I outlined in my third chapter
the role played by the Union des Latins d'Amérique (ULA) in publicizing Camacho's tolerant attitude in Canada, which eventually
influenced closer diplomatic ties. Members of religious communities
in Mexico also discussed with their associates abroad how the situation was evolving in their country and these exchanges were
reported in their publications. For example, the Jesuit monthly
review *Relations*, published by the École sociale populaire, played
this part in Quebec. From their first publication in January 1941 to
the end of the Guadalupan jubilee year of 1945, *Relations* published
thirty-four articles on the situation in Mexico.[55] These reports discussed the Synarchist movement, the controversy around article 3
of the Constitution (on socialist education), and the dangers
of Protestant proselytism, but overall the reports emphasized the
"renouveau religieux" reinvigorating the Catholic Church. The Jesuit
Joseph Ledit, one of the editors of *Relations*, made the most important contribution in reporting on the Catholic Church in Mexico and
Latin America.[56] But for a wider Catholic audience in the US, it is the
report on the situation in Mexico produced by the Inter-American
Committee of the Catholic Association for International Peace (LAC)
in 1944 – a branch of the US National Catholic Welfare Council
(NCWC) – that played a crucial role in raising awareness about the
strength of the *modus vivendi*.[57]

This publication attempted to take stock of the religious situation
in Mexico before the important Guadalupan commemoration the
following year. The report was produced under the supervision of
Richard Pattee, a scholar who was born in the United States and lived
nearly twenty years in Latin America. In the mid-1940s, Pattee became
very active in promoting a North American Catholic rapprochement.[58] He not only pushed for closer Catholic collaboration between
the US and Mexico, but he promoted French Canadian-Mexican relations as well, even lobbying the Canadian government to facilitate
links between universities in Quebec and Mexico.[59] As mentioned
in the previous chapter, he was a close collaborator of Rodulfo Brito
Foucher and played a crucial role in establishing relations between
Université Laval and Universidad Nacional Autónoma de México.
He later became Université Laval's leading Hispanist.

His report called the attention of the US Catholic community to the significant improvements made in Mexico. "The Catholic Revival in Mexico," the report's title, summarized the intended message. Nevertheless, this document cautiously stated that "anti-religious sentiment is ever latent" in this country.[60] Pattee explained that the nature of anticlericalism in Mexico was both a source of worry and an opportunity: "The deceptive characteristic of Mexico is precisely the fact that anti-clericalism gives the impression of a deeprooted [sic] and dogmatic hatred of the Church. Nothing could be further from the truth. Their anti-clericalism is rather secularism – the desire to prevent religion from having an influence on the public and social life of the country. Priest haters of the first order are among the most precipitate to seek the sacraments upon their deathbed."[61] According to Pattee, Mexico's political class felt compelled to restate their revolutionary credentials by hastily presenting motions reaffirming anticlerical positions from time to time.[62] These brusque gestures ended up provoking radical members of Catholic groups. Pattee nonetheless shared his conviction that ecclesiastical authorities – in Mexico and in the US – would now see through this cosmetic anticlericalism and support the *modus vivendi* for what it truly was.

The American scholar gave various reasons why Catholics should be optimistic about the situation in Mexico. First among many was "the intellectual revival."[63] According to Pattee, considerable Catholic influence at UNAM had survived the persecution thanks to the effort of the rectors Antonio Caso, Rodulfo Brito Foucher, and Manuel Gómez Morín. This enabled "Thomistic thought [to hold] an established and honourable place in the curriculum."[64] Neo-Thomistic thought was a crucial building block of the Latin American Catholic revival at the time, enabling Catholic scholars to solve dilemmas inherited from the Catholic Modernist Crisis by distinguishing a worldly order understood by reason from spiritual ends coming under the experience of faith.[65] Pattee himself contributed to this influence by facilitating the translation of Charles de Koninck's works in Spanish and convincing Rodulfo Brito Foucher to invite the neo-Thomist philosopher from Université Laval to lecture at UNAM.[66] Yet, as Pattee observes, the full scope of this Catholic restoration could be found elsewhere, "in the reviews, journals, in the appearance of an increasing number of Catholic writers, and in the remarkable continuation of the humanist tradition which is deeprooted in Mexican culture."[67] One statistic published by Roberto Blancarte concerning Catholic publications expresses the magnitude

of this editorial effort: in a limited number of years at the turn of the
1940s, "more than 66,000,000 bulletins and magazines [were pub-
lished] for a country of 20,000,000 inhabitants."[68] The Church's
publication effort was impressive enough, but Catholic participation
in secular media also contributed to the maintenance of the Church's
counter-hegemonic voice. The author of the IAC report listed the
Catholic intellectuals who collaborated in those publications. It is
worthwhile to note that an important number of them contributed
to Mexico City's main newspapers like *El Universal* and *Novedades*.[69]

Yet, the various branches of Mexican Catholic Action (ACM)
mainly stimulated the editorial effort of the Church. "'Catholic
Action' is today one of the main forces in Catholic life in Mexico...
without taking into account the affiliated bodies, [it] has at the present time 400,000 members."[70] Pattee said that the strength of the
women's section of the ACM was particularly impressive. Having
successfully lived through persecution, women had developed an
acute sense of adaptability to confront revolutionary pressures. This
strength was nurtured in "*Cultural Femenina*, founded in 1926
under the immediate direction of a most remarkable Catholic lay-
woman, Sofía del Valle... [The] thorough grounding in Catholic philosophy, apologetics, and action" provided to women in their courses
gave a crucial impetus to ACM activities.[71] At the beginning of the
1940s, the ACM was in a position to maximize the opportunities
offered by Camacho's national unity campaign, while delineating a
clear Catholic alternative on cultural and social issues. With their
publications providing a platform to spread Catholic ideas and its
unrivalled size, the organization had an enormous capacity to mobilize the masses in support of symbolic actions.

A quick examination of *Juventud*, the monthly magazine published by the Juventud Católica Femenina Mexicana (JCFM), supports this contention. The publication – aimed at women under
35 years old – uncompromisingly embraced the rhetoric of *unidad
nacional* after Mexico declared war on the Axis. From July 1942 to
the end of the year, Sofía del Valle wrote a monthly column on the
stakes of this war for Mexican Catholics, emphasizing a Catholic
inner sense of patriotism and trustworthiness.[72] She argued that
Catholic women served their patriotic duty best because they were
good mothers first.[73] Guadalupe Gutiérrez de Velasco, the magazine's chief editor, wrote in another article: "In this work of national
rapprochement, in this work where we are all working to brandish

our patriotism, in order to awaken the consciousness of our fellow Mexicans and unite our hearths in this effort of national consolidation, the J C F M – which has never been indifferent to Mexico's social problems – wholeheartedly dedicates itself with great enthusiasm to cooperate in this work of national rapprochement."[74] The J C F M, along with other groups of the A C M, claimed it was in a unique position to mobilize people in support of the government's war effort, the more so because they shared an intimate connection with the most important symbol of *mexicanidad*, the Virgin of Guadalupe. They wrote in *Juventud* that "our nationality shall never be overcome as long as the Tepeyac remains the spiritual centre of our nation, and as long as our Mother the Virgin of Guadalupe inhabits it."[75] It is under the protection of *la morenita* that Catholic groups negotiated their access to the public sphere, organizing congresses and pilgrimages in honour of the Virgin, and framing these activities within Camacho's national unity campaign and the pan-American concord the war imposed.

El Año Jubilar Guadalupano: Archbishop Luis María Martínez y Rodríguez and Symbolic Politics during the Camacho Years

Catholics – from the Cristeros to the A C M – never stopped using the image of Guadalupe as symbolic capital to influence the balance of power between the Church and the State. But this practice engendered different reactions. For example, the pomp of the 400th anniversary celebrations of the Virgin's 1531 appearance to Juan Diego had provided anticlerical groups with a pretext for launching brutal attacks against Catholic groups.[76] The restoration of public acts of faith in the streets of Mexico during the six years of Manuel Ávila Camacho's presidency was more peaceful, but public display of religiosity did provoke violence every so often. Pattee reported on this: "The popular feeling of faith is so keen that it is almost impossible to avoid religious activities in public. The Eucharistic Congresses have been, unhappily, one of the causes of certain conflicts with the authorities, precisely because of their greater visibility."[77] Of course, visibility was the point of public affirmations of faith; but religious authorities were not supposed to formally plan unconstitutional acts. Yet overall, the federal government turned a blind eye to them when they happened and did not tolerate violent response to public outbursts of religiosity. With time, the stakeholders of Camacho's national unity campaign hoped the country would become impervious to a limited religious comeback in the public sphere.

One way to facilitate this process was to provide even greater visibility of religious activities, turning them into pan-national undertakings or organizing acts of faith publicized by international media. The planning of the 1945 Marian festivities fell into both categories. Mexican ecclesiastical authorities declared the period between 12 October 1944 and 12 October 1945 to be a jubilee year commemorating the fiftieth anniversary of the Virgin's crowning as Queen of Mexico.[78] They called for special ceremonies to be held in the nation's churches on the twelfth of each month in honour of the Mexican virgin. Guadalupan congresses, special contests, and "Guadalupan-historic" conferences were planned throughout the country.[79] The organizers of the special commemoration were also anticipating numerous pilgrimages from Mexico's various dioceses to reach Mount Tepeyac. Finally, the apex of the festivities would occur in the week preceding 12 October; people from all over the Americas were expected to congregate in Mexico City, at the renovated basilica on the Tepeyac, to proclaim their allegiance to Guadalupe and thank her for "preserving Mexico and the rest of Latin America from the most disastrous consequences of this war which is destroying the world at this sombre hour."[80] The Virgin would be crowned again in a grandiose ceremony on 12 October. The whole hemisphere would then kneel before the Mexican virgin and accept her protectorate by naming her "Empress of the Americas."

For the nationalistic appeal of this event to succeed, Mexican religious authorities had to secure the enthusiastic participation of North American ecclesiastics. The Mexican Catholic Church did not object to the prospect of using the celebrations to put its privileged connections with modern North America on display. It was especially important for them to make an impression in Mexico City: US citizens demonstrating their utmost respect for the ultimate symbol of Mexican identity, the Virgin of Guadalupe, would accomplish this. The ACM's president, Martín del Campo, wrote to Archbishop Martínez a month before the publication of the pastoral letter telling him: "One thing North American Catholics could do in our country to counterbalance the work of Protestant propagandists is to come to Mexico, in sufficient numbers, with the avowed goal of cooperating in the defence of Mexican Catholicism... Allow me, Your Excellency, to tell you that I believe it would have the greatest impact on our people to see a 'gringo' on his knees, at the Virgin Mary's feet, saying in proper English or bad Spanish: The Catholic religion is the true one."[81] Martín del Campo's desires were answered – multiple times – during the high point of the jubilee year in Mexico.

In the end, it seems that Richard Pattee's report set the stage for the enthusiastic participation of North American dignitaries in the 1945 celebrations. In 1910, US ecclesiastics let the Vatican know of their objection to extending the Virgin's protectorate to all of the Americas – confining her to *Latin* America.[82] Now, nineteen prelates from the US accepted the invitation of the archbishop of Mexico City, Luís María Martínez, to come to Mexico and embrace the new symbolic title granted to the Virgin of Guadalupe by the pope, that of Empress of the Americas. For those in Mexico who (like communist-leaning anticlericals or fascist-leaning Catholics) would have accused the Church of pandering to US interests, Archbishop Martínez had a surprise: Canadian prelates took the foreign delegations' centre stage since Martínez specifically invited the archbishop of Quebec City, Jean-Marie-Rodrigue Cardinal Villeneuve, to act as papal legate for the commemoration.[83] An alternative model of North American modernity was invoked during the commemoration, one that could be beneficial to Mexico, it was argued, if only the country relied more on pan-American networks of Catholic solidarity.

CARDINAL VILLENEUVE AND THE GOLDEN JUBILEE: UNCONSTITUTIONAL CELEBRATIONS AND CHURCH-STATE RECONCILIATION

The parallel between the 1895 and 1945 celebrations speaks volumes. In both instances, the festivities associated with the coronation were used to express Church-State reconciliation without formalizing the rapprochement with official signatures. The 1945 organization of the week preceding 12 October was almost an exact replica of the event it commemorated. The Second World War festivities definitively marked the end of a political era in Mexico, since the revolutionary government lent its full support to the event by guaranteeing its execution. In contrast to the celebrations held during the Porfiriato, the 1945 commemoration had an assertive public tone: outbursts of religiosity in Mexico City's streets were numerous and uncontrollable. Participants in the celebrations decidedly cast the Virgin of Guadalupe as the ultimate emblem of *mexicanidad* and the country's most tangible contribution to pan-American harmony. The public image of the revolutionary government broadcast by this event was never closer to the first meaning of the word "revolution." Detractors pointing to the numerous unconstitutional actions perpetrated during the 1945 festivities grumbled that by letting Catholics take over the streets of the capital, the Revolution had come full circle.

The Impact of Jean-Marie-Rodrigue Cardinal Villeneuve's Visit and His Role as Papal Legate

With the exception of the strong opposition to the celebrations of some Mexican periodicals like *Tiempo*, criticism was relatively muted for the most important portion of the festivities, a time when Mexico was the centre of attention of the Catholic world.[84] The presence of Cardinal Villeneuve played an important part in this process. Luis María Martínez specifically wanted the archbishop of Quebec City to be named papal legate *a latere* for the commemoration because of their common effort strengthening North American Catholicism during the war: both had made an essential contribution to the war effort by convincing their recalcitrant flocks to support the Allies; both had also facilitated the establishment of academic connections between Mexican universities and French Canadian Catholic institutions to counterbalance US hegemony.[85] Quebec's reputation for staging events that attracted the attention of the Catholic world was well-established, and Villeneuve himself had been appointed as papal legate twice before. Martínez therefore petitioned Pope Pius XII to name the Primate of the Church in Canada papal legate for the commemoration in Mexico and sent Mgr Miguel Darío Miranda y Gómez twice to Quebec City in 1944 and 1945 to discuss plans with diocesan authorities. Martínez then delegated Antonio Santacruz – none other than the leader of La Base, the UNS's shadow directorate – to Quebec's capital to make the final arrangements.[86] As papal legate for these festivities, the archbishop of Quebec City was the first cardinal ever to set foo on the land of *la Virgen morena*, therefore becoming the highest Vatican representative visiting Mexico up to that point.[87] Visas were granted for the trip on 28 September 1945 by Ambassador Francisco del Río Cañedo to Cardinal Villeneuve, Paul Nicole

(Villeneuve's secretary), Armand Corriveau (Villeneuve's chamberlain), Archbishop Alexandre Vachon (archbishop of Ottawa), and Arnele Power (Mgr Vachon's secretary).[88]

The cardinal's coming to Mexico was an important event. Mexican newspapers relayed the information that on 5 October 1945, "when *J.M. Rodrigo Villeneuve* crossed the rio Bravo on the international bridge between Laredo, Texas and Nuevo Laredo, Mexico, a cardinal entered our national territory for the first time."[89] Villeneuve was undoubtedly the focal point of the celebrations – notwithstanding, of course, the exposure given to the Virgin of Guadalupe herself. D.A. Brading noted this fact: "It was the presence of the apostolic legate, Cardinal J.M. Rodrigo Villeneuve (sic), archbishop of Quebec, which aroused public enthusiasm. The first prince of the Church to visit Mexico, he was gratified by his warm reception and in return praised Mexicans for their heroism and their aptitude for the arts and sciences; predicted a 'brilliant destiny' for the country; and saluted Mexico City as 'the Athens of the New World.' By and large, the Mexican press lavished praise on the event, since a leading newspaper described the proceedings as an example of 'civilized human coexistence,' so that, at a time when much of Europe was governed by sectarian obscurantism, 'our country is a light, an island of civilized tolerance.'"[90] It is interesting to note that Villeneuve's declarations echoed the discourse on Mexico the ULA articulated in Quebec.[91]

But the cardinal's visit enthralled Mexican Catholics for another reason: his stature ensured a definite protection for the public expression of religiosity. Masses of people followed him in the streets of Mexico, along with the *charros* escorting him.[92] A newspaper reported that "close to half a million Catholics gathered to welcome him... and the few who were lucky enough to come close to him heard the cardinal say: 'Mexico is the fulfilment of the miracle of faith.'"[93] Another newspaper asserted that "the presence of the cardinal, the pope's other self... brought greater magnificence and solemnity to the celebrations, ultimately strengthening and rooting for good Mexicans' deep veneration for the Virgin Mary."[94] Finally, Eduardo Tellez maintained on the front page of *El Universal* that Villeneuve's presence at the ceremonies resulted in "an apotheosis without parallel in the history of Mexican Catholicism."[95] The effect of his stay in Mexico undoubtedly showed Mexicans and the whole world the strength of the *modus vivendi*, as virtually every single law limiting the public display of religiosity and Catholic symbolism was broken by hundreds of thousands of Catholics every day for over a week. For this reason, the *Gaceta Oficial del Arzobispado de México* proudly reported that the crowds shouted "*viva la Virgen de Guadalupe, viva el cardenal, viva el presidente Camacho!*"[96] Whether Camacho's name was heard often or not, the Church's official publication in the diocese of Mexico made sure it was recorded.

The president was lauded while Catholic interests were cast in a favourable light, to the detriment of their old foes. Considering the political distance travelled in the course of Church-State reconciliation, Catholic authorities could be thankful. The presidency gave them enough latitude to organize the celebrations to their liking, including exacting subtle symbolic revenge against anticlerical forces. The cardinal's reception in Mexico, worthy of the most important ambassadors, is an example of this. To paraphrase Brading on the 1895 celebration, the arrival of Villeneuve created a stir in Mexico City because, rather than being lodged in a hotel, he was welcomed into the home of a very wealthy Catholic.[97] Newspapers noticed that Guillermo Barroso's residence was not only the most luxurious in the capital, but it was the old mansion of a close collaborator of Calles, Luís León. Some Catholic publications mentioned that this fact constituted an ironic reversal of history. *Relations*, the Jesuit monthly magazine in Quebec, wrote: "So, Luís León's luxury was used to honour the papal legate. Father Pro must have turned in his grave."[98] Still, Villeneuve himself never bragged publicly about this symbolic twist.

The cardinal nevertheless met with Mexico's most dynamic Catholic representatives, controversial or not. Carlos Septién García, a founding member of the Unión Cultural México-Canadá Francés (UCMCF) and director of PAN's official publication, *La Nación*, was the first lay person Villeneuve officially received in a private audience, along with the paper's editors. The cardinal then welcomed the representatives of the *Acción Católica de la Juventud Mexicana* (ACJM). According to their publication *Acción*, the ACJM's chaplain introduced the young *acejoteros* to Villeneuve saying, "Here are the combatants." The chaplain then added, "Here we are: those who fought in the Militant Church, and those who shed their blood to defend the Church's religious freedom." The report mentioned that the cardinal was deeply moved by this encounter, responding with emotion "my dear sons, my dearest sons... your mark of respect has touched my heart."[99] If Villeneuve privately maintained relations

5.1 Barroso's palace. The house of Catholic industrialist Guillermo Barroso in Las Lomas, which was one of Mexico's richest residences, was where Cardinal Villeneuve was lodged during his stay in the country. (Archives de l'Archidiocèse de Québec, Fonds Jean-Marie-Rodrigue Villeneuve, O M I)

5.2 Cardinal Villeneuve with the Barroso family. Only the oldest son is missing from this picture of Cardinal Villeneuve posing with the Barroso family. (Archives de l'Archidiocèse de Québec, Fonds Jean-Marie-Rodrigue Villeneuve, O M I)

with people known for religious violence – like the infamous Madre Conchita, the alleged "intellectual author" of Álvaro Obregón's murder – his public contacts were definitively with Catholic voices of compromise.[100] These meetings were publicized in advance, and the media covered glamorous encounters like those with the ladies of the ACM's women's sections or those with the various Catholic dignitaries present in Mexico.

If criticism of the government was to be found, it had to be decoded from the symbolism associated with certain actions the planning committee took or it had to be read into messages proclaiming the intrinsic virtues of the Church's social project. Villeneuve himself never directly attacked governmental positions on issues relating to religious liberties. On the contrary, the cardinal delivered a message of peace in Mexico, stating that he was glad to note the undeniable progress achieved in favor of the Church's position. He mentioned at various times that he was impressed by the profound faith in God he witnessed in Mexico, and he showed his appreciation for the impressive festivities organized to honour the Virgin of Guadalupe. This is not to say that Catholics did not publicly intervene to pressure the government on certain issues. But speakers rarely took the floor directly on their behalf. To express that the *modus vivendi* could go further and that Catholics needed more leeway, they used oblique critiques of Mexico's *status quo* by singing the praises of North American Catholicism.

North American Catholicism out on Display:
Welcoming the French Canadian Delegation

Those who planned the final weeks of the Guadalupan jubilee year provided an opportunity for the representatives of the main groups participating in the celebrations to express themselves. Before the actual coronation on 12 October 1945, twelve days were dedicated to specific geographical areas involved in the festivities.[101] On each day, special processions were organized and masses were celebrated at the basilica where dignitaries from an honoured region preached sermons. From 30 September to 7 October, various Mexican dioceses took centre stage: Yucatan, Puebla, Monterrey, Durango, Oaxaca, Guadalajara, Morelia, and Mexico. The organizers also planned to dedicate special days to other parts of the world from 8–11 October: first was Spain and the Spaniards in the Americas;

then on the ninth Canada together with France and Holland were honoured; the next day was the US and England; and finally on the eleventh was Latin America as a whole. Notwithstanding the climax of 12 October, the sermons given on the days dedicated to the US and Canada drew the most intense attention of Mexico's press. It is on these days that the contributors to the festivities articulated most clearly the Virgin of Guadalupe's pan-American appeal. Indirect criticism of the status quo of Church-State relations could be deciphered by the readers of Mexico City's main newspapers from their reporting on the dignitaries' interventions at the basilica.

As stated above, it was important for Mexican Catholics to publicize their privileged relations with North American co-religionists. Mexican collaboration with the Allies' war effort magnified the impact of the sermons preached at the basilica on the days devoted to the US and Canada. The Mexican government wanted the country to be perceived as being an integral part of North America, and the numerical presence at the festivities of prelates from the US and Canada (alongside Mexican dignitaries) strengthened the Church's nationalistic appeal. This explains in part why Camacho's government tolerated public outbursts of religiosity and indirect criticism articulated by foreign prelates. Therefore, the press reported in detail on what was said during these special activities since it touched a chord with their readership.

The US delegation was headed by the bishop of Erie, John Mark Gannon, who also was at that time chairman of the US Bishop's Committee for the Montezuma Seminary (a seminary in New Mexico established during the conflict with the revolutionary State to ensure continued training of Mexican students for priesthood). Gannon and many of his compatriots made noted contributions to special events held during the festivities.[102] The archbishop of San Antonio, Robert Lucev, was one of them. Catholic connections between San Antonio and Mexico were solid and age-old, so when Lucev took the floor, his sermon was particularly meaningful. What he said during the celebrations of 10 October was reported in the newspapers of the capital the following day:

In recent times, the enemies of God and religion have won many victories. In some moments, in some places, the Church's voice was almost stifled. Her rightful public purpose in the life of nations was negated... Recently, political leaders have discovered

the uses of democracy. But Catholic theologians have preached
its virtues for centuries. They say that lasting peace must be
based on justice. Since its very beginning our Church has taught
nothing but that... More than ever, our national leaders will
need divine guidance to maintain this frail and unstable peace.
[A symbol of peace] appeared on Mount Tepeyac 414 years ago,
and we finally arrive here as humble pilgrims to kneel down in
front of her image to honour and praise her, thanking her for
everything she has done for our Western Hemisphere, and fer-
vently asking her to be our patron and queen for years
to come.[103]

In the first part of his sermon, Lucev's was making an explicit reference to the European context, but many Mexicans could apply
his observations to the period of persecution in their country. As for
the second part, other North American prelates directly echoed his
speech, saying that the hour of America had come thanks to the
Virgin of Guadalupe's protection, and that she embodied tolerance
in its fullest sense. Deep down, the ACM's president Martín del
Campo must have thought, mission accomplished.

Lucev's sermon aptly demonstrated the US prelates' utmost respect
for Mexico's most important symbol of identity. But Catholic stakeholders used the example of French Canada to greater effect to
express how the *modus vivendi* could provide more leeway to the
Church's social project. Villeneuve travelled to Mexico with an
important contingent of prelates from all over the country: the archbishops of Edmonton, Moncton, Montreal, and Ottawa were there
along with the bishop of Bathurst and the superiors of the
Dominicans, the Franciscans, the Holy Cross Fathers, the Oblates,
and the Indian Missions to Northwestern Canada. Mgr Cyrille
Gagnon, rector of Université Laval, Ernest Côté, commander of
Quebec, and André Turcot, Mexico's honorary consul in Quebec
City, were also part of the delegation. This contingent was representative of Canadian Catholicism, highlighting the country's multicul-
tural nature; yet it was the similarities with its French-speaking
counterpart that found an echo in the Mexican context.

The sermons preached on the day dedicated to Canada made this
clear. The contributors specifically sang the praises of Catholic
Quebec since, they argued, this North American Latin society could
be an inspiration to Catholic Mexico. The sermon the Jesuit Julio

Vértiz Burchard preached – in which he welcomed the Canadian prelates to Mexico – is a good example.[104] Vértiz spoke in the name of the Mexican Catholic Church: "I believe these superb Guadalupan celebrations would have been somewhat darkened or they would have lacked, at least, one of their most spectacular example of magnificence had this shinning ray of the most splendid light failed to reach us. This light from old France, which without ever knowing Jacobin terror or radical secularism's oppression, has come to possess Human and Christian values unsurpassed in any other nation on this earth; and all this only by following the evolution of its Catholic and French essences."[105] Of course, messages welcoming foreign dignitaries could easily slide into panegyrics (especially in the desire to honour the papal legate for the crowning of a religious icon). Yet, it is easy to understand why Catholic clerics worldwide would have envied the situation of the Church in Quebec: education, health care, and other social programs for its French-speaking majority were administered by the Catholic Church; denominational trade unions, credit unions, and cooperatives almost exclusively structured its workforce and provided for its network of support; and, finally, the ratio of priests per inhabitant in the province was second only to Italy, one in 586.[106] Quebec could indeed look like a part of *ancien régime* France from a Mexican point of view, with the particularity that this Catholic nation benefited from all the advantages of a modern North American economy at the same time.

Vértiz detailed this point by arguing the model of a traditional social order Quebec offered was not incompatible with the modernization of a Latin society like Mexico:

Yes, French Canada offers an incomparable example where individual freedoms are achieved without neglecting the austere dignity of traditional religious customs; where families, prominently chaste and fecund, benefit from all the advantages of the holy sacrament of matrimony; where a wonderful organization triumphs in Catholic schools, in Catholic media, and in the most powerful radiation of a missionary movement; where religious life proliferates in a variety of affluent institutions set up to fulfill all the needs of a Christian society; where their essentially constructive, progressive and dynamic Catholicism leads all kinds of popular and social activities, particularly those associated with workers – Oh, glorious JOC [Young Catholic Workers, a

specialized branch of Catholic Action] the simple evocation of
your name honours me! – where, finally, through the strictest
practice of true democracy guaranteeing civil and political liberties, the purest Christian spirit came to permeate the whole body
of institutions, laws and public administrators governing it.[107]

The argument that the Catholic Church effectively acclimatized
French Canadians to the practice of democracy, guaranteeing civil
liberties, was used against its detractors in the country who argued
that religious structures – especially Catholic ones – inhibited the
modernization of Quebec. But for traditionalists in the province of
Quebec and abroad, the success of social programs administered by
the Church was proof they provided an alternative model of modernization, one specifically appropriate for Latin societies.

To emphasize the usefulness of the French Canadian example in
Mexico, Vértiz ended his message by underlining the cultural proximity of both people: "[How] rich in suggestions is this fruitful
exchange, this joint tribute to the Virgin by two people equally loved
by Mary and equally burdened by the cross! Oh French and Catholic
Canada, Kingdom of Mary on earth, shining son of the eternally
shining France, Latin brother, cherished brother, in the name of
Mexico and in the name of the Holy Virgin of Guadalupe, queen of
Mexico, welcome!"[108] Beyond the embellishments and excessive fervour, there are two points in Father Vértiz's message that I think are
particularly important. First, the Jesuit clearly expressed to a Mexican
audience that the French Canadian traditional social order did not
threaten projects of modernization; it could therefore serve as an
inspiration for the country. In other words, governmental tolerance
could be extended to allow a greater social role for the Catholic
Church without jeopardizing the Revolution's contemporary ideals,
especially those concerning economic progress and the well-being of
the working class. The second aspect is the representation of French
Canada as the inheritor and guardian of French culture in the
Americas. This was done to capitalize on a *sensibilité commune*
expressed through a shared sense of Catholic and Latin identity.
Canadian prelates supported this point by saying that French Canada
– this Latin society in the midst of a British Dominion north of the
US – constituted the perfect bridge for Latin Americans toward North
American modernity. Authoritarianism was not the only way Latin
nations could adapt to the new economic reality imposed by industrialization: the French Canadian example proved it.

This discourse reveals that prelates attempted to pressure the government without endangering the *modus vivendi* by using a symbolic politics of their own. They did not put forth a negative message about the *status quo* to ask for more flexibility regarding the Catholic Church. Instead, they did the opposite: they broadcasted a very positive message about Canada – the country's new diplomatic partner – contrasting its radically different social arrangement with the situation in Mexico. At the same time, North American dignitaries made reference to the pan-American appeal of the Virgin of Guadalupe. Doing so was obviously strengthening the Mexican Catholic Church's nationalist credentials at a time when US hegemony in the region seemed irreversible. The enthusiastic international coverage of the commemoration, which displayed the strength of Catholic ties of solidarity in the Americas, weighed heavily in favour of this argument.

Further Considerations on the Commemoration's Coverage

By and large, the Mexican and international press coverage of the event was very positive. There is no point repeating that various complaints were sent to President Camacho by groups like the Instituto Social Continental.[109] Private denunciations might have been numerous, but the government (and the international community) turned a deaf ear to their demands. If the Catholic Church and the revolutionary government wanted to publicize their reconciliation, they used the media very effectively to achieve that objective. This accomplishment garnered crucial support for their cause.

The commemoration benefited from the greatest international visibility a religious event taking place in Mexico had ever had. It has to be said first that Cardinal Villeneuve's travelling by car and train from Quebec to Mexico City was widely covered by the press along the way, calling the attention of the US public to the festivities south of the border.[110] But this international dimension was reinforced by the Church's astute usage of mass media in Mexico. Activities were often planned as media events. Ecclesiastical authorities made sure all the available technologies – press, radio, cinema – were used to publicize their message. For example, on 12 October, they used the radio to broadcast the pope's message to the crowd gathered at the basilica live from the Vatican, a first in the history of the Church in Mexico.[111] The coronation was also filmed and distributed to foreign dioceses, giving larger international scope to the event.[112]

Consequently, the feeling of reconciliation evoked by the festivities reached a broader public than just Catholic stakeholders in Mexico.

Newspapers throughout North America relayed this message of concord and agreed on the success of the coronation, and Catholic publications in Mexico enthusiastically reported on this interest. They seemed particularly satisfied by the coverage the celebrations received in the papal legate's province. Messages broadcast in Quebec usually went along the following lines: "Seven years ago, Mexico was going through a period of religious persecution; four years ago, no priest would dare to wear his Roman collar in public. Now, Mexico City has just organised the most astonishing religious demonstration America has seen since the Eucharistic Congress of Buenos Aires."[113] This is exactly the type of message the supporters of the government's national unity campaign hoped for. Indeed, reports like this made Camacho's Mexico look like a place of civilized tolerance. Catholic publications pointed out that this perception had wider implications than the simple recognition of the reestablishment of religious freedom. After the horrors of the Second World War, Mexico had just crowned a brown Virgin as a symbol of peace and fraternity, a *mestiza* Virgin. Catholic clerics made sure international acknowledgement of this fact was known in their country.

The interpretation of the coronation's meaning in Quebec once again supported their objectives. Mexicans were informed of the parallel special celebrations held in Quebec City on 12 October. Of course, these festivities were covered by the Quebec City press as well. People could read Joseph Ledit's sermon preached for this occasion. The Jesuit used it to articulate a plea against racism – favourably positioning the Catholic Church on this issue: "Through her motherly sweetness, Our Lady of Guadalupe teaches us that all the races of the world can rightfully benefit from her protection; that a vanquished people should never lose hope, since the conquerors ought to bow in front of a force which is infinitely gentle but strong enough to smash their pride – in other words, the strength of a mother. With her decision to appear to a poor Indian, choosing him to be her ambassador to the archbishop of Mexico, Our Lady demonstrated the absurdity of racism and reaffirmed the unity of humankind."[114] Ledit was not the only one to point this out. The ULA's president and honorary president, Dostaler O'Leary and Olivier Maurault, also used the Mexican example to condemn racism

– stating for their part that the Latin and Catholic identity they defended could not be interpreted otherwise. Ledit's sermon was reported in Mexican Catholic publications. The article he published on the Virgin in the magazine of *L'École sociale populaire* was also reproduced in Mexico in the ACM's *Boletín del Asistente Eclesiástico* under the title "La Virgen Americana."[115] Ledit's argument gave credence to the contentions of the Mexican Church that the country could claim some form of moral ascendency over the continent through the glory of the Virgin of Guadalupe.

Quebec's political class had good news in store for Camacho's national unity campaign as well. The Guadalupan celebrations earned the Mexican government official congratulations from Quebec's lieutenant-governor and the whole cabinet of Premier Maurice Duplessis. The press in Mexico reported this with interest, mentioning as well that the government of Quebec asserted that the whole province was at one with the people of Mexico in honouring the Virgin of Guadalupe. The commemorative album of the golden jubilee commented on this support and concluded on its significance: "This way, there was at least one State – and one among the most civilised and democratic – that was officially with us 'in praying to the Virgin of Guadalupe,' congratulating the '*Presidente de Méjico*' and the whole Nation for these splendid days of celebration that went through without a hitch. [We] must sincerely be grateful [to our government] for this event which constituted the most dazzling and resounding plebiscite of national unity the history of our country has ever had."[116] It is true that the 1945 Marian celebrations portrayed Catholic groups as being at ease in this revolutionary country. The commemoration definitively showed the nation and the world that the tacit mutual tolerance between the Catholic Church and the Mexican government was not simply based on hearsay. President Camacho might not have been ready to go as far as explicitly supporting the festivities – for example, by putting in an appearance – but foreign governments could still congratulate him for his crucial collaboration. For the purpose of strengthening the *modus vivendi*, that was sufficient.

CONCLUSION

The 1945 festivities did not cause the *modus vivendi*. It was rather a grandiose celebration of its accomplishment, which, when carefully deconstructed, demonstrates the necessary steps required to sustain it. In many ways, the golden jubilee represented a cathartic moment of reconciliation between the Catholic Church and the modern Mexican State. The fact that this cleansing of bad feelings was accomplished by staging a similar version of the 1895 crowning is a testimony to the depth of this new concord. Much like the 1895 event, the 1945 Guadalupan celebration was intended for national and international audiences. In this case, however, the international audience was not a mere spectator. The participation of foreign dignitaries in the festivities in Mexico and the coverage of their participation seen in their home countries were essential parts of the spectacle, a spectacle that saw the Virgin and the Cardinal, national unity, and pan-American harmony performed on the stage of Mexican politics for all to see.

The politics of religion in Second World War Mexico required a difficult balancing act. We have seen in this chapter the political and cultural distance the Mexican State and the Catholic Church were ready to cover to make concessions. Achieving and maintaining peace in the conflict between anticlerical and Catholic forces necessitated an astute use of symbolic politics. The religious and revolutionary aesthetics that triggered symbolic violence and physical attacks in the 1920s and 1930s needed to be recoded in order to defuse their inflammatory potential. To prevent destabilization, the Mexican government and the Catholic Church had to find a middle ground without alienating their grass roots. They discovered that figurative concessions on both sides – one accepting a limited comeback of religion in the public sphere, the other supporting the government's national unity crusade – could become leverage to build and sustain a *modus vivendi*. The nationalistic symbolism associated with the Virgin of Guadalupe became a discursive point of convergence where their institutional interests met. The Church argued that *she* personified the soul of Mexico. The State maintained that good *guadalupanos* respected the legitimate authority of the country the Virgin embodied.

The pan-American situation helped them in this endeavour. In thi time of war, the whole continent had to come together and openly challenging the established order was out of the question. This chapter has illustrated how Cardinal Villeneuve's participation in the Marian celebrations provided a secure opportunity for Catholics to express disagreement by framing it as constructive criticism strengthening the larger framework of national unity. It was by asserting that the nation would benefit from a pan-American network of Catholic solidarity and by singing the praises of the contrasting social arrangement of Canada, that ecclesiastical authorities were able to argue in favour of further leeway for the Church in Mexico.

Conclusion

The Second World War was a major turning point in world history, a moment that helped redefine national identities and reshape international relations. In North America, Canada acquired a new international status, Mexico turned over a new leaf on conflicting social relations with Catholic groups, and both countries reconfigured their ties to the United States. On the margins of this scenario, French Canadian nationalists and Catholic militants in Mexico tried to make geopolitical relations more favourable to their sociocultural struggles. The fact that Catholic authors in both nations came to see these struggles over cultural identity as interconnected enabled them to use events showcasing expressions of solidarity as political capital. As we have seen, the balls and congresses organized by the Union des Latins d'Amérique, the student and dignitary visits at UNAM's summer school and Quebec's Catholic institutions, and the transnational character of the fiftieth anniversary celebration of the Virgin of Guadalupe's crowning, constituted occasions to underline the role political outsiders could play in the establishment of good connections with diplomatic partners. In some ways, the organizers of these encounters attempted to influence the national balance of power by positioning themselves as key actors on the scene of pan-American affairs. The episodes of transnational collaboration analyzed in this book represented, to paraphrase Bruce Curtis (discussing Lord Durham's strategy of comportment), efforts to perform grandeur "brought visibly to bear upon the field of... political relations."[1] But did this strategy also contribute to the attainment of specific local goals? Could social groups who felt marginalized by the government acquire enough symbolic capital to influence the political process?

It is impossible to settle this question once and for all. Proving that symbolic gestures and cultural acts are decisive factors in resolving a complex situation is tricky. It is indeed difficult to confirm that reconfiguring a discourse of identity or putting a group's connections with prestigious foreign sympathizers on display on the national scene has direct implications favouring local objectives. Nevertheless, I highlighted various examples of the role played by Quebec and Mexico's civil societies in influencing official diplomatic interactions, and I analyzed their implications for Canadian and Mexican politics, revealing that these situations did in fact convince federal authorities to take a stand – albeit not always publicly. When the endeavours of groups from French Canadian and Mexican civil society were judged potentially subversive, authorities reacted by trying to co-opt their transnational agenda or silence it; when federal administrators considered that the government could benefit from the situation, they allowed them to organize these encounters autonomously. Of course, making cultural compromises with a dissatisfied social group could constitute a politically profitable move, especially since Canadian-Mexican relations were not really the main concern of either country's foreign policy.

Which begs the question: do the French Canadian-Mexican episodes of collaboration analyzed in this book, the *prise de parole* and symbolic actions of these groups and the resulting diplomatic controversies, still have resonance today? Considering the short-lived importance of this transnational exchange, should we simply describe such episodes as interesting but insignificant footnotes of history? After all, once the war was over, the connections established did not lead to a long-lasting reconfiguration of north-south political interaction. The half-hearted attention Latin America got from Ottawa before the 1940s did not significantly change with the beginning of the Cold War, Canada aligning its foreign policy on a North Atlantic axis rather than a pan-American one.[2] I conceded at the beginning of this book that, for the most part, the interactions studied did not in themselves change the course of history. In retrospect, contacts – like Mexican diplomats cozying up to French Canadian nationalists or Catholic militants inviting religious dignitaries from Quebec to Mexico – might have helped tip the balance in specific instances, but they still count for little in the grand scheme of things.

Yet, they are symptomatic of deeper group dynamics relating to
majority-minority relations in Canada and Mexico. The episodes of
collaboration analyzed also shed light on the inter-connectedness of
national histories and provide an example for analyzing early cultural forms of international relations, early cultural forms that question the premises of the long-held view in academia that economic
and political motivations can explain the evolution of diplomatic
relations between Canada and Mexico. Indeed, re-framing a discourse of identity so that it impinges on national politics and building strategic alliances with foreign sympathizers to influence the
balance of power are common strategies used by marginalized
groups to confront hegemonic control; Canadian and Mexican
authorities had to react to these strategies during the war. The emergence of *latinité* as a discourse of identity in Quebec or the Mexican
Catholic Church's new outlook on "North American" democracy
and economic modernization were symbolic stances meant to have
an impact on the political process. It was hoped that this impact
would produce potential improvements in the social position of
French Canadian nationalists and Mexican Catholic militants.
However, the transnational collaborations analyzed in this book
resulted in mixed results more often than not – at times quite different from the intentions of their organizers. Yet, even the interactions
that could be qualified as "failures" constitute enlightening illustra-
tions of the way power relations were (re)produced in Canada and
Mexico. They point to new dynamics involving politically marginalized social groups and national authorities that were emerging during the war.

I explained earlier that Canadianists and Mexicanists can interpret
these transnational interactions differently, either as attempts to
secure a French Canadian voice in foreign relations (strengthening
along the way Quebec's position in the federation) or as a course of
action to use Catholic networking in North America to first denounce
religious persecution in Mexico and then to support the Church-
State *modus vivendi* (improving at the same time the image of the
Mexican government abroad and the perception of the Catholic
Church at home). These different interpretations can sway the final
assessment we have on the outcome of civil society's transnational
collaboration and the relative importance we give to governmental
reaction to it. As a result, I will present my final observations separately on the intertwined histories analyzed.

An Original but Disquieting Prise de Parole: French Canada's Latinité at a Crossroads

I mentioned at the outset that one question I would pay particular attention to is whether or not the crafting of an imagined community reaching across national borders could advance local demands. The promotion of Latin identity in U L A activities provided the best insights to investigate this. Indeed, their original take on Quebec's *américanité* – latinizing this trait of national character by promoting widespread continental relations with Spanish- and Portuguese-speaking countries – constituted a shrewd way to counter French Canada's cultural isolation at the beginning of the war. According to a British diplomat quoted by the Canadian Ministry of External Affairs, this vision of French Canadian *latinité* could have been used to sanitize the British Empire's image in Latin America. The U L A's leadership claimed that they were willing to serve as ambassadors for the anglophone majority, providing only that they could broadcast freely their own understanding of *Canadianess*, which meant speaking out as French Canadians on the international scene.

In this scenario, the performance of grandeur would bear fruit for French Canada's reputation first and foremost, something many decision-makers in Ottawa were wary of. Furthermore, the way pan-American relations were presented during U L A activities – a view channelled through the disadvantageous socio-political relations French Canadians had to cope with in North America – was also problematic for Ottawa. For example, the External Affairs' staff saw this presentation of pan-American relations as potentially harmful to what they considered to be the country's best interests. Indeed, the presentations made at U L A events revealed that a hegemonic/counter-hegemonic model of social interaction was used to decode power relations between Anglo and Latin America, and between English and French Canada. In forging alliances in the Americas, French Canadians were attempting to solve their own national dilemma: how could francophone Quebec assert its identity while remaining an integral part of a country where anglophones formed the majority of the population? The answer U L A's spokespersons proposed was to re-contextualize French Canada's cultural struggle into a broader civilizational framework, one that had an impact on Canada's foreign relations. They successfully called Ottawa's attention to the issue of Canadian-Mexican relations, even positioning themselves as knowledge-brokers for a while. But the freedom they were granted to organize goodwill missions between both nations was curtailed because of diplomatic imbroglios resulting from the way they presented their country's identity abroad. Yet, for a while, the U L A diffused the language of French Canadian national assertion on the international scene decades before the Gérin-Lajoie Doctrine was crafted to legitimize Quebec's authority to act internationally in its fields of provincial competence.

Despite the ephemeral political use of *latinité*, this episode reveals a new approach concerning identity politics in Canada, an approach born from the desire among Quebec's francophone population to be considered as a *majority*, and therefore, as equals to English Canadians in the federation. For many, the idea that the Confederation put the two "founding people" on a par was all but a broken dream, since French Canadians were treated as an ethnic minority outside Quebec and as second-class citizens in the province's economic structures. Something had to be done to reposition francophones on the political scene. U L A spokespersons wanted to break that predicament by establishing linkages with the largest cultural group in the Western Hemisphere, a group that was given some deference in North America under Roosevelt's Good Neighbor Policy. This strategy did not work directly, but it enabled nationalists and the government in Quebec City to articulate new ideas concerning the province's political role in the Americas and to contemplate in passing what the symbolism associated with acting as Québécois on the international scene would be like. However, these ideas were nipped in the bud as a result of O'Leary's removal from the U L A's presidency and the 1944 electoral defeat of Godbout's Liberal Party.

One constraint with studying this struggle of ideas, however, results from the fact that *latinité* never constituted a well-articulated ideology in Quebec, but remained at the discursive level of a deeply-felt sentiment (a feeling of being part of a larger Catholic civilization). It cannot be said that this discourse of identity had specific literary canons like *québécitude* would have later on. Nevertheless, I contend that the *prise de parole* by members of the U L A in favour of Latin identity is symptomatic of an emerging distinctive structure of feelings (to use Raymond Williams' concept).[3] In many ways, the sudden interest in this discourse during the war constitutes a prelude to the expression of a neo-nationalist ideology at the turn of the 1960s. The course of action adopted during the Quiet Revolution, and the symbolic politics involving foreign sympathizers used by the Parti Québécois (PQ) thereafter, echoed the actions taken by the ULA to broadcast a distinct French Canadian identity in Mexico in the 1940s. As an illustration of that parallel, Quebec-Mexico's political connections even made a comeback, haunting federal-provincial relations half a century later.

Indeed, a controversy surrounding the triangular diplomatic relation of Quebec-Mexico-Canada resurfaced when the PQ attempted to draw diplomatic support south of the Rio Grande. From the late 1970s on, the State of Quebec developed independent relations in the region, opening a Délégation générale du Québec à Mexico.[4] Once again, Mexico City became a point of contention between the federal and provincial governments. The symbolic conflict over those links reached a peak when the candidate of the PAN in the 2000 election won the presidency, marking the end of the Partido Revolucionario Institucional's seventy year rule over Mexico. Vicente Fox, the elected candidate, then officially invited the leader of the PQ and Premier of Quebec, Lucien Bouchard, to his historic inauguration as president. The Liberal government of Jean Chrétien in Ottawa did not appreciate this polite gesture. As his administration argued, Quebec was not a sovereign state, and the premier of a province should not stand alongside the Americas' heads of state as an equal. Through political and diplomatic pressures, the Canadian government succeeded in having Bouchard's invitation to the official ceremony revoked.[5] The potential political capital the PQ could have drawn from this prestigious event was unacceptable in the eyes of Prime Minister Chrétien. As we have seen in various chapters of this book, the use of symbolic politics to further Quebec's goal without Ottawa's approval was disallowed, unless the provincial government was ready to confront the federal administration on that issue. On the subject of symbolic politics, Prime Minister Chrétien once declared: "Our country is sick of symbolic politics, and… it may die from this disease. In symbolic politics, unlike ordinary politics, everything becomes a matter of black and white. Positions are turned into sacred ideals on which no compromise is possible… So I would ask all of us in the next few months to be careful in our assessments and our rhetoric, to avoid emotionally laden language and symbolic politics that could destroy this country. We cannot allow Canada to die of symbolic politics."[6] Chrétien's plea was disingenuous. What federal authorities want – in Canada as much as anywhere else – is to gain the upper hand and control the meaning associated with symbolic politics. After all, Chrétien's administration designed the sponsorship program (the infamous plan to plaster Quebec's public sphere with symbols of the Canadian federation) at the same time he made the above declaration.

Thus, symbolic stances and actions have direct repercussions on the political landscape. The designation "Latins d'Amérique" crafted in the 1940s by French Canadian nationalists did not necessarily entail a reconfiguration of federal-provincial dynamics like the emergence of a Québécois identity would later on. But, by some means, the experience of the Second World War constituted a way to test the waters of a new kind of identity politics involving foreign sympathizers. In the 1960s, Quebec was pro-active in establishing independent cultural relations with the francophone world, forcing Canada to move in the same direction to recover this symbolic space. In this way, nationalists made sure that if Quebec and Canada had "dirty linen to wash," they could be supported by "natural" allies who would take notice.[7] Carlos Calderón's intervention on behalf of the French Canadian students (getting a pledge from the Canadian government that international communications in French would be allowed during their stay in Mexico) constitutes a fascinating precedent to Québécois nationalists' efforts to get foreign officials' support for their cause. The end result, however, is in line with Chrétien's observations: the Canadian government's handling of the situation – flip-flopping on its promise – indicates that symbolic politics with nationalist groups from Quebec has always been perceived as a slippery slope.

Consequently, after the Church-State conflict in the 1920s and 30s, we get the impression that Mexico City was more adroit than Ottawa in using symbolic politics to its own advantage. Canada seemed to have lagged behind Quebec and Mexico in establishing north-south connections. In the 1940s, the impulse to promote Canadian-Mexican relations mostly came from cultural associations in Quebec's civil society rather than decision-makers in Ottawa or the English-speaking business community. As for Mexican diplomats, they sought early on to establish formal ambassadorial links with this British Dominion. They were finally able to put pressure on Ottawa when they backtracked from their anticlerical revolutionary appeal and followed the lead of the UCMCF in Mexico, establishing connections with French Canadian nationalists from Université de Montréal and Université

Laval. Using the transnational social networks of Catholic groups was an efficient avenue to call Canada's attention to their requests. By and large, Ottawa looked to be a passive participant in this triangular relation, reacting to diplomatic breakthroughs rather than taking the lead in occupying that symbolic space.

Symbolic Politics in Mexico: The Way out of the Church-State Impasse

If anything, the Mexican use of symbolic politics directly contradicts Chrétien's assertion. Since the end of the 1930s, symbolic politics has been characterized by shades-of-grey positions rather than being "a matter of black and white." Of course, Mexico had gone through a period in which symbolic violence constituted a serious motive for launching violent attacks against opponents and their social agenda. But while symbolic acts often resulted in bloodshed in the late 1920s and early 1930s, they also became the solution for finding a way out of the paralysing religious conflict. Once the government overcame the recurring threats of a coup d'état, and once the State solidified its corporatist foundations, the leading bodies of Mexico were in a position to make an astute use of symbolic politics to bring about a truce with Catholic opponents of the regime (and put an end to the international pressures resulting from the mobilization of Catholics around the World against religious persecution). The Catholic Church and leading conservative groups agreed to this course of action as they saw that a rapprochement with the State could safeguard their institutional interests. They worked out a tacit agreement of mutual respect that helped them recode the controversial symbolism of the interwar period, finally enabling a limited comeback of religious iconography in Mexico's public sphere during the Second World War. Symbolic politics played a crucial role in this course of action. Cultural historians have noted before that "ritualized politics of public celebrations" have supported the consolidation of power in Mexico, and that "Mexico's entry into Second World War in May 1942 reinforced this process of patriotic identification."[8] As my research shows, this strategy also worked in favour of a rapprochement between the government and Catholic militants in the early 1940s. In Canada, however, it seems that the French Canadians' practice of symbolic politics resulted instead in widening the gap with federal authorities.

Could we explain this discrepancy by arguing that the stakes were higher in Canada? After all, French Canadians had a real power base in Canada's second-most populous province. The strategic positioning of nationalist groups from Quebec, along with the rise of nationalist political parties like the Bloc Populaire, gave the impression that the Canadian federation's foundations might be at risk in the French-speaking province. In the 1940s, part of the Canadian Ministry of External Affairs' staff thought that the ULA's rhetoric of Latin affinities was a smokescreen for separatism and pro-fascist leanings (an impression Ambassador del Río Cañedo apparently shared). Collaboration with such individuals was out of the question for them. Nevertheless, Canada's situation was not bleaker than Mexico's. To start with, the conflict opposing revolutionary anticlericals and Catholic fundamentalists in Camacho's Mexico remained bloodier than nationalists' skirmishes with federal authorities in Canada. Middle-class dissatisfaction and Catholic mobilization also posed a non-negligible threat at the beginning of Camacho's *sexenio*, and it was common knowledge that prominent members of UNAM's conservative circles had pro-fascist inclinations. Yet, the context of the Second World War was successfully used to justify holding out an olive branch to Catholic militants, discrediting remaining counterrevolutionaries along the way. Two observations can be drawn from this incongruity: first, there was an inability (or lack of goodwill) in Canada to imagine a way out of cultural binaries opposing the federal government to patriotic groups from Quebec; and second, Catholic militants and the government of Manuel Ávila Camacho were ready to find common ground to finally achieve "national unity."

In point of fact, the episodes of informal collaboration between Catholic militants and representatives of the government attest to the extent to which Mexico's political landscape was shifting in the early 1940s. I provided many examples to demonstrate how comfortable Catholics felt under Camacho as a result of cultural concessions made by his regime – and the coverage of the coronation celebrations, this cathartic moment of reconciliation between the Catholic Church and the Mexican State, certainly demonstrated that. Yet, stabilizing this changeover without substantially reforming the 1917 Constitution or awakening anticlerical intolerance was not a given. Enforcing the *modus vivendi* meant walking a political tightrope, both for Catholic and revolutionary authorities alike.

Catholic and conservative groups were granted substantial leeway, but on one condition: their actions could not destabilize the government's national unity campaign. Rodulfo Brito Foucher learned this at his expense. Conservatives had to test the government's limits without forcing the authorities to overtly go against their revolutionary credentials. Episodes like Brito Foucher's ouster served to calibrate the margin of manoeuvre these groups had and consequently adjust their actions to uphold the Church-State rapprochement. Over time, Catholic groups learned to re-contextualize religious imagery to signify the nation's open-mindedness and tolerance, legitimizing its reappearance in Mexico's public sphere.

In this endeavour, the image of the Virgin of Guadalupe constituted a genuine asset. The Catholic clergy and lay associations like the J C F M toiled over positioning that symbol as an essential building block of the government's national unity campaign. Moreover, the archdiocese of Mexico City, the A C M, and associations like the U C M C F re-framed the Virgin of Guadalupe's nationalist appeal in the context of wartime continental collaboration. With the help of sympathizers from Canada and the US, they organized public events like the fiftieth anniversary of the Virgin's coronation to draw the attention of a North American audience and, therefore, of the Mexican government. The prestige associated with Cardinal Villeneuve's visit (the first cardinal to set foot in Mexico) and the magnificence of religious ceremonies where an important number of North American dignitaries participated along with Mexican and Latin American clergy, guaranteed the success of the event and a safe return of Catholic symbolism to the nation's public sphere. After all, no revolutionary leader could sincerely deny the fact that seeing a "gringo" kneeling down at Guadalupe's feet constituted a potent nationalistic image; unfortunately for them, only the Church could raise this type of symbolic capital. But the Church's performance of grandeur in the early 1940s did reflect on the Mexican State. President Camacho even received direct congratulations from Catholic authorities and foreign officials (such as Quebec's premier and his cabinet) for the success of the event. At the end of the day, the religious iconography that triggered attacks in the 1920s and 1930s was successfully reconfigured to signify Catholic support of the Revolution and contribution to good pan-American relations at the beginning of the 1940s. Alan Knight notes: "The war thus offered superb terrain on which to build the national consensus to which the regime was committed and to which the United States now also contributed – not, as in 1938, as the external enemy but as a fellow-democracy and military ally."[9] My findings demonstrate that Canada played a complementary role in this process.

To conclude with a cliché, we could say that it takes two to tango, but that would be forgetting the active role played by the North American audience in this Mexican act. Nevertheless, governmental and Catholic authorities were ready to make a deal, providing that this was a legally non-binding agreement. On the one hand, the Mexican government granted Catholics substantial leeway to organize cultural activities, even refusing to intervene when numerous anti-constitutional acts were performed during the golden jubilee. We can safely deduce from episodes like this that Mexico's political landscape undeniably experienced a radical reconfiguration during the war, with Catholics being able to secure a safe space in Mexico's public sphere. On the other hand, the larger context of Catholic militants' collaboration with the State points to a second inference: the willingness of Mexico's conservative middle class to endorse the State's semi-authoritarian scheme. Indeed, Catholic groups did not succeed in crafting a completely autonomous space for organizing a counter-hegemonic social project. The actions analyzed in this study indicate that many decided instead to accept becoming minority partners in the authoritarian regime – some directly collaborating with the government, others leading an unthreatening opposition. This point supports Alan Knight's observation that "much of the dissident right of 1940 was incorporated into official politics."[10] After the abrogation of socialist education in 1946, a resolutely anti-communist, conservative nationalism became a point of agreement enabling the interests of Catholic groups to converge with those of the State. This is not surprising considering that the *modus vivendi* they crafted and upheld in the previous years was ultimately celebrated by re-enacting the Virgin of Guadalupe's crowning that, half a century earlier, had symbolized the Church's reconciliation with the Porfirian regime – the very regime the Revolution brought down.

Final Remarks

Back in the undulating countryside of Notre-Dame-de-la-Guadeloupe, Quebec, the inhabitants of the newly created parish heard of the "magnificent" welcome Cardinal Villeneuve received in

Mexico. Like many Catholics in French Canada, they certainly rejoiced to learn that their *Latin* brethren were no longer being "persecuted" by their government.[11] They thanked *Guadalupe* for that. Two other parish churches were named in honour of *la morenita* in Quebec at the turn of the 1970s and 1990s: one was inspired by the inroads made by Liberation Theology and the other was created to minister to Latin American immigrants in Montreal. Still, the Virgin of Guadalupe did not become a symbol of identity in Quebec, as some people had hoped for. Despite what the author of *Histoire des apparitions de Notre-Dame-de-la-Guadeloupe* claimed, this French Canadian connection with *Guadalupe* did not result in many believers associating closely with this religious icon.

It is unclear if the large image of the *Virgen de Guadalupe* decorating the church's façade inspired the inhabitants of La Guadeloupe to join the province's missionary effort, but this parish produced an important number of missionaries for a small village of a thousand souls. By 1995, the commemorative album of the fiftieth anniversary of the parish's foundation reported that thirty-one people born in La Guadeloupe became members of religious orders and eleven became missionaries, many going to Latin America. It has to be said that the French Canadian missionary effort in Latin America experienced a sharp increase from the end of the Second World War to the beginning of the 1970s, reaching close to 2,000 people working in the region. Among these, Father Herman Morin of La Guadeloupe even went back to the land of *Guadalupe* and became an important instigator of the charismatic movement in the state of Guerrero.[12] This way, Mexico and Latin America remained common references in Quebec's public sphere in the following years, mostly because of the rise of the tourist industry, the popularity of Latin American music, and above all the intense missionary effort in the region. On that last subject, Ross Harkness noted in the pages of Toronto's *The Star Weekly* in 1951: "There is under way a Canadian invasion of Latin America that may have more effect on the way of life of the people of this southern continent than all the economic missions of other countries put together. It is a peaceful invasion by Canadian priests and nuns, mostly French-Canadian, and it is at the personal request of the Pope who has circularized Canadian dioceses asking them to spare as many priests as possible for the task of rejuvenating the spiritual life of Latin America."[13] Pope Pius XII and Pope John XXIII did indeed ask the Canadian clergy to revive Latin American

Catholicism since religious authorities believed that this continent was "sinking into paganism."[14] Since little is known about this missionary effort, ongoing research should help us have a better understanding of their actions in Latin America and their impact on generating solidarities between French Canada and Latin America; the impressions brought back in Quebec's public sphere of this politically tumultuous region also remain to be thoroughly investigated. There is interesting work underway to delineate these experiences (Catherine LeGrand's recent publications in *Globe* and *Études d'histoire religieuse* come to mind here or Catherine Foisy's PhD dissertation), but further investigations should give us new insights.[15] A methodical survey of the Mexicans studying in Quebec's seminaries from the Second World War on and a clearer understanding of the first French Canadian members of religious orders who went to Cuernavaca to acquire language skills at Ivan Illich's Centro Intercultural de Documentación should also shed new light on the transnational networks under review in this book.[16]

In the same vein, the use Mexican diplomats and officials made of Catholic social networks in Canada, either by sending relatives to study in religious schools or by collaborating with Catholic associations, merits careful attention. The evidence presented in this study points in the direction of a particular dynamic involving representatives of the revolutionary government and religious institutions in far-away Canada. However, I was not able to assess the intentionality of certain moves. For example, it seems that Carlos Calderón willfully collaborated with Dostaler O'Leary's association for political gain (something representatives of the Canadian Ministry of External Affairs blamed him for after the 1944 controversy involving Canadian students). Although it is certain that this collaboration forced Ottawa to pay attention to Mexican diplomacy in Quebec, I was not able to verify if it constituted a conscious strategy devised by Calderón since his personal archives are closed at the Acervo Histórico Diplomático de la Secretaría de Relaciones Exteriores de México.

Regardless of these uncertainties, one thing is sure: influential members of the U L A deeply appreciated Calderón and Brito Foucher. In the aftermath of the Mexican incidents, both individuals were honoured separately by the association in Montreal at events that garnered the attention of the press – Brito Foucher even received an honorary degree from Laval University. In those instances, their contribution in fostering continental relations respectful of small nations was underlined. We know what the Canadian federal government and the Mexican ambassador in Ottawa thought of these individuals' contacts in Quebec. It would be instructive to know if the controversies they were involved in ever reached the ears of US stakeholders in pan-American affairs. What did the Americans think of the convoluted histories linking French Canadian nationalists and Mexican Catholic militants? Was their perception of the situation influenced by the looming Cold War? After all, the shadow of Uncle Sam was always in the background of these transnational dealings: no direct connection could have been established during the war between the French Canadian and Mexican civil societies had their representatives been denied access to the US railway system linking Montreal and Mexico City.

Still, the US played a supporting role at best; the impulse to establish the north-south cultural connections described here came from political minorities in Canada and Mexico, which had to display inventiveness in order to legitimize their endeavours at first. To a certain extent, we could say that the most dynamic forces seeking to modernize Canadian-Mexican relations and establish transnational connections during the Second World War were groups associated with traditional values and nationalist ideas. Indeed, the deep alienation felt by French Canadians and Mexican Catholics during the 1910s, 1920s, and 1930s prompted them to seek alliances with foreign sympathizers and even reconsider the parameters of their national identity. Therefore, on the periphery of Washington's centre of power, French Canadian and Mexican advocates of a shared Latin and Catholic ethos were engaged in an active re-imagining of socio-political relations, weaving the fabric of a connected history of cultural struggles in an effort to craft an alternative pan-Americanism that would generate better leverage with their respective governments. Whether or not this leverage resulted in concrete gains, this endeavour ultimately demonstrates how ideas about foreign linkages often start with local concerns, and how identities are contextual and malleable – even for those defending the uniqueness of a specific cultural heritage.

Acronyms

AACM	Archivo de la Acción Católica Mexicana
AAQ	Archives de l'archevêché de Québec
ACM	Acción Católica Mexicana
ACJM	Asociación Católica de la Juventud Mexicana
ACRLG	Archives du centre de recherche Lionel-Groulx. These archives are now located at the BANQ
AGN	Archivo General de la Nación
AHDSRE	Acervo Histórico Diplomático de la Secretaría de Relaciones Exteriores de México
AHAM	Archivo Histórico del Arzobispado de México
AHUNAM	Archivo Histórico de la Universidad Nacional Autónoma de México
AUL	Archives de l'Université Laval
AUM	Archives de l'Université de Montréal
BANQ	Bibliothèque et Archives nationales du Québec
CCM	Comité Canada-Mexico
CIAA	Canadian Inter-American Association
CIDA	Canadian International Development Agency
CNCT	Confederación Nacional Católica del Trabajo
CNE	Confederación Nacional de Estudiantes
CROM	Confederación Regional Obrera Mexicana
GIRA	Groupe interdisciplinaire de recherche sur les Amériques
HEC	École des hautes études commerciales
IAC	Inter-American Committee
JCFM	Juventud Católica Femenina Mexicana
JEC	Jeunesse étudiante catholique

JOC	Juventud Obrera Católica
JP	Jeunesses patriotes
K of C	Caballeros de Colón/Chevaliers de Colomb/Knights of Columbus
LAC	Library and Archives Canada
LNDLR	Liga Nacional de la Defensa de la Libertad Religiosa
MAC	Fondo documental Manuel Ávila Camacho
NAFTA	North American Free Trade Agreement
NCWC	National Catholic Welfare Council
PAN	Partido Acción Nacional
PAU	Pan American Union
PQ	Parti Québécois
PRI	Partido Revolucionario Institucional
PRM	Partido de la Revolución Mexicana
RCMP	Royal Canadian Mounted Police
SEP	Secretaría de Educación Pública
UCMCF	Unión cultural México-Canadá francés
UDCM	Unión de Damas Católicas Mejicanas
ULA	Union des Latins d'Amérique
UNAM	Universidad Nacional Autónoma de México
UNEC	Unión Nacional de Estudiantes Católicos
UNPF	Unión Nacional de Padres de Familia
UNS	Unión Nacional Sinarquista
US	United States of America

Notes

INTRODUCTION

1 To state that French Canadian culture is one of the "Latin" cultures of the Americas might be surprising to some. Of course, there are important differences nowadays between Québécois and Latin American cultures. Nervertheless, in its largest sense, being culturally Latin has always meant speaking a Latin language, coming from a nation whose roots went back to a Mediterranean European culture, and being Roman Catholic. In this sense, French Canada has always been Latin. In addition, the influence of ultramontane ideology on society and the transmission of a humanist tradition that glorified Greco-Latin civilization – common in Quebec's academic life before the 1960s – strengthened these Latin foundations. These cultural markers provided the underpinnings of an identity that differentiated French Canadian from Anglo-Protestant culture.

2 Armstrong and Nelles, *Southern Exposure*; Cuff and Granatstein, *Canadian-American Relations in Wartime*; Secretaría de Relaciones Exteriores Instituto Matías Romero de Estudios Diplomáticos, ed., *Canadá y México*; Granatstein, *Canada's Foreign Relations*; Granatstein, *Canadian Foreign Policy since 1945*; Hillmer and Granatstein, *Empire to Umpire*; Holloway, *Canadian Foreign Policy*; Mace, "Les relations du Québec avec l'Amérique latine"; Melakopides, *Pragmatic Idealism*; Lorenzo Meyer, *Su majestad británica contra la revolución mexicana*; Murray, "Canada's First Diplomatic Missions in Latin America"; Ogelsby, *Gringos from the Far North*; Rochlin, *Discovering the Americas*; Schiavon, Spenser, and Vázquez Olivera, *En busca de una nación soberana*; Schuler, *Mexico between Hitler and Roosevelt*; Stevenson, *Canada, Latin America, and the New Internationalism*. The history of Canadian-Mexican

relations has often been written from the viewpoint of political science. Various studies also include information on Canadian-Mexican connections as footnotes to Canada-US relations or Mexican diplomacy toward the British Empire. This is not surprising considering that Canadian-Mexican relations remained economically and politically marginal up until the signing of NAFTA.

3 A few good examples of this literature are: Behiels, Cook, and Martel, *Nation, Ideas, Identities*; Coleman, *The Independence Movement in Quebec*; Handler, *Nationalism and the Politics of Culture in Quebec*; Lacombe, *La rencontre de deux peuples élus*; Mann, *The Dream of Nation*; Ryan, *Penser la nation*.

4 Some good studies on the conflict between Catholic groups and the Revolutionary State are: Galeana de Valadés, ed., *Relaciones Estado-Iglesia*; Meyer, *La Cristiada*; Butler, *Popular and Political Identity in Mexico's Cristero Rebellion*; Reich, *Mexico's Hidden Revolution*; Vaughan and Lewis, *The Eagle and the Virgin*.

5 De Certeau, *La Prise de parole*, 175. The concept of "prise de parole," which states that discursive stands can be actions in themselves, was developed by Michel de Certeau. The expressions "speaking out," "taking the floor," or "capture of speech" can be used, but I believe they do not translate the full dimension of the concept in French. As a result, I will regularly use the concept in French, much like I will do for the concept of *américanité*. For an English translation of the concept, see De Certeau and Giard, *The Capture of Speech*.

6 Read French Canadians. The name *Canadiens* was used to identify the French-speaking population of the Province of Quebec, the administrative unit created out of New France by the Royal Proclamation of 1763. After the 1791 Constitutional Act, creating Lower and Upper Canada, the name *Canadiens* was still used for the francophone population. French Canadian was used more broadly after the British settlers also identified as Canadians (establishing a distinction between the French and English-speaking population of the country), but the word *Canadiens* remained as a popular reference to the French-speaking population.

7 Garibi Tortolero, *Histoire des apparitions de Notre-Dame de la Guadeloupe*, 29. All translations in this book from French or Spanish sources are mine, unless otherwise mentioned. My PhD dissertation can be consulted for the original quotes in French and Spanish.

8 Joseph and Nugent, ed., *Everyday Forms of State Formation*.

9 Inspiring literature is emerging on the role of domestic and symbolic politics in Canada, influenced by post-colonial studies and Pierre Bourdieu's

insights. A few good examples are: Curtis, "The 'Most Splendid Pageant Ever Seen'"; Nelles, *The Art of Nation-Building*; and Radforth, *Royal Spectacle*. As for Mexico, historians have made significant contributions to our understanding of the connections between cultural politics and nation-building projects. Three good examples are: Fein, "Everyday Forms of Transnational Collaboration"; Tenorio-Trillo, *Mexico at the World's Fairs*; and Vaughan, *Cultural Politics in Revolution*. It is also worth noting that studies of Mexican relations with Latin America do emphasize the importance of symbolic politics to stimulate those linkages. Two good examples are: Yankelevich, "América Latina en la agenda diplomática de la revolución mexicana"; and González González, "México ante América Latina."

10 By French Canadian nationalists, I do not necessarily mean separatists like two of the main actors I am studying here, the brothers Dostaler and Walter O'Leary. By French Canadian nationalists, I simply mean those who identified French Canada as their *patrie* and lobbied for public recognition of Canada's two 'founding' nations, rather than blending everybody into a completely amalgamated Canadian identity. The leading intellectual figure of French Canada in the interwar period, Lionel Groulx, summarized this position by promoting the idea of the French State. As Pierre Trépanier explained, Groulx's ideological position was not incompatible with the Canadian federation, since for the cleric – who never directly supported separatism – this idea meant "serving the [French Canadian] nation or using the provincial State to promote national assertion" (see Gougeon, "Entrevue avec Pierre Trépanier," in his book *Histoire du nationalisme québécois*, 89–104). Concerning the designation "Catholic militants," I have to mention that Catholicism continued to constitute the religion of the overwhelming majority in Mexico after the Revolution. Nevertheless, the Constitution of 1917 and the ending of the Cristero War (1929) effectively confined the political affirmation of Catholics to the margins of Mexican affairs of State. Fighting for the Catholic Church to play a wider social and cultural role categorized someone as a Catholic activist. I could have used the label "católicos intransigentes" like a significant part of the historiography does in regards to the ultra-conservative Catholic right, but it seemed to me that the term militant was more inclusive in the context of my study to integrate a wider spectrum of Catholic opposition and negotiation with the revolutionary State.

11 Trudeau, *Federalism and the French Canadians*, 208. In Mexico, Catholic groups were still routinely characterized as counter-revolutionaries in

the 1940s, despite the actual rapprochement with the State. For example, see Pattee and Inter-American Committee, eds., *The Catholic Revival in Mexico*.

12 While the influence of intellectuals and capitalists has been acknowledged in studies analyzing the professionalization of Canada and Mexico's external relations in the interwar period, these works still tend to downplay the influence of other sectors of civil society in the process. A few examples are: Granatstein, *The Ottawa Men*; Hall, *Oil, Banks, and Politics*; Owram, *Government Generation*; Schiavon, Spenser, and Vázquez Olivera, *En busca de una nación soberana*; Schuler, *Mexico between Hitler and Roosevelt*.

13 Adrian Bantjes rightfully points out that, "judging from the recent political and moral assertiveness of the Mexican Roman Catholic Church and laity, and the shrill responses of clerophobes, Catholicism is alive and well in post-*priísta* Mexico. During his momentous and ultimately successful bid for the presidency in 2000, PAN candidate Vicente Fox unfurled the banner of the Virgin of Guadalupe, Mexico's most powerful symbol of national identity. Soon after Fox's inauguration, *panistas* in various states ... launched moralistic campaigns ... and passed legislation penalizing women seeking abortion after being raped." Bantjes, "Religion and the Mexican Revolution," 223–4.

14 Trudeau, *Federalism and the French Canadians*, 211.

15 Aird, *André Patry et la présence du Québec dans le monde*; Balthazar, Bélanger, and Mace, *Trente ans de politique extérieure du Québec*; Paquin, ed., *Histoire des relations internationales du Québec*; Mesli, "Le développement de la 'diplomatie éducative' du Québec," 115–32.

16 Trudeau, *Federalism and the French Canadians*, 211.

17 Dorion-Poussart, "Le développement des relations Québec-Mexique"; Gay, *Les élites québécoises et l'Amérique latine*; Mace, "Les relations du Québec avec l'Amérique latine."

18 Armony, "Des Latins du Nord?," 30. In this citation, Armory is quoting Gay, *Les élites québécoises et l'Amérique latine*, 324. It is interesting to note that if this appraisal of the literature finds an echo in Manuel Garibi Tortolero's quote mentioned above, the subject of Tortolero's book, the Virgin of Guadalupe, contradicts the assessment of this literature, as Gay states that this language of direct filiation between French Canadians and Latin Americans "symbolically expulsed the Indo-American and Afro-American populations from the history of Latin America," ibid., 325.

19 Gay, *Les élites québécoises et l'Amérique latine*, 34.

20 Bouchard, *Genèse des nations et cultures du nouveau monde*, 215.

21 Although this situation was contested by the left and various liberals in
Quebec, strict opposition to clericalism was very difficult to express in the
province between the downfall of the *Rouges*' radical liberalism in the late
1860s to the late 1940s. Bernard, *Les Rouges*; Lamonde, *L'heure de vérité*;
Lamonde, *Louis-Antoine Dessaulles*; Lévesque, *Éva Circé-Côté*; Racine,
L'anticléricalisme dans le roman québécois.

22 Wilkie, *Statistics and National Policy*, 56; Dominion Bureau of Statistics,
Report of the Eight Census of Canada, 289.

23 Marie Couillard, Patrick Imbert, and Daniel Castillo Durante, three professors of literature from the University of Ottawa, have compared the
ideological affinities of French Canada and Latin America in a number of
studies. Couillard and Imbert, "Canada, Argentine et Amérique latine au
dix-neuvième siècle"; Couillard and Imbert, *Les Discours du Nouveau
Monde au XIXe siècle au Canada français et en Amérique latine*; Imbert,
Trajectoires culturelles transaméricaines; Imbert and Castillo Durante,
L'interculturel au cœur des Amériques. Licia Soares de Souza and Nova
Doyon have done the same for Quebec and Brazil. Doyon, *Formation des
cultures nationales dans les Amériques*; Soares de Souza, *Utopies améric-
aines au Québec et au Brésil.*

24 For examples of studies comparing Canada and the Southern Cone, see:
Adelman, *Frontier Development*; Avni, *Canada, Argentina and the Jews
until World War II*; Makabe, "The Theory of the Split Labor Market";
Mayo and Sheinin, *Es Igual pero Distinto*; Platt, *Social Welfare*; Platt and
Di Tella, *Argentina, Australia, and Canada*; and Solberg, *The Prairies and
the Pampas.*

25 At the moment of writing these pages, the historiography of the French
Canadian missionary effort in Latin America is still embryonic. Foisy, "Des
Québécois aux frontières"; Gauthier, *Femmes sans frontières*; Gauthier
and Lord, *Engagées et solidaires*; Goudreault, "Les missionnaires canadiens à l'étranger"; Groulx, "Le Canada français en Amérique latine";
Groulx, *Le Canada français missionnaire*; LeGrand, "L'axe missionnaire
catholique entre le Québec et l'Amérique latine"; LeGrand, "Réseaux
missionnaires québécois"; Robillard, *Aventurières de l'ombre.*

26 Granger, *Le lys et le lotus*; LeGrand, "Cultural Approaches to Canadian-
Latin American Relations."

27 Catherine Foisy and Catherine LeGrand, in particular, have published
informative research on that subject.

28 This defensive discourse, however, did not prevent Premier Duplessis from
continuing Premier Taschereau's laissez-faire policies regarding foreign
investments. Therefore, the ideological isolationism of his administration

was more cosmetic than anything else: US capitalists kept playing a crucial role in Quebec's economy as they did in the rest of the country. Jones, *Duplessis and the Union Nationale Administration.*

29 Yvan Lamonde has thoroughly analyzed this period characterized by a deep "intellectual and spiritual crisis." Lamonde, *La modernité au Québec.*

30 Bélanger, *L'apolitisme des idéologies québécoises*, 349, 361.

31 Comeau, "Lionel Groulx, les indépendantistes de *La Nation* et le séparatisme," 85.

32 Ibid., 93.

33 Ibid., 87.

34 Comeau, *Le Bloc populaire.*

35 Dupont, "L'américanité québécoise ou la possibilité d'être ailleurs," 189–91.

36 Morisset, *L'identité usurpée*; Melançon, "La littérature québécoise et l'Amérique"; Morisset and Waddell, *Amériques.*

37 Ibid., 191–8. Monière and Vachet, *Les idéologies au Québec*; Rocher, Gaucher, and Rocher, *Le Québec en mutation.* Thériault, "Chronique des Amériques." See also Daniel Gay's introduction in his study on the Québécois élite's attitudes toward Latin America. Gay, *Les élites québécoises et l'Amérique latine.*

38 Bouchard, *Quelques arpents d'Amérique*; Bouchard, *Genèse des nations.*

39 Lamonde and Bouchard, *La nation dans tous ses états*; Lamonde and Bouchard, *Québécois et Américains.*

40 As Lamonde explains, Americanization and *americanité* are not exact synonyms. While the first concerns French Canadians' direct acculturation to the American way-of-life, a consequence of the growing influence US capital and culture exerted in twentieth century Quebec, the second refers to the idiosyncratic adaptation of this French-speaking nation to the continent, encompassing along the way the cultural influences resulting from sharing this territory with other societies. Lamonde, *Allégeances et dépendances*; Lamonde, *Ni avec eux ni sans eux.* I use the concept of *americanité* to better reflect how Quebec identity developed through its own cultural synthesis of North American influences.

41 Bellavance, *Le Québec au siècle des nationalités*; Cuccioletta, *L'américanité et les amériques*; Cuccioletta, Côté, and Lesemann, *Le grand récit des Amériques*; Ducharme, *Le concept de liberté au Canada à l'époque des révolutions atlantiques*; Harvey, *Le Printemps de l'Amérique française*; Jolivet, *Le vert et le bleu.*

42 For a good example, see Thériault, *Critique de l'américanité.*

43 Thériault, "Chronique des Amériques," 136.

44 Thériault, "Mais qu'a bien pu vouloir nous dire Robert Lepage?," 12–13.
45 Benessaieh, ed., *Transcultural Americas*; Bernd and Peterson, ed., *Confluences littéraires Brésil-Québec*; Chanady, *Entre inclusion et exclusion*; Danaux and Doyond, "Dossier – Enjeux et modalités des transferts culturels"; Doyon, *Formation des cultures nationales dans les Amériques*; Lesemann and Côté, ed., *La construction des Amériques aujourd'hui*; Nareau, "La revue *Dérives* et le Brésil"; Nareau, *Double jeu*; Nareau, "Coopération, réseautage et Liaison"; Nepveu, *Intérieurs du Nouveau Monde*; Morisset, *L'identité usurpée*; Soares de Souza, *Utopies américaines au Québec et au Brésil*.
46 García Canclini, *Hybrid Cultures*, 46.
47 Perin, *Ignace de Montréal*.
48 Ceballos Ramírez, *El catolicismo social, un tercero en discordia*; Ceballos Ramírez, "La Conciliación, los Arreglos y la Reforma Constitucional"; Ferretti, *Brève histoire de l'Église catholique au Québec*; Ferretti, *Entre voisins*; Harvey, s j, "L'influence de la pensée sociale de l'Église au Québec," 108–28; Super, "'Rerum Novarum' in Mexico and Quebec"; Voisine et al., *Histoire du catholicisme québécois*.
49 Torres Septién, *La educación privada en México*. French Canadian bishops encouraged a similar crossing a few decades before. See Laperrière, *Les congrégations religieuses*.
50 Blancarte, *El pensamiento social*.
51 Jean Meyer's latest book is the best example of this: Meyer, *La cruzada por México. Los católicos de Estados Unidos y la cuestión religiosa en México*.
52 For two classical interpretations of the Mexican Revolution, see Knight, *The Mexican Revolution*; Hart, *Revolutionary Mexico*.
53 Meyer, *La cruzada por México*.
54 Meyer, *La Cristiada. El conflicto*, 314–32. For an excellent critical counterpoint to Meyer's take on the Cristiada, cf. Butler, *Popular and Political Identity in Mexico's Cristero Rebellion*.
55 García Ugarte, "Los católicos y el presidente Calles."
56 Assad, *El laboratorio de la revolución*. Another Mexican state that had been strongly influenced by anticlericalism was Yucatán. Savarino, *Pueblos y nacionalismo*.
57 Contreras, *Rodulfo Brito Foucher (1899–1970)*.
58 Blancarte, *Historia de la Iglesia Católica en México*, 34–8.
59 Vaughan, *Cultural Politics in Revolution*; Burke, "The University of Mexico and the Revolution," 252–73; Loaeza, *Clases medias y política en México*, 73.

60 Juan Ortega, SJ, *Noticias de la Prov. De México*, México, D.F., N° 77,
    January 1938, Archivo Histórico de la Provincia de México de la
    Compañía de Jesús.
61 See, among others, Blancarte, *Historia de la Iglesia Católica en México*,
    59; Brown, "Mexican Church-State Relations"; Meyer, "An Idea of
    Mexico"; Michaels, "The Modification of the Anti-Clerical Nationalism."
    Regional studies of *Cardenismo* have nuanced the portrayal of anticleri-
    calism by showing that conciliation was a reality before this move:
    Bantjes, *As if Jesus Walked on Earth*; Becker, *Setting the Virgin on Fire*.
    Still, some scholars have also argued that reconciliation only concretely
    happened during the presidency of Manuel Ávila Camacho: Hernández
    García de León, *Historia política del sinarquismo*; Loaeza, "Los orígenes
    de la propuesta modernizadora de Manuel Gómez Morín."
62 Blancarte, *Historia de la Iglesia Católica en México*, 58.
63 Joseph, Rubenstein, and Zolov, "Assembling the Fragments," 8. The
    authors continue stating that "despite (and, in important ways, owing to)
    the economic dislocations generated by World War II, 1940 is often also
    hailed as the onset of the country's prolonged 'miracle' of economic
    growth, which continued through the 1960s."
64 Sherman, *The Mexican Right*, 129.
65 Smith, *Talons of the Eagle*, 78.
66 Niblo, *War, Diplomacy, and Development*, 123.
67 McNair Jones III, "'The War has brought Peace to Mexico,'" and Rankin,
    "*¡México, La Patria!*"
68 Rankin, "Mexico: Industrialization through Unity."
69 Nye and Keohane's research – being extremely important for the develop-
    ment of the neoliberal school of thought – primarily relates to the impact
    multinationals can have on international relations. Nevertheless, this
    research opens the door for considering other types of nonstate interna-
    tional actors. Nye and Keohane, "Transnational Relations and World
    Politics," 329–46.
70 Levitt and Khagram, "Constructing Transnational Studies," 9.
71 Stoler, "Matters of Intimacy as Matters of State," 896.
72 Darnton, *The Great Cat Massacre*.
73 Thanks to Mathieu Lapointe for mentioning to me the debate following
    Darnton's publication. For the controversy, see Chartier, "Texts, Symbols,
    and Frenchness"; LaCapra, "Chartier, Darnton, and the Great Symbol
    Massacre"; Mah, "Suppressing the text: The metaphysics of ethnographic
    history in Darnton's Great Cat Massacre."
74 Bourdieu, *Langage et pouvoir symbolique*, 59–60.

75 Foucault, *Surveiller et punir*, 36.

76 Foucault, "Nietzsche, la généalogie, l'histoire," 1004.

77 Edelman, "Political Language and Political Reality"; Edelman, *Politics as Symbolic Action*; Edelman, "Symbols and Political Quiescence." I also have to say that I agree with Ulf Hedetoft when he states that symbolic politics is, in a way, "about representation, projection, persuasion, signals, and appearance – the opposite (or complement) of a *Realpolitik* built on interests and problem solving. In another, however, it is concerned, sub-stantively, with moulding identities, building trust and legitimacy, and (re) creating solidarities and homogeneities that are, or are felt to be, under threat – whether from above or below, from within or without." Hedetoft, "Symbolic Politics and Cultural Symbols," 591.

78 When I stated above that the expressions "speaking out," "taking the floor," or "capture of speech" are pretty close to the original intent but do not translate the full dimension of the concept in French, I especially meant it regarding de Certeau's assertion that a *prise de parole* represents a concrete action in itself, not a simple rhetorical device. The concept gives another dimension to the notion of discursive agency. De Certeau, *La Prise de parole*, 175.

CHAPTER ONE

1 Letter from ambassador Francisco del Río Cañedo to Jesús J. Gónzalez Gallo, "secretario particular" of President Manuel Ávila Camacho, 24 May 1944, Archivo General de la Nación (AGN), Fondo documental Manuel Ávila Camacho (MAC), vol. 978, exp. 577, 1/66.

2 For an informed discussion of the concept of *sensibilité commune* and its application to Mexican history, see Siller, *México Francia*. The *sensibilité commune* developed with Quebec related to a French/Spanish Catholic heritage rather than the revolutionary and scientific heritage described in Pérez Siller's book.

3 Armstrong and Nelles, *Southern Exposure*.

4 Letter to O.D. Skelton from Merchant Mahoney, 4 January 1941, Library and Archives Canada (LAC), RG25, vol. 2854, Exchange of diplomatic representatives between Canada and Mexico – Proposals.

5 Murray, "Canada's First Diplomatic Missions in Latin America," 167.

6 Rochlin, *Discovering the Americas*.

7 Rankin, "Mexico: Industrialization through Unity," 21.

8 Rochlin, *Discovering the Americas*, 21.

9 Moreno, *Yankee Don't Go Home!*, 10.

10 This constituted a disappointment for Latin American countries and
    French Canadian nationalists alike. For a good discussion on the
    Canadian and American ambivalence toward the inclusion of Canada in
    the Pan American Union/Organization of American States, see: Miller,
    "Canada and the Pan American Union"; Murray, "Canada's First
    Diplomatic Missions in Latin America"; Podea, "Pan American Sentiment
    in French Canada"; and Rochlin, *Discovering the Americas*, 12–32.
11 Rochlin, *Discovering the Americas*, 14–15; Geneviève de la Tour Fondue,
    "Jean Désy."
12 Faber, "La hora ha llegado," 68.
13 See for example Royal Canadian Mounted Police, Secret Report,
    18 March 1942, LAC, RG 146, vol. 3260, dossier 42-01-26, L'Union
    culturelle des Latins D'Amérique, pte 2.
14 Bernard, *Les Rouges*.
15 The concept of *elites définitrices* was developed and used by Fernand
    Dumont to describe the genesis of Québécois society. It underlines the role
    of the literate petite-bourgeoisie in marking the boundaries of French
    Canada's imagined community. Despite its disregard for the role played by
    popular culture in the definition of the nation, this concept is useful for
    understanding the imagination of transnational affinities between French
    Canada and Latin America studied in this research, as this process largely
    excluded the popular classes. Dumont, *Genèse de la société québécoise*.
16 That French Canadian nation, although notionally pan-Canadian, was
    really centred on the Province of Quebec. Michel Bock adequately demon-
    strated that the notion of a French Canadian nation extended well beyond
    the boundaries of the Province of Quebec, at least for a nationalist like
    Lionel Groulx, to include even Franco-American communities. This
    extended conception of the imagined community never negated the contin-
    gencies of political power in North America but did recognize Quebec –
    the only province where francophones form the majority of the
    population – as the national homeland and the only place where French
    Canadians could exert some direct control on politics. Bock, *Quand la
    nation débordait les frontières*.
17 The 1791 Constitutional Act transformed the Province of Quebec into
    Lower and Upper Canada, which later became Quebec and Ontario. The
    1840 Act of Union united the two colonies into the Province of Canada.
    The British North America Act created, in 1867, a federal system in which
    powers are shared between the Dominion of Canada and the provinces.
    Quebec and Ontario then became separate provinces again.
18 Quoted by Lamonde, *The Social History of Ideas in Quebec*, 77.

19 Ibid.
20 Lamonde, *The Social History of Ideas in Quebec*, 171.
21 See Durham, *Lord Durham's Report*.
22 Perin, "L'Église et l'édification d'une culture publique au Québec," 261.
23 Susan Mann aptly points this out in *The Dream of Nation*: "Defeated in
    rebellion and condemned as an inferior race meriting only assimilation,
    French Canadians suddenly burst forth with extraordinary energy, enthu-
    siasm, tenacity, and vigour. They revived and remodeled their political
    institutions and thereby undermined the assimilationist purpose of the
    union. For example, they succeeded in bringing the executive under the
    control of the assembly, thus solving the most vexing pre-rebellion politi-
    cal problem. They even achieved an elective legislative council, if only for
    a short period, 1855 to 1867. They shook out their religious lethargy and
    gave form and substance to the faith and the church. They organized a
    school system and municipal institutions. They scrutinized their civil law,
    queried its basis in the *Coutume de Paris* and amended it according to the
    Code Napoléon. They produced a generation of historians, novelists, even
    would-be philosophers; they formed national, cultural, educational, and
    political interest groups. They investigated agricultural practices, orga-
    nized the settlement of areas of the Eastern Townships, and opened regis-
    try offices. They gave the green light to canal development along the St
    Lawrence and the red light to the seigneurial system, abolishing it in 1854.
    And they did it all, or most of it, in French, in spite of Durham." Mann,
    The Dream of Nation, 82.
24 Those words were pronounced by Mgr Louis-François Laflèche in 1866.
    Quoted in Wade, *The French Canadians*, 340.
25 Perin, *Ignace de Montréal*, 51–94.
26 Ibid., 33–4.
27 It has to be said that Radical liberalism did not completely disappear in
    Quebec after the defeat of the Patriotes. However, despite the *Rouges'*
    mobilization, it was progressively marginalized. Yvan Lamonde writes:
    "The most obvious failure of radical liberalism under the union was due
    to the reaffirmation of moderate liberalism, the liberalism of La Fontaine
    and Cartier as well as Hector Fabre, which, as much as Mgr Bourget and
    the Catholic Church or Étienne Parent, undermined radical liberalism and
    paved the way for Laurier. Laurier's strategy in 1877 consisted of ridding
    liberalism of its radical anticlericalism and clearly identifying the
    Canadian liberal tradition with English reform liberalism rather than
    French revolutionary liberalism." Lamonde, *The Social History of Ideas in
    Quebec*, 424.

28 Meyer, "Les Cristeros (1926–1929)," 164. As for lay associations, Silvia
    Marina Arrom gives the following example: "Despite the triumph of the
    Liberal Reform, the second half of the nineteenth century witnessed a
    Catholic revival embodied in new lay organizations that recuperated many
    public spaces for the church and deepened the commitment of the faithful.
    Yet even the historians who recognize the existence of a 'Catholic
    Restoration' in Porfirian Mexico have missed its gendered dimension. The
    Ladies of Charity were at the forefront of Catholic activism. These lay vol-
    unteers created a national network of local chapters, called 'conferences,'
    that mobilized thousands of philanthropic women in dozens of Mexican
    cities and towns to help the poor while simultaneously reinforcing their
    faith. In addition to their devotional activities, the Ladies offered extensive
    educational and welfare services that by the late nineteenth century
    reached a clientele numbering in the hundreds of thousands." Arrom,
    "Mexican Laywomen Spearhead a Catholic Revival," 52.
29 Lacasse, "L'intervention française au Mexique et l'opinion publique au
    Québec"; Larrinaga, "L'intervention française au Mexique vue par les
    principaux journaux canadiens-français."
30 Le Moine, "L'aventure mexicaine de quelques Québécois," 256–8.
31 Faucher de Saint-Maurice, De Québec à Mexico, 2:181.
32 Beaugrand, "Anita: souvenirs d'un contre-guérillas," Mélanges, 140.
33 Ibid.
34 Rajotte, "De Québec à Mexico de Faucher de Saint-Maurice. Une tentative
    de voyage vers soi," 94.
35 Rajotte, "De Québec à Mexico de Faucher de Saint-Maurice: entre la fidé-
    lité à une tradition de lecture et la recherche d'originalité," 264.
36 Ibid. As for Faucher's negative descriptions of Mexican towns, its inhabit-
    ants, and their cultural practices, see Faucher de Saint-Maurice, De
    Québec à Mexico, 1:78, 1:104, 1:113, 1:133–42, and 2:6. The author does
    have good words, however, for the beauty of the city of Puebla and the
    superiority of Mexican saddles: Ibid., 1:190–232 and 2:132.
37 Ibid., 1:105.
38 Ibid., 1:168 and 1:201–2.
39 Ibid., 1:183.
40 He claims a "lost Algonquine tribe was found in Yucatan." Ibid., 1:154–5.
41 Ibid., 2:118.
42 Ibid., 2:117.
43 Ibid., 1:162 and 2:66.
44 Ibid., 2:167–91.
45 Ibid., 2:6.

46 Ibid., 2:168.
47 Interestingly, Faucher does not blame France at all.
48 Ibid., 1:181.
49 Faucher de Saint-Maurice, *Notes pour servir à l'histoire*, 222–3. Quoted in Le Moine, "L'aventure mexicaine de quelques Québécois," 261.
50 Delâge, *Le pays renversé*, 296–8; Greer, "Iroquois Virgin," in Greer and Bilinkoff, *Colonial Saints*, 235–50.
51 Groulx, *Le Canada français missionnaire*, 380.
52 Bourassa, *Le Canada apostolique*, 381.
53 Groulx, *Le Canada français missionnaire*, 81.
54 Bourassa, *Le Canada apostolique*, 127. The contact between the two had been established while Mgr Bourget was in Rome. There he met Mgr Checa, archbishop of Quito, who ultimately made a request in the name of the president.
55 Howe, "García Moreno's Efforts to Unite Ecuador and France."
56 Lamonde, *Histoire sociale des idées au Québec*, 446.
57 Quoted in Bourassa, *Le Canada apostolique*, 130–1.
58 LeGrand, "Cultural Approaches to Canadian-Latin American Relations." This would be especially true in the second half of the twentieth century, after missionaries had more contact with the harsh inequalities afflicting Latin America's popular classes.
59 For example, see Bourassa, *Le Canada apostolique*, 127–8. As for the expression the "twin heirs of the Enlightenment," I borrowed it from Grandin, *The Last Colonial Massacre*, 189.
60 Ceballos Ramírez, *El catolicismo social, un tercero en discordia*.
61 Torres Septién, *La educación privada en México*, 56.
62 Those schools, despite being private, were initially free (ibid., 57).
63 The French communities that relocated because of anticlericalism in France also played an invaluable role in organizing Quebec's educational system at a time when the State was largely absent from this field. For a fuller discussion of the impact of the anticlerical laws in France on Quebec's school system, see the three volumes of Laperrière, *Les congréga-tions religieuses*.
64 Jean-Paul Trudel, "La Culture Gréco-Latine et le Bloc Latin d'Amérique," Section canadienne Union Culturelle des Latins d'Amérique, ed., *Rapport complet: Journées d'Amérique latine, 1943*. This report can be found at Library and Archives Canada (LAC), RG 25-A-3-B, vol. 4196, Union of Cultures of Latin America. A copy is also housed at the Archives du Centre de recherche Lionel-Groulx (ACRLG), P40/C4, 5, Congrès annuel de l'ULA, 1943.

65 This categorization excludes the other British territories, notwithstanding
    the US. Brazil also experienced a progressive and peaceful independence.

66 Donneur, "L'émergence de la politique étrangère canadienne," in his book
    Politique étrangère canadienne, 7–13.

67 "José María Morelos's 'Sentiments of the Nation,'" in Mills, Taylor, and
    Lauderdale Graham, *Colonial Latin America*, 397–400. Important ethnic
    and regional identities persist to this day. Still, the idea of a Mexican
    national identity predates that of a Canadian national identity, as Canada
    did not have someone like José María Morelos promoting nationalism at
    the beginning of the century. Of course, French Canadians (the original
    Canadiens) did develop a national consciousness early on in the late eigh-
    teenth or early nineteenth century. For more information on the emergence
    of the sentiment of nationalism in Quebec, see Bouchard, *Genèse des
    nations* and Dumont, *Genèse de la société québécoise*.

68 Barajas Durán, "Retrato de un siglo," 126.

69 Anderson, *Imagined Communities*. For a critic of that thesis, cf. Lomnitz-
    Adler, *Deep Mexico, Silent Mexico*. Néstor García Canclini also notes that
    national consolidation was never truly achieved. He writes: "The liberal
    oligarchies of the late nineteenth and early twentieth centuries acted as if
    they constituted states, but they only ordered some areas of society in
    order to promote a subordinate and inconsistent development; they acted
    as if they formed national cultures, and they barely constructed elite cul-
    tures, leaving out enormous indigenous and peasant populations, who
    manifest their exclusion in a thousand revolts and in the migration that is
    bringing 'upheaval' to the cities." García Canclini, *Hybrid Cultures*, 7.

70 In the volatile political context of post-independence Mexico, where the
    presidency was violently contested and political leaders barely lasted lon-
    ger than a year in office, the Pastry War of 1838 strikes out as a particu-
    larly preposterous episode of imperialist intervention in Mexico's internal
    affairs. That year, the remonstrance of a French pastry cook named
    M Remontel, who claimed his business in Mexico City had been ravaged
    by political protest, led king Louis-Philippe to ask for retribution, ulti-
    mately sending a fleet to block all Mexican ports on the Atlantic. Mexico
    then declared war on France.

71 If this is true especially for the Southern Cone, Mexico was also integrated
    in this British system despite US's economic interests. For example, see
    Lorenzo Meyer, *Su majestad británica contra la revolución mexicana*.

72 This was the first pan-American organization sponsored by the US. Latin
    Americans previously attempted different schemes to link new republics
    together. Simón Bolívar's 1826 Congress of Panama is perhaps the most

famous of these projects of pan-American cooperation. However, the conflict opposing liberals and conservatives, and the influence of competing neo-colonial powers represented insuperable hurdles.

73 Coerver and Hall, *Tangled Destinies*, 37–8.

74 Casey, "The Creation and Development of the Pan American Union."

75 Great Britain nonetheless maintained a significant influence in the Southern Cone and, of course, over Commonwealth territories.

76 The shift of influence from European culture (mainly British) to American in Mexican elite circles has been compellingly analyzed by Beezley, *Judas at the Jockey Club*.

77 Hall, *Oil, Banks, and Politics*. Lorenzo Meyer, *Su majestad británica contra la revolución mexicana*.

78 Coerver and Hall, *Tangled Destinies*, 56.

79 Schuler, *Mexico between Hitler and Roosevelt*, 37.

80 Ibid., 13.

81 For a good discussion of Mexico's cultural diplomacy with Latin America, see: González González, "México ante América Latina"; Yankelevich, "América Latina en la agenda diplomática de la revolución mexicana."

82 Murray, "Canada's First Diplomatic Missions in Latin America," 163.

83 Needless to say that none of the English-speaking colonies joined the Pan American Union before it transformed itself into the present-day Organization of American States in 1948. Most started to join the organization in the late 1960s, after gaining independence.

84 Humphrey, *The Inter-American System*, 6. Quoted in Miller, "Canada and the Pan American Union," 29.

85 Gutiérrez-Haces, *Procesos de integración económica en México y Canadá*, 9. Teresa Gutiérrez-Haces portrays Canada and Mexico's situation as characteristic of peripheral nations.

86 Berger, *The Sense of Power*. Relations with the United States were not completely rejected, of course. Canada had a reciprocity treaty with the US in the nineteenth century, and trade and investment between both nations were priority concerns for the parliament in Ottawa. Yet, the ties with the Empire were given priority over any new geopolitical reordering of the Americas.

87 Ogelsby, *Gringos from the Far North*.

88 Armstrong and Nelles describe well the paradox of the vigour of Canadian investments in Mexico juxtaposed with commercial and diplomatic apathy: "A close inspection of the goods traded, however, brings into question any suggestion of a direct linkage between investment and trade. In 1911 Canada's exports to Mexico consisted overwhelmingly of

two raw materials, grain (64 per cent) and coal (25 per cent). Only 11 per cent of Canadian exports were manufactured goods. In this category iron and steel, whisky, cordage, newsprint, and drugs were the principal items of trade. Mexico exported coffee, henequen, and asphalt to Canada. Natural products accounted for an overwhelming 95.5 per cent of Mexican exports. Thus when Canada and Mexico did open up trading links during the high point of Canadian investment in Mexican utilities early in the twentieth century, Canadian exports to Mexico resembled Canadian exports to the rest of the world. Basically the two countries exchanged raw materials where each had an absolute advantage, wheat for coffee." Armstrong and Nelles, *Southern Exposure*, 280.

89 The authors explain this number represents the book value of assets controlled by Canadian companies (ibid., 252–3).
90 Ibid., 7.
91 Ibid., x–xi.
92 Ibid., 283.
93 Ibid., 282.
94 Ibid., 271.
95 Ibid., 185. Lorenzo Meyer, *Su majestad británica contra la revolución mexicana*, 23–4. Ogelsby, *Gringos from the Far North*, 154–81.
96 Lorenzo Meyer, *Su majestad británica contra la revolución mexicana*, 23–4.
97 Ibid., 296.
98 Hall, *Oil, Banks, and Politics*; Meyer, *Su majestad británica contra la revolución mexicana*.
99 Armstrong and Nelles, *Southern Exposure*, 277.
100 Ibid., 226.
101 Ibid., 283.

CHAPTER TWO

1 Guy Laperrière, "Le congrès eucharistique de Montréal," 22.
2 Quoted in Guy Laperrière, "Le congrès eucharistique de Montréal," 33.
3 Quoted in Mark G. McGowan, *The Waning of the Green*, 245.
4 Quoted in Guy Laperrière, "Le congrès eucharistique de Montréal," 33. The translation in English is quoted in Kennedy, *Liberal Nationalisms*, 170.
5 A motion was presented afterward at the Quebec legislature by the MP of Lotbinière, J.N. Francoeur, asking Parliament to consider breaking the 1867 Confederation pact. Although it was quickly dismissed, the conflict

that generated it continued to define Canadian politics and ethnic relations between French and English Canada for generations to come.
Linteau, Durocher, and Robert, *Histoire du Québec contemporain*, vol. 2,
598–600. See also, Bonenfant and Falardeau, "Cultural and Political
Implications of French-Canadian Nationalism."

6 Bourassa, *La langue française au Canada*, 46–7. Bourassa also gave the
   example of Argentina to expose the advantages of full independence for
   Canada. Bourassa, *Independence or Imperial Partnership?*, 53.
7 Bourassa, *Hier, aujourd'hui, demain*, 162.
8 Bourassa, *La langue française au Canada*, 46–7.
9 Meyer, "Les Cristeros (1926–1929)," 170.
10 Meyer, "An Idea of Mexico," 282.
11 Padilla Rangel, "Anticlericalismo carrancista," 450.
12 Ibid., 457.
13 Lynch, *New Worlds*, 246. Lynch further explains that "his government
    inaugurated a new purge of religion, and even an abortive attempt, with
    the connivance of two reprobate priests, to contrive a schism and a
    national Church."
14 Buchenau, *Plutarco Elías Calles*, 141.
15 Blancarte, *Historia de la Iglesia Católica en México*, 37–42.
16 Young, "The Calles Government and Catholic Dissidents," 69–81.
17 Ibid., 80.
18 Ibid., 69–70. The full quote reads: "Cristero-era exiles included both cleri-
    cal and lay Catholic dissidents. Between 1926 and 1929, up to 2,500
    Mexican religious, including priests, nuns, monks, seminarians, bishops,
    and archbishops, either fled or were deported to the United States. Over
    the same period, dozens of prominent Mexican Catholic political leaders
    left Mexico as well; they included leaders of the *Asociación Católica de
    Juventud Mexicana*, the *Liga Nacional Defensora de la Libertad Religiosa*,
    and the Mexican Knights of Columbus."
19 Meyer, *La cruzada por México*. Meyer explains the opposition to the
    Catholic cause in detail from pages 71 to 78.
20 Despite the fact that the K of C crossed the Rio Grande during the Pershing
    punitive expedition in 1916, Catholics in Mexico saw the association not
    as part of Yankee imperialism (as in Quebec), but as another useful instru-
    ment to organize lay religious life in the country. As for its collaboration
    with Acción Católica Mexicana (ACM), there are various documents stat-
    ing the benefits of that collaboration explicitly in the Catholic Action
    archives at Universidad Iberoamericana. See Archivo de la Acción Católica
    Mexicana (AACM), 7, 1, Caballeros de Colón, 1930–1936.

21 Meyer, *La cruzada por México*, 127–218.

22 Ibid. Also, see Redinger, *American Catholics and the Mexican Revolution, 1924–1936*.

23 Lapointe and Vézina, "El México rojo y la Cristiada."

24 Lynch, *New Worlds*, 250.

25 Miguel Agustín Pro was beatified on 25 September 1988 by Pope John Paul II. He is considered a martyr by the Catholic Church.

26 Juan Ortega, s j, *Noticias de la Prov. De México*, México, D.F., N° 77, January 1938, Archivo Histórico de la Provincia de México de la Compañía de Jesús.

27 Martínez, "Prologo," in Antonio Dragon, s j, *Vida intima del padre Pro*, iii-xiii. The original book in French was translated in Spanish by Rafael Martínez del Campo and was republished many times.

28 Dragon, s j *Le Père Pro*.

29 Young, "The Calles Government and Catholic Dissidents," 71.

30 Jean Meyer explains that being a non-believer, Gorostieta fought first and foremost for the "pleasure of adventure and for vengeance." Meyer, "Les Cristeros (1926–1929)," 175.

31 Dragon, s j, *Au Mexique Rouge*, 17.

32 Ibid., 39–40.

33 Lévesque, *Éva Circé-Côté*; Lévesque, *Virage à gauche interdit*.

34 Yvan Lamonde explains that the economic and social crisis in the 1930s favoured the resurgence of secularism in Quebec. Lay Catholics started to ask for their right to "express themselves and take decisions." Lamonde, *L'heure de vérité*, 13.

35 Dragon, s j, *Pour le Christ-Roi*.

36 Ibid., 14

37 Shumway, "Hispanism in an Imperfect Past," 293.

38 Dragon, s j, *Pour le Christ-Roi*, 12–13.

39 We can also note that Dragon's perspective on Hispanic culture is very different from the "Anglo-American tradition [which was] marked by a profound and abiding anti-Hispanic bias." Shumway, "Hispanism in an Imperfect Past," 289.

40 Dragon, s j, *Pour le Christ-Roi*, 20.

41 Ibid., 19.

42 Ibid., 31, 69–70.

43 Ibid., 49.

44 Ibid., 126.

45 Ibid., 145. It should be noted that the guilt of Miguel Pro was never proven; he was summarily executed by the police without due process.

46 Ibid., 98.

47 Interestingly, Jean Meyer also agrees with that assessment. When asked in an interview about "the fundamental significance for Mexican history of the Cristiada," Meyer answered: "I think that it's a confirmation of what was said many centuries before by Tertullian, that the blood of the martyrs is the seed of the Christians. I met a lot of priests, older than I or my generation, and a lot of bishops, now of my generation, that all were sons of Cristeros. And the Mexican Catholic Church has been, for many years, the only Church in Latin America, which is 100 per cent native. Mexico never had, and still, has no problem of vocations, and really I think that it was not of course a voluntary gift of the Mexican revolutionary government, but the fact of the persecution was confirmation of the Mexican people in his Catholic faith." Cullinan Hoffman, "The History behind 'For Greater Glory.'" *National Catholic Register*, 29 May 2012.

48 Albert, "Sens et enjeux du martyre: de la religion à la politique," 17–25.

49 Dragon, s j, *Pour le Christ-Roi*, 164.

50 Lynch, *New Worlds*, 250.

51 Dragon, s j, *Pour le Christ-Roi*, 180.

52 This appraisal seems to be different from what Italian prelates wrote back then, as it was not characterized by the same "sentiment of superiority." Meyer, "Les Cristeros (1926–1929)," 188.

53 Dragon, s j, *Pour le Christ-Roi*, 174.

54 Fournier, *Communisme et anticommunisme au Québec*, 53. Referring to André-J. Bélanger's book *L'apolitisme des idéologies québécoises*, Fournier also mentions that the Catholic *École sociale populaire*, led by the Jesuit Joseph-Papin Archambault, published "56 leaflets and pamphlets spreading anticommunist ideas from March 1931 to August 1935." Ibid., 150.

55 Ibid., 55.

56 He also specifies that "Unionists like Madeleine Parent were forced into exile. This dissident committed the 'crime' of organizing strikes of clothing and textile workers in Montreal and Valleyfield, Cardinal Leger's fief. Accused of sedition by the Duplessis government, she had to leave Quebec in the depths of the 'grande noirceur.'" Beaudet, *Une brève histoire de la solidarité internationale au Québec*, 40.

57 Dragon, s j, *Au Mexique Rouge*, 29.

58 Ibid., 121.

59 Ibid., 122.

60 *The Globe* (Toronto), 15 December 1927. Quoted in Ogelsby, *Gringos from the Far North*, 183–4.

61 *The Globe* (Toronto), 16 December 1927. Quoted in ibid., 186.

62 Ibid., 197.

63 The Mexican diplomat Luis Quintanilla noted in 1943: "it becomes apparent that the contention for a *Latin* America finds no demographic ground. I do not have before me the percentages of people of Latin extraction among the populations of the United States and Canada, but important sections of these two countries are, demographically speaking, more Latin than many of our republics." Quintanilla, *A Latin American Speaks*, 7.

64 Aillón Soria, "La política cultural de Francia," 71–5.

65 As mentioned above, these tensions were caused, among other things, by the hanging of Louis Riel (the Métis leader) in 1885, the negation of schooling rights for francophones outside Quebec, the Canadian involvement in imperial wars opposed by the French Canadian population, and the Conscription crisis in 1917.

66 *Canada, House of Commons Debates*, 1935, vol. III, 2287. Quoted in Podea, "Pan American Sentiment in French Canada," 335.

67 Bourassa, *Le Canada apostolique*. Podea also mentions Bourassa's articles on Latin America in her review of French Canadian sentiments in favour of the Pan American Union. Podea, "Pan American Sentiment in French Canada."

68 Lacroix, "Lien social, idéologie et cercles d'appartenance."

69 Ibid., 51.

70 Ibid., 54.

71 Jean-Philippe Warren sums up what corporatism represented for these Québécois reformers. Warren, "Le corporatisme canadien-français comme 'système total.'"

72 Jones, *Duplessis and the Union Nationale Administration*.

73 ACRLG, P40/C2, 9, Correspondance du Comité central des Jeunesses patriotes du Canada français, 18 mars 1936–12 janvier 1950. See also Noël, *Lionel Groulx et le réseau indépendantiste* and Lamonde, "Dostaler O'Leary," 125.

74 Robert Rumilly quotes O'Leary's criticism of Duplessis: "Dostaler O'Leary, being younger, criticized Maurice Duplessis, who led a real nationalist movement in the impasse of politics.'" Rumilly, *Maurice Duplessis et son temps*, 352.

75 "Nous voulons un dominion autonome, catholique et français, dans le Québec," [La Patrie], 15 May 1937. A copy of this article can be found in ACRLG, P40/C1, 1, Causeries, conférences et allocutions, 15 mai 1937–18 mai 1939.

76 Membership card of the Jeunesses Patriotes, ACRLG, P40/C2, 2, Documents officiels des Jeunesses patriotes du Canada français.

77 Shumway, "Hispanism in an Imperfect Past," 293.

78 Robert Comeau, "Paul Bouchard," 109.

79 Ibid.

80 Bélanger, *L'apolitisme des idéologies québécoises*, 268.

81 Dostaler O'Leary, "La liberté du Conclave," ACRLG, P40/B, 2, Coupures de presses d'articles de Dostaler O'Leary, 19 juin 1935–1 mai 1966. See also P40/A, 4, Correspondance personnelle de Walter-Patrice O'Leary, 10 février 1937–30 août 1978.

82 Camillien Houde, a populist (and very popular) mayor of Montreal, Canada's metropolis at the time, was jailed from 1940 to 1944 for opposing the National Registration Act. Walter O'Leary and Paul Bouchard were both known separatists and had opposed conscription publicly, suggesting the French Canadian population should not cooperate with the war looming ahead.

83 Letter by Norman A. Robertson to Commissioner S.T. Wood of the Royal Canadian Mounted Police, 31 October 1942, LAC, RG 146, vol. 3260, dossier 42-01-26, L'Union culturelle des Latins D'Amérique, pte 2. Part of the documentation in the RCMP files was censored. I am not able to completely assess if Walter O'Leary was interrogated in Mexico as a result of Skelton's request.

84 Letter by Hector Allaire to Walter O'Leary, 13 July 1944, ACRLG, P40/A, 5, Correspondance générale de Walter Patrice O'Leary, 5 octobre 1938–1 avril 1980.

85 Letter by Paul Bouchard to Walter O'Leary, 11 October 1941, ACRLG, P40/A, 4, Correspondance personnelle de Walter-Patrice O'Leary, 10 février 1937–30 août 1978. The letter was written in Spanish.

86 Like O'Leary, he would become a member of the *Unión cultural México-Canadá francés*. ACRLG, P40/C4, 1, Documents officiels de l'Union des Latins d'Amérique, 16 mai 1944–14 mars 1945.

87 Armour Landry, Rencontre avec le peintre Stanley Cosgrove Morel au Mexique, 29 November 1941, ACRLG, P40/C4, 4, Rapports d'activités de l'Union des Latins d'Amérique, 29 novembre 1941–27 mai 1947. It is mentioned in Landry's article that O'Leary helped Cosgrove to establish contacts with influential people in Mexico, facilitating access to this particular academy. A fellow member of the *Unión México-Canadá francés*, José Garci,dueñas, also contributed in letting Cosgrove regularly access the collection of paintings at the National Museum, where he worked. Finally, it is also important to note that the journalist Armour Landry was a top organizer of the ULA in Montreal.

88 Ibid. Stanley Cosgrove, like the O'Leary brothers, is considered (and viewed himself as) a French Canadian despite his anglophone name.

French was literally Cosgrove's and the O'Leary's mother tongue, as they both had French Canadian mothers. Walter and Stanley used their French Canadian last name in Mexico to follow the Hispanic tradition of using the last name of the father and mother. Walter often signed his letters as Walter-Patricio O'Leary-Rodier, and Stanley was referred to as Stanley Cosgrove-Morel.

89 Interview with Gratia O'Leary, Walter's widow, was conducted at her house in Montreal on 14 February 2006. When I interviewed her, I noted that a beautiful painting representing the hybridization of Indians and Spaniards in Mexico, painted by Orozco, adorned the vestibule of her house. As for the reference of Walter meeting with the muralists at art exhibits, Landry mentions it in his article on Cosgrove, where he says that Orozco helped the French Canadian painter to organize an exhibit of his work at the Benjamin Franklin Library in Mexico during the War. The *Nouvelle Librairie française* of Mexico, for its part, was an important meeting place for intellectuals and francophiles. When French Canadian students visited Mexico in 1944, they organized a cocktail to welcome the students and introduce them to their audience. Maurault, *Le Mexique de mes souvenirs*, 140.

90 In the paper he gave *in absentia* during the 1943 *Journées d'Amérique latine* organized by the ULA in Montreal – his brother's wife read his presentation – he celebrated the "independence" exhibited in the paintings of the muralist movement and their ability to craft a uniquely Mexican style. Union Culturelle des Latins d'Amérique, ed., *Rapport complet: Journées d'Amérique latine, 1943*.

91 History of the Association, *Unión cultural México-Canadá francés*, ACRLG, P40/C4, 1, Documents officiels de l'Union des Latins d'Amérique, 16 mai 1944–14 mars 1945.

92 Ibid. Many were or became famous literary or intellectual figures in Mexico.

93 Ibid.

94 For Mgr Martínez, see the letter sent by Walter to his brother Dostaler where he describes him as a "revolutionary" (in the sense of the *Jeunesses Patriotes*), 18 January 1940, ACRLG, P40/A, 1, Correspondance de Dostaler O'Leary, 18 juin 1931–30 juin 1944.

95 Ibid.

96 The content and significance of that collaboration will be analyzed more in detail in chapter three. Chapter two focuses more specifically on the transnational discourse of Latin identity in the Americas articulated in the Union's gathering. Unfortunately, I do not have sufficient primary

sources from the UCMCF to discuss the members' contribution to this identity construction in Mexico.

97 The association used as a maxim in the heading of their official correspondence: "Para el desarrollo de la cultura Greco-Latina en América" [Favouring the development of Greco-Latin culture in the Americas], ACRLG, P40/C4, 4, Rapports d'activités de l'Union des Latins d'Amérique, 29 novembre 1941–27 mai 1947. Three of the founding members became members of the *Real Academia Española* (Manuel Alcalá, Antonio Gómez Robledo – who became Latin America's most famous Hellenist – and José Rojas Gacidueñas). Manuel González Montesinos later incorporated the *Academia mexicana de la lengua* as a member, while José Luis Martínez became its director. http://www.academia.org.mx/historia.php.

98 [Association of Mexican Catholic Youth] Castellanos Pinzón and Curiel, eds., *Jalisco en el siglo XX. Perfiles*, 188–94. Quoted in "Jaliscienses distinguidos," http://www.jalisco.gob.mx/nuestroedo/muro/gomezrob.html.

99 [National Union of Catholic Students]

100 See, http://www.pan.org.mx/?P=revista_nacion.

101 Manuel González Montesinos was part of Guisa y Azevedo's inner circle of friends. See Loaeza, "Poderoso caballero, III," in *Las niñas bien.*

102 Memorándum para información del Señor Presidente, AHDSRE, III/1329/9/1940–1966, Establecimiento de Relaciones Diplomáticas entre México y Canadá. Correspondencia, informes y recortes de periódicos norteamericanos y canadienses.

103 Rubenstein, *Bad Language, Naked Ladies, and other Threats to the Nation.*

104 All the documentation directly pertaining to the UCMCF was found in the ACRLG in Montreal. A few documents concerning Walter O'Leary's activities in Mexico were also found at the AHDSRE. Brito Foucher's collection at *Archivo histórico de la Universidad Nacional Autónoma de México* (AHUNAM) also contains documents relating to the organizations of student exchanges between Quebec and Mexico. I found various documents on the Canada-Mexico group, supervised by the UCMCF and the ULA who organized the first student exchange programs between Montreal and Mexico City. I analyze the substance of these exchanges in more detail and expand a bit more on the UCMCF's role in Mexico in the next chapter – to the extent documentation has allowed me to do so.

105 Many cultural activities were planned in the UCMCF's constitution. The role of this association, according to the constitution, was supposed to be as all-embracing as the role the ULA played in Montreal. There was some

mention in the documents of events organized in Mexico to publicize the transnational affinities between French Canada and this country. However, unlike similar happenings in Montreal, I cannot assess participation in them. Nor can I offer an estimation of the UCMCF membership in Mexico during the war. The only conclusive documentation pertaining to the association in Mexico relates to the creation of the association and its organization of student exchange programs.

106 [Good girls] This phrase was coined by Soledad Loaeza to described girls from the Mexican high society. Loaeza, *Las niñas bien.*

CHAPTER THREE

1 Dostaler O'Leary, Closing statement of the 1942 Latin American days in Montreal, ACRLG, P40/C4, 6, Causeries, conférences et allocutions prononcés dans le cadre des activités de l'Union des Latins d'Amérique, 9 novembre 1942–19 février 1944.

2 Dostaler O'Leary, Conference given during the 1943 Latin American days in Montreal, ACRLG, P40/C4, 5, Congrès annuel de l'Union des Latins d'Amérique 1943.

3 The total membership is assessed from ULA documentation and Maurault's publication. It is possible that many "members" were actually "sympathizers" who sporadically attended their activities. Maurault, *Par voies et par chemins de l'air*, 226.

4 See ACRLG, P40/A, 5, Correspondance générale de Walter Patrice O'Leary, 5 octobre 1938–1 avril 1980, and P40/A, 4, Correspondance personnelle de Walter-Patrice O'Leary, 10 février 1937–30 août 1978.

5 Actually, Walter felt that Dostaler was taking too much time and was neglecting his demands from Mexico. In a few letters, insults were exchanged, but the association was nonetheless formed four months after the Mexican branch. See for example, ACRLG, P40/A, 1, Correspondance de Dostaler O'Leary, 18 juin 1931–30 juin 1944.

6 Pax Romana is the official name of the International Movement of Catholic Students. Ana María Bidegain claims that it was at their international congress in New York, in 1939, that French Canadian and Latin American Catholic students first established concrete contacts. Bidegain de Uran, "La organización de movimientos de juventud de Acción católica en América latina." Daniel Johnson attended this congress. He later made a presentation entitled "Collaboration entre étudiants latins dans Pax Romana" at the 1943 *Journée d'Amérique latines* organized by the Union.

7 Of course, Drapeau became most famous for his campaign for public morality and against corruption in the 1950s and subsequently for being mayor of Montreal for twenty-nine years.

8 Constitution of the ULA, ACRLG, P40/C4, 1, Documents officiels de l'ULA, 16 mai 1944–14 mars 1945. I am deducing Jean-Marie Parent and Reynald Pelletier's academic affiliation from Walter and Dostaler's correspondence.

9 It has to be said that the Mexican founding members had a better intellectual standing than those from Montreal. Conversely, the French Canadian founding members in Quebec had more political impact throughout their careers than their colleagues in Mexico. Still, the members of the Mexican and French Canadian branches of the UCMCF had both academic and political standing.

10 This comparison could be somewhat unfair to Mexico, as I do not have enough data to fully track the evolution of the directorate of the UCMCF there.

11 Constitution of the ULA, ACRLG, P40/C4, 1, Documents officiels de l'ULA, 16 mai 1944–14 mars 1945. For the 1943 committee see Union Culturelle des Latins d'Amérique, ed., *Rapport complet: Journées d'Amérique latine, 1943*. In its surveillance of the ULA, the RCMP agent described in detail Manolita del Vayo's personality, dress, character, and daily activities. Royal Canadian Mounted Police, Secret Report, 15 May 1942, LAC, RG 146, vol. 3260, dossier 42-01-26, L'Union culturelle des Latins D'Amérique, pte 2.

12 ACRLG, P40/C4, 8, Correspondance de l'ULA, 6 avril 1942– 11 avril 1945.

13 Constitution, ACRLG, P40/C4, 1, Documents officiels de l'ULA, 16 mai 1944–14 mars 1945.

14 Draft for the constitution of the ULA, ibid.

15 The rationale for this point was that if Mexicans could gain the sympathy of a portion of the Canadian population (the French Canadians), foreign relations with this British Dominion would be facilitated.

16 O'Leary, *Séparatisme, doctrine constructive*.

17 This was done after O.D. Skelton specifically asked to know the whereabouts of Walter O'Leary in Mexico and the nature of the association he was forming with his brother in Montreal. Letter by Norman A. Robertson to Commissioner S.T. Wood of the Royal Canadian Mounted Police, 31 October 1942, LAC, RG 146, vol. 3260, dossier 42-01-26, L'Union culturelle des Latins D'Amérique, pte 2.

18 This promise was primarily made to Quebec, since conscription during the First World War brought ethnic strife that seriously threatened the future political stability of Canada.

19 For this statistic, see Conrad and Finkel, *Canada: a National History*, 423. As for the reference to the "two solitudes," this comes from a Hugh MacLennan's novel with this title addressing French-English relations in Quebec.

20 Mémoire sur la section canadienne de l'Union culturelle des Latins d'Amérique, ACRLG, P40/C4, 1, Documents officiels de l'ULA 16 mai 1944–14 mars 1945.

21 Canadian Latin-American Association Formed in City, *The Ottawa Journal*, Ottawa, 15 October 1942.

22 Mémoire sur la section canadienne de l'Union culturelle des Latins d'Amérique, ACRLG, P40/C4, 1, Documents officiels de l'ULA, 16 mai 1944–14 mars 1945. In its surveillance of the ULA, Mercier-Gouin's attitude and dress were described in detail. Royal Canadian Mounted Police, Secret Report, 18 February 1943, LAC, RG 146, vol. 3260, dossier 42-01-26, L'Union culturelle des Latins D'Amérique, pte 2.

23 Royal Canadian Mounted Police, Secret Report, 24 February 1943, LAC, RG 146, vol. 3260, dossier 42-01-26, L'Union culturelle des Latins D'Amérique, pte 2.

24 Royal Canadian Mounted Police, Secret Report, 19 October 1943, LAC, RG 146, vol. 3260, dossier 42-01-26, L'Union culturelle des Latins D'Amérique, pte 2.

25 A news clipping about this event can be found in their archives. The article also mentions that the consuls from Brazil, Chile, France, Guatemala, Haiti, Spain, and Portugal were present. "Belle réussite des journées pan-latines de Montréal," *Le Canada*, 26 January 1942. LAC, RG 146, vol. 3260, dossier 42-01-26, L'Union culturelle des Latins D'Amérique, pte 2.

26 After Maurice Duplessis came back to power in 1944, relations between Quebec City and Ottawa were often confrontational over questions of constitutional authority to act in cultural and social fields of activities. On the one hand, Quebec strongly reacted to Ottawa's attempts to finance schooling in the province and other social programs of provincial authority. On the other, Ottawa reacted negatively to the creation of a national flag for Quebec in 1948, and the Tremblay commission on the future of constitutional questions from 1953 to 1956. In the subsequent decades, a move by Quebec or Ottawa in a shared field of activity would be answered by the other level of power with an equivalent action to maintain

its ground. See Coleman, *The Independence Movement in Quebec*. See also Martin, "Quebec Defines this Country."

27 De Certeau, *La Prise de parole*, 175.

28 Granatstein, *A Man of Influence*.

29 William Ferdinand Alphonse Turgeon was an Acadian with close connections with Liberal circles, who had a successful career as Chief Justice in Saskatchewan before retiring in 1941 to serve in Canadian diplomacy. He became Canada's first ambassador to Argentina that year. Turgeon, "Turgeon, William Ferdinand-Alphonse (1877–1969)." In 1944, he was also named as the first Canadian ambassador to Mexico. Boletin para la prensa, México, D.F., 16 de marzo de 1944, AHDSRE, III/1329/9/1940–1966, Establecimiento de Relaciones Diplomáticas entre México y Canadá. Correspondencia, informes y recortes de periódicos norteamericanos y canadienses.

30 Memorandum for N.A. Robertson prepared by W.A.F. Turgeon, 16 February 1943, LAC, RG25-A-3-b, vol. 5753, Union culturelle des Latins d'Amérique.

31 Royal Canadian Mounted Police, Secret Report, "L'union Culturelle des Latins D'Amerique," 29 January and 6 February 1942.

32 Memo written by N.A. Robertson, 22 November 1943, LAC, RG25-A-3-b, vol. 5753, Union culturelle des Latins d'Amérique.

33 Ibid.

34 Letter to N.A. Robertson from W.A.F. Turgeon, 19 June 1943, LAC, RG25-A-3-b, vol. 5753, Union culturelle des Latins d'Amérique.

35 In this sense, the simple fact that members of the ULA were speaking out and asserting French Canada's difference in front of an audience that included representatives of Latin American countries could be considered subversive by some officials from Ottawa.

36 Memo written by N.A. Robertson, 22 November 1943, LAC, RG25-A-3-b, vol. 5753, Union culturelle des Latins d'Amérique.

37 The double language used by the ULA is a strategy long associated with religious discourse. See, de Certeau, *La Prise de parole*, 140–1.

38 Letter by Mgr Olivier Maurault to Louis Bilodeau, 6 December 1944, ACRLG, P40/C4, 10, Correspondance de l'ULA, 18 décembre 1943–6 décembre 1944.

39 Union Culturelle des Latins d'Amérique, ed., *Rapport complet: Journées d'Amérique latine*, 1943.

40 Letter to N.A. Robertson from W.A.F. Turgeon, 19 June 1943, LAC-, RG25-A-3-b, vol. 5753, Union culturelle des Latins d'Amérique. David

Kelly and W.A.F. Turgeon were British and Canadian ambassadors to
Argentina at the time of their discussion.

41 William Coleman appropriately summarizes the situation: "In the years
immediately following the Second World War, quite remarkably, the position occupied by French Canadians in the North American economy were
as minor as they had been in 1810. Virtually all the important industries
in the province and all the senior positions in the management were
owned by or held by English Canadians or Americans. For close to 150
years, the French Canadians had been absent from the centres of economic
power in their own land. This position of weakness had led elites… to
adopt humiliating political positions, to bargain for second-class places in
government, and to countenance feelings of inferiority on the one hand
and hallucinating messianism on the other. This seeming inability of
French Canadians to assert themselves economically over the years had
helped foster myths among English Canadians that cast the French as
lacking business sense, as lazy, simple, priest-ridden peasants." Coleman,
The Independence Movement in Quebec, 26.

42 Letter to N.A. Robertson from W.A.F. Turgeon, 19 June 1943, LAC,
RG25-A-3-b, vol. 5753, Union culturelle des Latins d'Amérique.

43 Ibid.

44 Dostaler O'Leary, "Ce que nous sommes?," Union Culturelle des Latins
d'Amérique, ed., *Rapport complet: Journées d'Amérique latine, 1943*.

45 The RCMP worried about potential fascist connections. In a report from
18 March 1942, an RCMP agent mentioned some people said Walter
O'Leary "was considered, in some quarters, to entertain pro-Fascist sentiments, and was alleged to have fled to Mexico, at the outbreak of the present war." Other reports tried to establish connections between the
O'Learys and an Italian editor whose newspaper was subsidized by Fascist
Italy, or tried to link ULA language courses to a similar system used by
Italian Consulates. Royal Canadian Mounted Police, Secret Report,
10 February, 18 March, and 22 June 1942, LAC, RG 146, vol. 3260,
dossier 42-01-26, L'Union culturelle des Latins D'Amérique, pte 2.

46 One report from the RCMP mentioned: "My observations as to subversive
activities apply more, I suppose, to the organizers of the movement in
Montreal than to those in Ottawa where all the members apparently are
serious and respectable persons." Royal Canadian Mounted Police,
Censorship co-ordination committee, Press Censorship, 25 March 1942,
LAC, RG 146, vol. 3260, dossier 42-01-26, L'Union culturelle des Latins
D'Amérique, pte 2. See also, LAC, RG25, vol. 2854, Exchange of diplo-
matic representatives between Canada and Mexico – Proposals, and

RG25-A-3-b, vol. 5753, Union culturelle des Latins d'Amérique. "Journées d'Amérique latine," memorandum prepared by [R. Chaput] for N.A. Robertson, March 1943, LAC, RG25-A-3-b, vol. 5753, Union culturelle des Latins d'Amérique.

47 See Armour Landry's letter to Walter O'Leary, 22 April 1942, ACRLG, P40/C4, 9, Correspondance de l'Union des Latins d'Amérique, 31 janvier 1940–27 mars 1953.

48 Letter by Armour Landry to Walter O'Leary, 22 May 1942, ibid.

49 Carlos Calderón and Thomas Irving, "Canada and Latin America: An Outline for Activities for the Canadian Inter-American Association," LAC, RG25, vol. 2854, Exchange of diplomatic representatives between Canada and Mexico – Proposals.

50 Writing on the literature about the "affinities of race, religion and culture" characteristic of the period between the years 1920 and 1950, Daniel Gay states: "Supporters of French Canada's 'international vocation' think they can do a better job than the English Canadians as interpreters of Ottawa's political thinking [in Latin America]." But the previous quote by the Mexican consul and the suggestion by a British diplomat to use French Canadians as examples of the Empire's fair-play attest that this pretense to serve as intermediaries was echoed by some foreign diplomats as well. See Gay, Les élites québécoises et l'Amérique latine, 266.

51 "A la Ligue panaméricaine," [La Patrie?], [s.m.], 1944.

52 Paul Bouchard was closely associated with the Cercle Cervantes upon his return to Quebec City after the war, as he was hired by Université Laval soon after. He became president of the club in the 1950s. See Archives de l'Université Laval (AUL), P40 Fonds Paul Bouchard.

53 Paul Baillargeon, president of Canada-Amérique latine, said during the congress: "We have collaborated with the Union Culturelle [des Latins] and the organization of the Journées d'Amérique latine." Paul Baillargeon, Union Culturelle des Latins d'Amérique, ed., Rapport complet: Journées d'Amérique latine, 1943.

54 Memorandum to William Lyon Mackenzie King prepared by [N.A. Robertson], 12 December 1941, LAC, RG25, vol. 2854, Exchange of diplomatic representatives between Canada and Mexico – Proposals.

55 Memo written by N.A. Robertson, 22 November 1943, LAC, RG25-A-3-b, vol. 5753, Union culturelle des Latins d'Amérique.

56 I am using the concepts of "gente decente" [decent people] and "bonne société" interchangeably in this chapter to express this fraction of the bourgeois class that asserted itself first and foremost through a shared sense of education, good manners, and professional respectability.

57 John George Lambton, the Earl of Durham, was mandated to report on
the 1837–38 Rebellions in Lower Canada. His account of the conflict
noted as root cause of the civil war a visceral hatred between the
Canadiens and the British settlers. Since he asserted the French Canadians
formed a people "without history and literature," he argued assimilation
was the best way to improve their lives and insure stability in Canada. See
Durham, *Lord Durham's Report.*

58 Dostaler O'Leary, Closing statement of the 1942 Latin American days in
Montreal, ACRLG, P40/C4, 6, Causeries, conférences et allocutions prononcés dans le cadre des activités de l'Union des Latins d'Amérique,
9 novembre 1942–19 février 1944.

59 For this influence in the United States, see Helen Delpar's excellent study:
Delpar, *The Enormous Vogue of Things Mexican.*

60 Monette, "Serie tango," in *El tango nómade*, 403. It is interesting to note
that conservative groups first opposed this cultural influence.

61 ACRLG, P40/C4, 11, Bulletin de l'Union des Latins d'Amérique, vol. 4,
no. 17, 31 décembre 1947.

62 The newspaper *Le Canada* reported that more than 300 people attended
this congress organized by the ULA. The 1943 report mentioned it as well.
Union culturelle des Latins d'Amérique, ed., *Rapport complet: Journées
d'Amérique latine, 1943.*

63 I am using the 1943 congress as a case example for two main reasons.
First, this is the congress following the 1942 plebiscite that Ottawa specifically wanted to monitor for its potentially seditious upshots. It is therefore
instructive to analyze the type of French Canadian nationalist discourse
articulated at this particular gathering. The second reason to use 1943 as a
case study is simply that it is the only year that a complete report remains
available in the archives. Speeches made at ULA gatherings were widely
reported in the press for other years as well, but a full report goes more in
depth, obviously, than newspaper articles on the subject.

64 Marcel Roussin, "L'Amérique du sud et les relations diplomatiques,"
Union Culturelle des Latins d'Amérique, ed., *Rapport complet: Journées
d'Amérique latine, 1943.*

65 François Hertel, "Notre Culture et ses retentissements possibles chez les
autres Latins d'Amérique," ibid.

66 Léon Mercier-Gouin, "Opening Statement," ibid.

67 Memo written by N.A. Robertson, 22 November 1943. LAC, RG25-A-
3-b, vol. 5753, Union culturelle des Latins d'Amérique.

68 Harvey, a journalist and novelist, author of *Les demi-civilisés* – a novel
brutally condemned by Catholic authorities – became a strong opponent

of clerico-nationalism and clericalism in the province. He gave an important speech on this topic in May 1945, entitled *La peur* [Fear], in which he denounced "clerical oppression." Lamonde, *L'heure de vérité*, 26.

69 Podea, "Pan American Sentiment in French Canada," 340.

70 Quoted in the section "Opinion" of Union Culturelle des Latins d'Amérique, ed., *Rapport complet: Journées d'Amérique latine, 1943*.

71 Lamonde, *L'heure de vérité*, 25, 27.

72 T.D. Bouchard had also previously defended Dostaler O'Leary in an article entitled "L'extrême gauche et l'extrême droite." In this article, Bouchard explained that both the far left and the far right despised him. He then mentioned that the attacks against O'Leary were also unjustified. T.D. Bouchard, "L'extrême gauche et l'extrême droite," [s.d.], A C R L G, P40/C1, 1, Causeries, conférences et allocutions, 15 mai 1937–18 mai 1939.

73 Letter from Dostaler O'Leary to Walter O'Leary, [1944], A C R L G, P40/C4, 9, Correspondance de l'U L A, 31 janvier 1940–27 mars 1953.

74 For the two previous references, see Union Culturelle des Latins d'Amérique, ed., *Rapport complet: Journées d'Amérique latine, 1943*.

75 Lucille Lévesque-O'Leary, ibid.

76 Jacques Melançon, under-secretary of Montreal Chamber of Commerce, made a presentation during the congress entitled "Notre situation économique en Amérique" where he underlined the importance of 'Latin' capital for an autonomous national life, ibid.

77 See for examples the extracts reprinted in the *Rapport complet des Journées d'Amérique latine, 1943*, op. cit., and the articles included in A C R L G, P40/C4, 12, Coupures de presse sur l'Union des Latins d'Amérique, 17 mars 1941–31 décembre 1976. The memorandum prepared for N.A. Robertson commenting on the 1943 Congress mentioned that: "the Montreal French-speaking press covered the congress, giving it first importance," memorandum prepared by [R. Chaput] for N.A. Robertson, March 1943, L A C, RG25-A-3-b, vol. 5753, Union culturelle des Latins d'Amérique.

78 Iris S. Podea also noted this point concerning Quebec media in 1948. Podea, "Pan American Sentiment in French Canada."

79 "Chez les Latins d'Amérique 720 nouveaux membres dans cette association," *La Patrie* (Montreal), n.d., A C R L G, P40/C4, 12, Coupures de presse sur l'Union des Latins d'Amérique 17 mars 1941–31 décembre 1976.

80 To practice languages, the U L A also organized a social circle where people got together to discuss and sing Latin American songs. A closer analysis of language courses and related deeds will be provided in the

following chapter, which focuses on student exchanges and other ULA social activities.

81 Union Culturelle des Latins d'Amérique, ed., *Rapport complet: Journées d'Amérique latine, 1943.*

82 Historical memo prepared by the ULA executive, ACRLG, P40/C4, 1, Documents officiels de l'ULA, 16 mai 1944–14 mars 1945.

83 "Latins d'Amérique," [La Patrie?], 11 February 1944, ACRLG, P40/C4, 12, Coupures de presse sur l'Union des Latins d'Amérique 17 mars 1941–
·   31 décembre 1976.

84 See ACRLG, P40/A, 1, Correspondance de Dostaler O'Leary, 18 juin 1931–30 juin 1944, and P40/C4, 9, Correspondance de l'Union des Latins d'Amérique, 31 janvier 1940–27 mars 1953.

85 Union Culturelle des Latins d'Amérique, ed., *Rapport complet: Journées d'Amérique latine, 1943.*

86 Daniel Johnson, "Collaboration entre étudiants latins dans Pax Romana," Union Culturelle des Latins d'Amérique, ed., *Rapport complet: Journées d'Amérique latine, 1943.*

87 Union Culturelle des Latins d'Amérique, ed., *Rapport complet: Journées d'Amérique latine, 1943.*

88 Oscar Drouin, ibid.

89 The type of foreign relations envisioned for the province of Quebec during the 1943 ULA congress and the following student exchanges with Mexico predated the establishment of similar programs with France in the 1950s (Association France-Canada) and the opening of a Maison du Québec à Paris in October 1961. For a larger discussion of the elaboration of Quebec's international relations, see Paquin, ed., *Histoire des relations internationales du Québec.*

90 William Coleman aptly describes the context in which this doctrine was elaborated in the 1960s and the strains it provoked with the federal government: "The pursuit of closer relations between Quebec and France brought to the political stage a new issue for dispute between the federal government and the government of Quebec. When Quebec and France signed an agreement to initiate the new program of co-operation in education in 1965, Gérin Lajoie, the minister of education of Quebec, stated that Quebec would pursue similar relations on its own in the future. He argued that Quebec should be able to act alone on the international stage in those areas that come under provincial jurisdiction in the Canadian constitution. Such a demand was not new to politics in Quebec. As early as 1949, in its brief to the Massey Commission, the Ligue d'Action natio-nale had suggested that provinces be able to deal on their own with

UNESCO on educational matters. Similarly, the CTCC had asked for a more important role for the provinces in the International Labour Organisation in the 1950s." Coleman, *The Independence Movement in Quebec*, 143–4.

91 Roger Duhamel, "Québec, phare de la civilisation française," *Le Devoir*, 31 March 1943. A copy of the article can be found, along with an English translation in LAC, RG25-A-3-b, vol. 5753, Union culturelle des Latins d'Amérique. Roger Duhamel was a member of the ULA.

92 Ibid.

93 Granatstein, *Canadian Foreign Policy since 1945*.

CHAPTER FOUR

1 The punning title of "*Amar te duele*" translates in English as "Love hurts/Loving *you* hurts." Sariñana, "Amar te duele."

2 It is also worth mentioning that since a substantial majority of students on the exchange trips were girls, the trips seemed to have provoked exhilaration rather than despair. Two examples convey this point. From a French Canadian point of view, a note from the ULA to a group of Mexican students attending a ball in Montreal on 27 January 1945, illustrates this point. It stipulated that they, the girls, "should not be accompanied, the college's directorate will introduce [them] to young Canadians." As far as Mexicans were concerned, a newspaper article from *Excelsior* exemplified this perception by making a crucial omission in their reportage. When the group of 125 Canadian students arrived in Mexico, their coverage focused only on the 100 girls of the group, mentioning that "Mexican authorities are collaborating in putting together celebrations to honour the Canadian girls." See, "Comunicado No 1 a los miembros de la Misión Cultural Mexico-Canadá," ACRLG, P40/C4, 3, Programmes d'activités de l'Union des Latins d'Amérique, 23 janvier 1942–25 janvier 1945; and "Cien Muchachas del Canadá Visitarán Nuestra Ciudad," *Excelsior*, [21 May 1944], ACRLG, P40/C4, 12, Coupures de presse sur l'Union des Latins d'Amérique, 17 mars 1941–31 décembre 1976.

3 By "traditionalist groups," I mean the people who adopted a counter-revolutionary stance in order to defend Catholic education. I am using the term traditionalist to encompass the Catholic and conservative factions at UNAM. To a large extent, Catholic and conservative could be used interchangeably to describe the groups opposing revolutionary reforms. Yet, I am sometimes using traditionalist as a neutral term because their project did not completely overlap. If Catholic academics and students were

almost always very conservative, the opposite was not true. For example, the conservative PAN that emerged out of the University conflict was not taking orders from the Catholic Church, and the Catholic Church did not blindly support the PAN. Therefore, I will sometimes use both terms to underline their conjoint mobilization, but I will more systematically use traditionalist to describe their struggle against State reforms in education. For a discussion of the relation between PAN ideologues and the Catholic Church, see Loaeza, "Los orígenes de la propuesta modernizadora de Manuel Gómez Morín." For the terminology used, see also Mabry, *The Mexican University and the State*.

4 For the sake of clarity, I will consistently use the acronym UNAM to refer to the University of Mexico, despite the fact that this institution gained its official autonomy in 1929.

5 Mabry, *The Mexican University and the State*, 29.

6 See Burke, "The University of Mexico and the Revolution."

7 *The Cosmic Race* is a cornerstone essay revaluating Mexico's mixed-racial and ethnic heritage. Written at the heyday of scientific racism, the *Cosmic Race* flipped many eugenic theories on their head to argue that miscegenation produces superior civilization. Mexico, for its miscegenation of indigenous and Spanish heritage is therefore portrayed in his essay as the chief nation indicative of the civilization offering the world's best hopes. This theory was used as a premise to craft a Mexican nationalism more respectful of the racial make-up of the country.

8 Michael Burkes contends that "their idealism and individualism were far removed from the pressing economic and social problems" of the Revolution, therefore making "confrontation between the university humanists and the hard-nosed, practical revolutionaries" unavoidable. Burke, "The University of Mexico and the Revolution," 254.

9 For the most exhaustive study on the subject, see Meyer, *La Cristiada*.

10 Vaughan, *Cultural Politics in Revolution*, 30.

11 On this subject, Mary Kay Vaughan writes: "Teachers were also cultural ideologues, crafting unity and legitimacy through the use of song, dance, theatre, and oratory, matching new revolutionary heroes and causes to local myth, legend, and artistic expression," ibid.

12 Espinosa, "Student Politics, National Politics." The association was first named National Catholic Student Confederation but changed its name to UNEC shortly after.

13 Burke, "The University of Mexico and the Revolution," 265.

14 The autonomy of UNAM was a major demand articulated by Manuel Gómez Morín, one of the most vocal representatives of the conservative

movement in Mexico and a founding member and principal organizer of the PAN. See Loaeza, "Los orígenes de la propuesta modernizadora de Manuel Gómez Morín."

15 One element of Bassols's reformist agenda that especially provoked the ire of Catholics was his plan to introduce sex-education classes in Mexican schools. See Espinosa, "Student Politics, National Politics," 546.

16 Vaughan, *Cultural Politics in Revolution*, 34–5.

17 Loaeza, "Los orígenes," 458.

18 Krauze, *La presidencia imperial*.

19 Contreras, *Rodulfo Brito Foucher*, 171.

20 Concerning his French Canadian ancestors, see "Bel hommage à la culture française," *Le Devoir*, 3 November 1944. See also, Doctorat d'honneur au Dr Rodulfo Brito Foucher, AHDSRE, II/823 (71)/15136, Brito Foucher, Rodulfo. Lic. (rector de la Universidad de Mexico).

21 Contreras, *Rodulfo Brito Foucher*.

22 Loaeza, "Los orígenes," 461.

23 The honorary title *Jefe Máximo* [First Leader] is used to describe the ascendancy of Calles over his party and the series of puppet presidents that followed him in office until the election of Lázaro Cárdenas in 1934. In the context of his speech in Guadalajara, *grito* can be translated as "call to arms."

24 *El Nacional*, 21 July 1934. Quoted in Meyer, "An Idea of Mexico," in *The Eagle and the Virgin*, 290.

25 Quoted in Vaughan, *Cultural Politics in Revolution*, 34–5.

26 Espinosa, "Student Politics, National Politics," 551.

27 The death of Rodulfo Brito Foucher's brother happened during the 1935 punitive expedition to Villahermosa against the regime of Tomás Garrido Canábal. Camp, *Mexican Political Biographies*, 44.

28 For a thorough presentation of Luis Chico Goerne's concrete actions, see Mabry, *The Mexican University and the State, 1910–1971*.

29 See Assad, "La rebelión cedillista o el ocaso del poder tradicional." See also Meyer, *El sinarquismo, el cardenismo y la iglesia*.

30 Mabry, *The Mexican University and the State*.

31 An enthusiastic US scholar noted that UNAM's Summer School had an important geopolitical role to accomplish in the aftermath of the First World War and the Mexican Revolution: "It was correctly perceived that the future success or failure of Western civilization on the American continent depends on whether the two forms of it, the Anglo-Saxon and the Latin, can cooperate and benefit by mutual contact without giving up any of their peculiar characteristics. The destiny of America lies in the

comprehension of the fact that mankind living on this continent should lead the rest of the world in the new era which is now beginning; an era in which human beings, regardless of what their evolution may have been in the past, must firmly resolve to abandon inhuman methods of settling their problems." Nykl, "Summer School of the Universidad Nacional de Mexico," 52.

32　On this subject, Mgr Maurault made some comments a decade later on the ongoing necessities for Mexican Catholics to build bridges with foreign co-religionists. He also revealed that his Mexican hosts informed him of the direct correlation between the harshness of religious repression in the 1930s and the increased frequency of pupils completing their education in religious institutions abroad. He wrote: "I was told that the program of the normal schools [was] unspeakable in particular. When Parliament passed laws that ruined the traditional religious education of the nation, legislators themselves hastened to send their children to colleges and convents abroad." Maurault, *Le Mexique de mes souvenirs*, 131–2.

33　The US exerted a crucial influence in the resolution of the two waves of the Cristiada, notwithstanding significant nativist and anti-catholic sentiments in the country. Meyer, *La cruzada por México*.

34　Brand, "United States-Mexican Scientific and Cultural Relations." Meyer, *La cruzada por México*.

35　This point is well illustrated by Linda Hall in her study of the paradoxical relation between the US government, American oil companies and financial institutions, and the Post-revolutionary State. See Hall, *Oil, Banks, and Politics*.

36　From the beginning of the Second World War, Josephus Daniels, the American ambassador in Mexico at the time, insisted on the necessity of solving the problem resulting from the nationalization of oil as soon as possible. It still took until 17 April 1942 to settle this question once and for all. For a detailed analysis of this process, see Lorenzo Meyer, *Las raíces del nacionalismo petrolero en México*.

37　Since the beginning of the twentieth century, private educational trusts (like the Rockefeller Foundation and the Guggenheim Fellowship) along with US governmental foundations financed academic projects in Mexico. The Good Neighbor Policy helped to offer a first systematization of US investment in academic connections and cultural endeavours during the 1930s. But in 1941, the Office of the Coordinator of Inter-American Affairs (OCIAA) was established under the governorship of Nelson Rockefeller to coordinate and facilitate pan-American dealings.

The OCIAA then established the Inter-American Educational Foundation in 1943 to orchestrate wide-ranging reforms related to educational programs. See for example Cueto, ed., *Missionaries of Science*; Fein, "Myths of Cultural Imperialism and Nationalism," in *Fragments of a Golden Age.*

38 Gabriela Contreras mentions that some publications in Mexico identified Rodulfo Brito Foucher and Julio Vértiz Burchard, SJ, among others, as members of a fifth column conspiracy. Contreras, *Rodulfo Brito Foucher*, 285.

39 Camacho even let the controversial old master return to the country to head the *Colegio Nacional*, an establishment modeled on the Collège de France. Vasconcelos founded this institution in 1943 with distinguished Mexican figures including Antonio Caso, Diego Rivera, and José Clemente Orozco. Krauze, *La presidencia imperial*, 60.

40 Quoted in Contreras, *Rodulfo Brito Foucher*, 287.

41 Quoted in Mabry, *The Mexican University and the State*, 184.

42 Castillo, "The Los Angeles 'Zoot Suit Riots' Revisited."

43 *Excelsior*, 26 June 1943. Quoted in ibid., 379.

44 This motto could be read directly under the UCMCF's emblem in official letters from the association. Examples can be found in ACRLG, P40/A, 4, Correspondance personnelle de Walter-Patrice O'Leary, 10 février 1937–30 août 1978.

45 I became aware of the importance of Quebecois publishers' distribution of French publications in Latin America through a paper given by Lüsebrink, entitled "Transferts culturels en temps de guerre." Maurault also briefly mentions this in his book published in 1947. Maurault, *Par voies et par chemins de l'air*, 214.

46 This translation was written for the Canadian Department of External Affairs. It originally comes from an article published in *El Economista*, Mexico, DF, 16 November 1941, LAC, RG25, vol. 2854, Exchange of diplomatic representatives between Canada and Mexico – Proposals.

47 Racine, *L'anticlericalisme dans le roman québecois*, 18.

48 Axelrod, *Making a Middle Class*. Shore, *The Science of Social Redemption*. This expertise was in part the result of receiving money from the same US foundations Mexican institutions did.

49 The telegrams exchanged between Ambassador Francisco del Río Cañedo and Manuel Ávila Camacho's secretarial staff, Jesus J. Gonzalez Gallo, reveal the prominence given to McGill University over Université de Montréal in attracting professors and students to Mexico. AGN, MAC, vol. 978, exp. 577, 1/66, Relaciones diplomáticas con Canadá, 1944.

50 For a glimpse at the leading English Canadian scientists courted to come to Mexico, see also LAC, RG77, vol. 157, National University – Mexico City General Correspondance 1944–1946.

51 Letter from Richard Pattee to Rodulfo Brito Foucher, 25 July 1942, AHUNAM, 3, 33, Rodulfo Brito Foucher. Please note that this fonds was not completely organized when I consulted it. Classification of documents in the collection might have changed since then.

52 Charles de Koninck would later come to Mexico to collaborate with UNAM professors, further strengthening this bond. See Brito Foucher's correspondence at AHUNAM, 3, 33, Rodulfo Brito Foucher.

53 O.H., "L'Amérique espagnole," *Le Devoir*, 7 March 1941.

54 Personal letter written by Georges Villeneuve to Walter O'Leary, 12 June 1941, ACRLG, P40/A, 4, Correspondance personnelle de Walter-Patrice O'Leary, 10 février 1937–30 août 1978.

55 Daniel Johnson, "Collaboration entre étudiants latins dans Pax Romana," Union Culturelle des Latins d'Amérique, ed., *Rapport complet: Journées d'Amérique latine, 1943*.

56 The actual number of students who went to Mexico remains unclear. Some sources indicate that the delegation included 25 students, while another mentions 16. See the following article quoted and various memorandums in ACRLG, P40/C4, 4, Rapports d'activités de l'Union des Latins d'Amérique, 29 novembre 1941–27 mai 1947.

57 "Llegarán del Canadá 16 universitarios," *Excelsior*, 18 December 1943.

58 Quebec City municipal council and the federal MP from Rivière-du-Loup also endorsed the project. Memorandum official Mexico-Canada Frances, ACRLG, P40/C4, 4, Rapports d'activités de l'Union des Latins d'Amérique, 29 novembre 1941–27 mai 1947.

59 Letter to the Rector of UNAM, Rodulfo Brito Foucher, 15 February 1943, AHUNAM, 3, 33, Rodulfo Brito Foucher. See also, Vienen Estudiantes de Canadá a Nuestro País, ACRLG, P40/C4, 12, Coupures de presse sur l'Union des Latins d'Amérique, 17 mars 1941–31 décembre 1976.

60 "Canada and Mexico Will Exchange Students," ibid.

61 "Llegarán del Canadá 16 universitarios."

62 The UCMCF's exhibits, conferences, and student missions were publicized in newspaper articles. There are also reasons to believe that articles published on this subject were outlined first by UCMCF members, a draft of the aforementioned article being present in Walter O'Leary's personal documents. Finally, members of the organization also directly collaborated with official organs of the State to brief them on Canada. For example, at the beginning of April 1942 an in-depth review of Canada was published

in the government official newspaper, *El Nacional*, where the editorial staff of this publication thanked a founding member of the U C M C F in Mexico, Alejo Loustau, for his collaboration with the article. They also recognized the collaboration of Armour Landry, a U L A member, for crucial information. "El Canada y la Guerra," *El Nacional*, 19 April 1942, Bibliothèque et Archives nationales du Québec (B A N Q), centre de Montréal, P97 Fonds Armour Landry / 100 0 013 01-05-003A-01 / 2004-07-001 / 3 [Mexique; 1957–1974].

63 The ambassador even mentioned at one point that the McGill delegation formed the majority of the student contingent. This seems highly unlikely, although sources are not conclusive. Mgr Maurault and other representatives from the U L A contradicted the ambassador at various points in their own communications, stating instead that the majority of students came from *Université de Montréal*. However, the list of participants in the 1944 trip that I have consulted makes no mention of the academic affiliation of students (except for one student from McGill). Comité Canada-Mexico, A C R L G, P40/C4, 7, Recrutement des membres de l'Union des Latins d'Amérique, 3 janvier 1941–1 septembre 1948. See also the correspondence between Ambassador Francisco del Río Cañedo and Manuel Ávila Camacho's secretarial staff, Jesus J. Gonzalez Gallo, A G N, M A C, vol. 978, exp. 577, 1/66, Relaciones diplomáticas con Canadá, 1944.

64 Comité Canada-Mexico, A C R L G, P40/C4, 7, Recrutement des membres de l'Union des Latins d'Amérique, 3 janvier 1941–1 septembre 1948.

65 This is mentioned informally in the letterhead of a correspondence between Hector Boulay and Manuel Ávila Camacho, 10 August 1944, A G N, M A C, vol. 978, exp. 577, 1/66.

66 "Les étudiants canadiens au Mexique," *Le Canada*, 19 June 1944.

67 "Reportage no. 71," (Canada: Office national du Film du Canada, 1944).

68 *Le bulletin de l'Union des Latins d'Amérique*, vol. 7, no. 29, 31 January 1950, A C R L G, P40/C4, 11, Bulletin de l'U L A.

69 "Les étudiants canadiens au Mexique," *Le Canada*, 19 June 944.

70 For example, excerpts of the article first published in *Le Canada* were reproduced in the *Journal Français du Mexique*, 29 June 1944, A C R L G, P40/C4, 12, Coupures de presse sur l'Union des Latins d'Amérique, 17 mars 1941–31 décembre 1976.

71 Letter from Ambassador Francisco del Río Cañedo to Jesus J. Gonzalez Gallo, 17 June 1944, A G N, vol. 978, exp. 577, 1/66, Relaciones diplomáticas con Canadá, 1944.

72 This is for the second trip organized by the U L A the following year, after the end of the war. I do not have full evaluation of the total price for the

Canadian trip in 1944. I do know, however, that the Mexican trip to Canada six months later cost between $1,000 and $3,000 (pesos) depending on lodging. *Bulletin de l'Union des Latins d'Amérique*, 30 October 1945, vol. 4, no. 8, A C R L G, P40/C4, 11, Bulletin de l'Union des Latins d'Amérique. Proyecto de un viaje anual de una misión universitaria mexicana a Canadá, A C R L G, P40/C4, 4, Rapports d'activités de l'Union des Latins d'Amérique, 29 novembre 1941–27 mai 1947.

73 Maurault, "Petits côtés d'un grand voyage," *Le Mexique de mes souvenirs*.

74 I have compiled most of my statistics for this section from information extracted from a list of 119 people going to Mexico that included their address, occupation, nationality, and age. I have added the names of five women to my statistics on gender from information on members of the trip extracted in personal letters and photos. Comité Canada-Mexico, A C R L G, P40/C4, 7, Recrutement des membres de l'Union des Latins d'Amérique, 3 janvier 1941–1 septembre 1948.

75 Maurault and O'Leary also contended that the vast majority of them were U L A members, but I could not corroborate this claim.

76 74.4 per cent of U L A members taking Spanish lessons at Université de Montréal were women. It was reported in Mexico that hundreds of French Canadians had taken Spanish lessons thanks to the association. The 1945–46 presidential report of the U L A mentioned that 275 students divided in ten different classes completed their Spanish classes in that year alone. Rapport du Président 1945–46, A C R L G, P40/C4, 4, Rapports d'activités de l'Union des Latins d'Amérique, 29 novembre 1941–27 mai 1947.

77 This parallels the role played by women in lay Catholic associations to redraw the confines of gender roles by expanding the "traditional" definition of domesticity. This process will be exposed more clearly in the following chapter.

78 In the case of secretaries and stenographers, learning Spanish could be a career-defining skill since it was perceived at the time that the post-war economy would provide bureaucratic employment in Montreal for trilingual staff in relation to inter-American affairs.

79 These last numbers include the men as well.

80 The small number of young men in their twenties in the delegation can be explained by the contingencies of the war. As a result of the age discrepancy, the average age of the men who went to Mexico was 28.5 years old.

81 [young Canadian women]

82 Letter from Jaime Torres Bodet to Jesus Gonzales Gallo, 22 June 1944, A G N, M A C, vol. 978, exp. 577, 1/66, Relaciones diplomáticas con Canadá, 1944.

83 "Afinidades culturales entre Mexicanos y Francocanadienses. El viaje de
    125 muchachas francocanadienses para la Escuela de Verano," A C R L G,
    P40/C4, 4, Rapports d'activités de l'Union des Latins d'Amérique, 29
    novembre 1941–27 mai 1947.

84 "Programa para recibir a los 125 Canadienses," A C R L G, P40/C4, 12,
    Coupures de presse sur l'Union des Latins d'Amérique, 17 mars 1941–31
    décembre 1976.

85 Maurault, *Le Mexique de mes souvenirs*.

86 Report on activities relating to the student mission by Ambassador W.F.A.
    Turgeon, 14 August 1944, L A C, RG-25 vol. 3275, Visit to Mexico of
    group of Canadian students, June 1944, January 1945, Summer 1945.

87 L A C, RG-25 vol. 3275, Visit to Mexico of group of Canadian students,
    June 1944, January 1945, Summer 1945.

88 Invitation, A H U N A M, 3, 33, Rodulfo Brito Foucher. Maurault, *Le
    Mexique de mes souvenirs*, 153–4.

89 Ibid., 109.

90 "Spectacles et fêtes," ibid.

91 Ibid., 25–6.

92 There is contradictory evidence whether this speech was delivered exactly
    with those words or not. Maurault presented a draft in the first chapter of
    his book *Le Mexique de mes souvenirs*.

93 "Au Mexique avec l'Union culturelle," *La Patrie*, 21 August 1944.

94 Maurault, *Le Mexique de mes souvenirs*, 160.

95 "Programa," B A N Q, centre de Montréal, P97, Fonds Armour Landry/100
    0 013 01-05-003A-01/2004-07-001/3 [Mexique; 1957–1974].

96 Ibid.

97 Mabry, *The Mexican University and the State*, 188.

98 Herzog, *Una historia de la Universidad de México y sus problemas*. The
    quote in Spanish reads: "este diablo ya se siente presidenciable."

99 Mabry, *The Mexican University and the State*, 184.

100 Ibid., 185.

101 Ibid., 188.

102 Ibid., 189. Actually, this assertion needs to be nuanced. The new organic
    law that governed U N A M from then on did not entirely subordinate the
    institution to the state. U N A M kept its autonomous status. However, the
    elections of rectors were "de-politicized" and rendered an aca-
    demic/bureaucratic decision.

103 My assessment of the significance of the rector's downfall tally with
    Contreras' analysis of the situation. Contreras, *Rodulfo Brito Foucher*, 313.

104 Maurault, *Le Mexique de mes souvenirs*, 154.

105 For a good analysis of the Catholic, nationalist, and bourgeois opposition to communism and socialism in Quebec during the interwar period, see Lévesque, *Virage à gauche interdit*.

106 Memorandum for Dr Keeleyside, 3 August 1944, LAC, RG 25 vol. 3275, Visit to Mexico of group of Canadian students, June 1944, January 1945, Summer 1945.

107 Letter from the Under Secretary of State for External Affairs, H.L. Keenleyside, to the Canadian Ambassador to Mexico, W.F.A. Turgeon, 5 August 1944, ibid. The student in question was Marie-Claire Kirkland who later became a member of the Legislative Assembly in the same riding as her father in 1961. With her victory, she became the first women elected to Quebec's Legislative Assembly (nowadays Assemblée Nationale). Comité Canada-Mexico, ACRLG, P40/C4, 7, Recrutement des membres de l'Union des Latins d'Amérique, 3 janvier 1941–1 septembre 1948. See also http://www.assnat.qc.ca/en/deputes/kirkland-marie-claire-3799/biographie.html.

108 Maurault, *Le Mexique de mes souvenirs*, 141.

109 Various documents discuss these points in LAC, RG 25 vol. 3275, Visit to Mexico of group of Canadian students, June 1944, January 1945, Summer 1945.

110 Letter from Ambassador Turgeon to the Secretary of External affairs, 14 August 1944, ibid.

111 Maurault, *Le Mexique de mes souvenirs*, 146–7. It has to be said that the delegation sang "La Marseillaise" on other occasions. A picture was taken with a group of students (but also including Walter O'Leary and Carlos Calderón) during the visit in Xochimilco on a typical Mexican boat decorated with the official motto of the Province of Quebec "Je me souviens." This event was organized by the Mayor of Mexico City in honour of dignitaries from Montreal. On the back of the picture, it was noted that the group sang songs in French and Spanish such as "Chevaliers de la table ronde," "Ô Canada," the Mexican National Anthem, "La Marseillaise," and "Alouette." It is written on the margins of this photograph that French Canada's motto was honoured in Mexico thanks to Carlos Calderón. ACRLG, P40/T1, 1, 3, Fête en l'honneur d'un groupe d'étudiants canadiens-français de passage à Xochimilco, au Mexique.

112 LAC, RG 25 vol. 3275, Visit to Mexico of group of Canadian students, June 1944, January 1945, Summer 1945.

113 Different members of the 1944 trip later reported the negative impact the O'Leary's politicking had on the overall success of the mission. Others simply said that the very composition of the group misrepresented Canada

in the first place, since the French Canadians were numerically overrepresented and Mexicans kept hearing French spoken. See ibid.

114 Maurault, *Le Mexique de mes souvenirs*, 147.

115 Maurault wrote on this subject. See, ibid.

116 The Mexican consul was honoured for his labour in favour of the French language at a dinner in March 1944 the ULA organized. The Mayor of Montreal and other prominent Quebec politicians assisted. Armour Landry had previously confided to Dostaler O'Leary: "he was able to ensure that telegrams in French could cross the Mexican border. This is a first step toward the recognition of Canadian bilingualism. He deserves congratulations." Letter by Armour Landry to [Dostaler O'Leary], 5 February 1944, ACRLG, P40/C4, 9, Correspondance de l'Union des Latins d'Amérique, 31 janvier 1940–27 mars 1953. See also "Adieux de M Calderon," *La Patrie*, 27 March 1944.

117 Letter by Mgr Olivier Maurault to Louis Bilodeau, 6 Decembre 1944, ACRLG, P40/C4, 10, Correspondance de l'ULA, 18 décembre 1943–6 décembre 1944.

118 Conversation with Mr Hector Boulay concerning the Visit of Canadian Students to Mexico in the Summer of 1944, LAC, RG 25 vol. 3275, Visit to Mexico of group of Canadian students, June 1944, January 1945, Summer 1945.

119 Letter from the Under Secretary of State for External Affairs, N.A. Robertson, to the Minister of Justice, Louis St-Laurent, 26 August 1944, LAC, RG 25 vol. 3275, Visit to Mexico of group of Canadian students, June 1944, January 1945, Summer 1945.

120 "Voyage enchanteur des étudiants au Mexique," *La Presse*, 19 August 1944. Maurault also discusses this point in Maurault, *Le Mexique de mes souvenirs*, 122.

121 See, http://archives.radio-canada.ca/IDC-0-103-1487-9973/annees40/1944/.

122 Maurault, *Le Mexique de mes souvenirs*, 147.

123 Maurault, *Par voies et par chemins de l'air*, 226.

124 In all likelihood, this is what happened in 1946 when the University of Havana invited a professor from this institution to teach a course entitled "Cultural Backgrounds of the French Canadians." Mgr Olivier Maurault put the University of Havana in contact with Raymond Tanghe, a professor of his institution that had participated at the 1942 Journée Pan-Latine organized by the ULA. The University of Havana was interested, but when he delivered the necessary papers that would have allowed him to go, Ottawa apparently refused. They required that the course be on Canada

and launched an extensive search in English-speaking institutions to find a replacement (despite the fact that Tanghe said he could adapt his course). Tanghe later bitterly commented to the Rector of the University of Havana: "Monseigneur Olivier Maurault has just informed me that the Canadian Government has appointed a professor of the University of British Columbia to lecture on 'Canada' at your Summer School. It is with deep regret that I miss this opportunity of making your acquaintance and of having the honor of lecturing at the University of Havana." Letter by Raymond Tanghe to José M. Gutiérrez, 14 June 1946, Archives de l'Université de Montréal (AUM), P7/A, 154, Correspondance 3–28 juin 1946. LAC also has a substantial file on the issue: LAC, RG 25-G-2 vol. 3836, University of Havana – Proposed visit by a Canadian University professor to summer session 1946.

125 Mace, "Les relations du Québec avec l'Amérique latine."

126 Urgel Mitchell actually said in a radio broadcast that his association from now on would "avoid all controversial issues and remain strictly neutral on political questions." Quoted in Podea, "Pan American Sentiment in French Canada," 342.

127 *L'Autorité*, 19 May 1945. Quoted in ibid., 341.

128 Lapin means rabbit in English and represents a moniker intended to belittle their gatherings as shallow and promiscuous. Ibid., 340.

129 Brito Foucher had been invited to speak there through connections with the UCMCF and Walter O'Leary. He gave a speech praising French Canada to the skies, and underlined the virtues of the Hispanic world and its model of miscegenation. Later, Dostaler O'Leary (in various instances) and Mgr Maurault would draw from this to argue that this open-mindedness toward race "gave other continents an admirable lesson in humanity." Maurault, *Par voies et par chemins de l'air*, 217. For Brito Foucher's speech see "Bel hommage à la culture française," *Le Devoir*, 3 November 1944. See also, ACRLG, P40/C4, 8, Correspondance de l'Union des Latins d'Amérique, 6 avril 1942–11 avril 1945.

130 *Le Canada français* 33, no. 4 (December 1945): 297–8. Brito Foucher visited many people during his stay in Quebec. For example, the program included discussions with: Charles de Koninck, André Turcot (honorary consul of Mexico in Quebec City), Alphonse-Marie Parent, Joseph Ledit, and the rector of Université Laval. Visite à Québec de M le Dr et de Madame Rodulfo Brito Foucher (20–29 octobre 1944), AHUNAM, 3, 33, Rodulfo Brito Foucher.

131 The universities are the Iberoamericana (administered by the Jesuits) and the Motolinia (administered by nuns). Doctorat d'honneur au Dr Rodulfo

Brito Foucher, A H D S R E, II/823 (71)/15136, Brito Foucher, Rodulfo. Lic. (rector de la Universidad de Mexico).

132 Ibid. Brito Foucher later referred to Mgr Cyrille Gagnon as a very good friend in a letter sent to Richard Pattee announcing his death. Letter from Rodulfo Brito Foucher to Richard Pattee, 28 February 1946, A H U N A M, 3, 33, Rodulfo Brito Foucher.

133 Letter from Ambassador del Río Cañedo to the President of Mexico concerning Brito Foucher's trip to Quebec, 31 October 1944, A H D S R E, II/823 (71)/15136, Brito Foucher, Rodulfo. Lic. (rector de la Universidad de Mexico). A copy can also be found at A H U N A M, III-701-6, Rodulfo Brito Foucher. Doctorado Honoris Causa.

134 There are a few documents in LAC relating to the Mexican reply to Canadian disappointment with the 1944 exchange where they essentially mentioned they wished to receive "real" students in the future. A few can also be found in the A H U N A M. Lettre by Francisco Villagrán to Rector Alfonso Caso, 26 February 1945, A H U N A M, fondos Alfonso Caso.

135 We could read in *La Presse* directly following the 1944 student trip that "the representatives of Camacho's government mentioned they were favourable to the *Union des Latins*' projects in supporting the exchange of professors and speakers between our two countries. Besides, another group of Mexican students should visit us again next summer." "Voyage enchanteur des étudiants au Mexique," *La Presse*, 19 August 1944. See also, "Un groupe d'étudiants mexicains viennent visiter notre province," *Le Canada*, 5 January 1945.

136 See UAM, P7/A, 150, Correspondance 1–29 février 1946.

137 In one case, the students were also supposed to visit other academic institutions during their trip in Quebec.

138 Viajes a Montreal de una Mision Cultural Mexicana, A C R L G, P40/C4, 4, Rapports d'activités de l'Union des Latins d'Amérique, 29 novembre 1941–27 mai 1947.

139 *Novedades*, 5 January 1945.

140 Interview with Eugenia Loaeza de Manhes, Mexico City, May 2006.

141 By and large, Mexicans favoured education in English in the Catholic establishments of Canada to improve their command of this language.

142 Comunicado No. 1 a los miembros de la Misión Cultural Mexico-Canadá, A C R L G, P40/C4, 3, Programmes d'activités de l'Union des Latins d'Amérique, 23 janvier 1942–25 janvier 1945.

143 Ibid.

144 "Les Mexicaines fêtés par l'Union des Latins," *La Presse*, 11 February 1945.

145 "Comunicado No. 1 a los miembros de la Misión Cultural Mexico-Canadá," A C R L G, P40/C4, 3, Programmes d'activités de l'Union des Latins d'Amérique, 23 janvier 1942–25 janvier 1945.

CHAPTER FIVE

1 Knight, "Popular Culture and the Revolutionary State in Mexico," 395.
2 Brading, *Mexican Phoenix*, 314.
3 *The Concise Oxford Dictionary of the Christian Church* defines this status as follows: "A personal representative of the Holy See who has been entrusted with a mission. *Legati missi* are legates sent to carry out particular tasks; those appointed for more exalted occasions came to be known as legates *a latere*, i.e. from the side of the Pope. *Legati nati* were the holders of certain important archbishoprics to whom legatine status was conferred on a stable basis; to some extent these powers survive in the office of certain primates. See also 'Apostolic Delegate and nuncio.'" *Oxford Dictionary of the Christian Church*. http://www.oxfordreference.com.
4 Hall, *Mary, Mother and Warrior*.
5 Nebel, *Santa María Tonantzin*, 312.
6 Napolitano, "The Virgin of Guadalupe," 97.
7 This is an abridged presentation of the Virgin of Guadalupe's symbolism in Mexico. For an in-depth look at the evolution of her meaning in this country, see Poole, *Our Lady of Guadalupe*. For a broader history of Marian devotion in the Spanish-speaking world, see Hall, *Mary, Mother and Warrior*.
8 This point was inspired by the discussion generated by the presentation of Jason Dyck's paper "Sacred Indigenismo: Francisco de Florencia's Patriotic Construction of the Indian" at the G T A Latin American Research Group, 19 September 2008.
9 Brading, *Mexican Phoenix*, 119.
10 Stafford Poole, *Our Lady of Guadalupe*.
11 Brading, *Mexican Phoenix*, 228.
12 Lomnitz-Adler, *Deep Mexico, Silent Mexico*, 47.
13 Ceballos Ramírez, *El catolicismo social, un tercero en discordia*.
14 Brading, *Mexican Phoenix*, 290.
15 This point was inspired by various papers given at the colloquium "El anticlericalismo en la América latina," held at the fifteenth annual congress of the Asociación de Historiadores Latinoamericanistas Europeos (A H I L A), Leiden, August 2008. See also: Ceballos Ramírez, *El catolicismo social, un tercero en discordia*.

16 Brading, *Mexican Phoenix*, 297.

17 Jean Fillion, a resident of Quebec City, had a peculiar devotion to the Virgin of Guadalupe and made two pilgrimages walking to Mexico City in the 1890s. Garibi Tortolero, *Histoire des apparitions de Notre-Dame de la Guadeloupe*, 31–2.

18 Brading, *Mexican Phoenix*, 297.

19 Cabanel and Durand, eds., *Le grand exil des congrégations religieuses françaises*.

20 Brading, *Mexican Phoenix*, 312.

21 Meyer, "An Idea of Mexico," 282–3.

22 Ibid., 282.

23 Ibid., 283.

24 Hall, *Álvaro Obregón*.

25 Aguirre Cristiani, "Presencia de la Iglesia Catlica en el Gobierno de Álvaro Obregón," in *Del conflicto a la conciliación*.

26 García Ugarte, "Los católicos y el presidente Calles."

27 Espinosa, "'Restoring Christian Social Order.'"

28 Ibid., 461. See also: O'Dogherty, "Restaurarlo todo en Cristo."

29 Jean Meyer makes an interesting description of González Flores's references to Gandhi's passive resistance strategy as an inspiration for his course of action. Meyer, "An Idea of Mexico," 283–6.

30 Meyer, *La Cristiada*.

31 Meyer, *La cruzada por México*, 298.

32 Blancarte, *Historia de la Iglesia Católica en México*, 33.

33 As stated in the previous chapter, the imposition of sexual education – rather than socialist principles – was the first policy to mobilize Catholic lobbies against the government.

34 Blancarte, *Historia de la Iglesia Católica en México*, 31.

35 Hernández García de León, *Historia política del sinarquismo, 1934–1944*. Loaeza, "Los orígenes de la propuesta modernizadora de Manuel Gómez Morín." Meyer, *El sinarquismo, el cardenismo y la iglesia*.

36 Pattee and Inter-American Committee, eds., *The Catholic Revival in Mexico*, 37–8.

37 Schuler, *Mexico between Hitler and Roosevelt*.

38 See, among others, Blancarte, *Historia de la Iglesia Católica en México*; Brown, "Mexican Church-State Relations"; Meyer, "An Idea of Mexico"; and Michaels, "The Modification of the Anti-Clerical Nationalism of the Mexican Revolution." Others have nuanced this position by studying the entrenched Catholic antagonism against the revolutionary government in the late 1930s, arguing that reconciliation concretely happened during the

presidency of Manuel Ávila Camacho: Hernández García de León, *Historia política del sinarquismo, 1934–1944*; Loaeza, "Los orígenes."

39 Blancarte, *Historia de la Iglesia Católica en México*, 59.

40 Ibid., 58.

41 Pattee and Inter-American Committee, eds., *The Catholic Revival in Mexico*, 14.

42 Ampudia, *La Iglesia de Roma*, 261.

43 Seditious traditionalist movements and legitimate conservative political opposition represented direct threats to the government. For a good example of seditious movement, see Assad, "La rebelión cedillista o el ocaso del poder tradicional."

44 For examples, see AGN, MAC, 433/211, Congreso eucarístico de Tepic, 1941; AGN, MAC, 433/388, Congreso eucarístico de Córdoba, 1943; AGN, MAC, 547, 4/19, Actos de culto externo, 1943; AGN, MAC, 547, 4/249, Templos católicos y ley de nacionalización, 1943.

45 AGN, MAC, 547, 1/9, Fiestas Virgen de Guadalupe, 1942–45. Others, for example, asked the president to sponsor their request to canonize Juan Diego. AGN, MAC 547, 5/13, Juan Diego, 1942.

46 AGN, MAC 547, 1/1, Protestas y felicitaciones a la Iglesia, 1940–45; AGN, MAC, 542, 1/130, Conflictos, 1945; AGN, MAC, 547, 2/9, Atropello con las autoridades, 1941; AGN, MAC, 547, 3/13, Protestación contra congreso eucarístico, 1945; AGN, MAC, 547, 4/148, Atropellos con las autoridades, 1942; AGN, MAC, 547, 4/271, Acusaciones Sinarquistas Santa Ursula, 1944; AGN, MAC 547, 5/17, Violación de la ley de cultos, 1943; AGN, MAC, 547, 5/24, Protesta celebración Virgen de Guadalupe, 1945.

47 This led to multiple reports of violent confrontation. It has to be said that tensions became worse with the break of Protestantism into rural Mexico. AGN, MAC, 542, 1/130, Conflictos, 1945; AGN, MAC, 542, 1/995, Atropellos sangrientos, 1943; AGN, MAC, 547/8, Conflictos evangélicos y católicos, 1945; AGN, MAC, 547, 1/4, Atropellos con evangélicos Conferencia, 1940–45; AGN, MAC 547, 1/12, Encuentros sangrientos, 1944; AGN, MAC, 547, 1/13, Encuentros sangrientos, 1946.

48 Kirk, "Election Day, 1940."

49 For the Ley de Nacionalizaciones, see Blancarte, *Historia de la Iglesia Católica en México*, 98–9. Catholics' leeway for organizing private education has been treated in the previous chapter. The rest of this chapter will cover the progressive re-insertion of Catholic symbolism in the public sphere.

50　For a good exposition of Camacho's concession/marginalization of the UNS, see Hernández García de León, *Historia política del sinarquismo*, 230–6, 67–76.

51　Rankin, "Mexico: Industrialization through Unity," in *Latin America during World War II*, 19.

52　Knight, "Rise and Fall of Cardenismo," in *Mexico since Independence*, 304.

53　Reich, *Mexico's Hidden Revolution*, 116.

54　The 1940 and 1950 Mexican censuses also indicate that the proportion of Mexicans identifying as Catholic increased from 96.6 to 98.2 per cent, while the number of priests in the Mexican population rose by 36 per cent during the same decade. Wilkie, *Statistics and National Policy*, 56–9.

55　Most of these articles were in the section entitled "Horizon international," a section which discussed two or three relevant international cases each month. The situation in Mexico stands out as one of the most important subjects for the era.

56　A section of Ledit's book *Rise of the Downtrodden*, was selected by James W. Wilkie and Albert L. Michaels for their book on the turmoil of the 1910–1940 period in Mexico. Ledit, SJ, "Sinarquismo Victory in Tabasco."

57　The NCWC was created to coordinate American Catholic activities during the First World War. It evolved as a pressure group which lobbied the government for Catholic inclusion in the US, and militated against nativist sentiments in the 1920s and 30s. Their denunciations of Catholic persecution in Mexico were important; they galvanized an originally divided Catholic public to make sure the US government would ultimately attempt to sway Mexico in settling the religious dispute. See, http://libraries.cua.edu/achrcua/ncwc.html and Meyer, *La cruzada por México*.

58　Pattee also collaborated with *Relations* in Quebec and published in its pages a few articles on the subject in the 1940s.

59　Letter by Richard Pattee to the Canadian Secretary of State for External Affairs, LAC, RG77, vol. 157, National University – Mexico City General Correspondence, 25-34-1, 1944–1946.

60　Pattee and Inter-American Committee, eds., *The Catholic Revival in Mexico*, 18.

61　Ibid., 14.

62　Ibid., 18.

63　Ibid., 21–32.

64　Ibid., 22.

65 Compagnon, *Jacques Maritain et l'Amérique latine*, 42.

66 De Koninck's works were translated by an influential Catholic intellectual, Gabriel Mendez Plancarte, director of *Abside*. "L'Université Laval et le Mexique," *Le Canada français* 33, no. 4 (December 1945): 297. Foucher also maintained a correspondence with de Koninck and invited him to U N A M. De Koninck also helped when Foucher received his honorary degree from Laval and visited Quebec. Letter from Rodulfo Brito Foucher to Charles de Koninck, 25 September 1944, A H U N A M, 3, 33, Rodulfo Brito Foucher.

67 Pattee and Inter-American Committee, eds., *The Catholic Revival in Mexico*, 22.

68 Blancarte, *Historia de la Iglesia Católica en México*, 66.

69 A few of these Catholic writers were also founding members of the U C M Ç F.

70 Pattee and Inter-American Committee, eds., *The Catholic Revival in Mexico*, 46–7.

71 Ibid., 31.

72 *Juventud*'s active support of the Mexican war effort probably started in July rather than June for publication reasons, Mexico having declared war against the Axis on May 22. For two good examples of Sofía del Valle's articles supporting the war effort, see: Sofía del Valle, "¡¡La patria en peligro!!," *Juventud* 12, no. 7 (July 1942): 12–13"; and "¿Qué es patria?," *Juventud* 12, no. 7 (August 1942): 9.

73 Sofía del Valle and María Luisa Herrasti, "Servir a la Familia es Servir a la Patria," *Juventud* 12, no. 10 (October 1942): 5, 26.

74 Guadalupe Gutiérrez de Velasco, "Acercamiento nacional," *Juventud* 12, no. 11 (November 1942): 5.

75 E. Castro, "Nuestra nacionalidad y la Virgen de Guadalupe," *Juventud* 12, no. 12 (December 1942): 5.

76 Blancarte, *Historia de la Iglesia Católica en México*, 35.

77 Pattee and Inter-American Committee, eds., *The Catholic Revival in Mexico*, 48.

78 "Carta pastoral colectiva del vble. Episcopado mexicano sobre la celebración del quincuagésimo aniversario de la coronación de ntra. Madre santísima de Guadalupe," in Romero, s J, ed., *Cincuentenario Guadalupano*, 15–19.

79 "Año Jubilar Guadalupano," *Juventud* 15, no. 2 (February 1945): 8–9.

80 "Carta pastoral colectiva del vble.," in Romero, s J, ed., *Cincuentenario Guadalupano*, 16.

81 Letter by Ignacio Martín del Campo to archbishop Luis María Martínez, 1 August 1944, Archives of the Acción Católica Mexicana (A A C M), 1, 5, Episcopado mexicano, 1943–1944.

82 Brading, *Mexican Phoenix.*

83 "L'Université Laval et le Mexique," *Le Canada français* 33, no. 4 (December 1945): 298.

84 The Manuel Ávila Camacho fonds nevertheless reveals that denunciations were numerous. A G N , M A C , 547, 4/299, Denunciación Instituto Social Continental, 1945; A G N , M A C 547, 5/24, Protesta celebración Virgen de Guadalupe, 1945.

85 The two archbishops had also worked to support the allied war effort. For further analysis of their contribution to academic connections, see previous chapter "The Poetics of Student Exchanges."

86 *Le Canada français* 33, no. 4 (December 1945): 297–8. My characterizations of La Base as a "shadow directorate" of the U N S does not do full justice to the intricacies of the linkages between both organizations. Nevertheless, it is Antonio Santacruz who named Salvador Abascal leader of the U N S in 1940 and "since its foundation, *la Unión Nacional Sinarquista* was indirectly controlled by Antonio Santacruz... from whom Sinarquist leaders received orders and funds to organise the movement." Hernández García de León, *Historia política del sinarquismo*, 168, 207.

87 Casillas, s J , *Jesuitas en México durante el siglo XX*, 272.

88 Visas de cortesía, A H D S R E , III/551.1 (71-0)/16207, Rodrigue Villeneuve, Jean Marie (Cardenal y Arzobispo de Quebec).

89 "S.E. el Cardenal Villeneuve Llega a Territorio Nacional," *Excelsior*, 5 October 1945.

90 Brading, *Mexican Phoenix*, 318.

91 Calling Mexico the "Athens of the New World" was in line with the way French Canadian-Mexican relations took form (see chapter three). For his part, Jesús Guisa y Azevedo, a member of the Mexican branch of the association, the *Unión Cultural México-Canadá Francés* (U C M C F), welcomed the cardinal in an article mentioning he was the best representative of the universality of the Church since he had Thomas Aquinas's Summa Theologica on his blazon. The humanist tradition definitely represented a meeting point of French Canadian and Mexican Catholic cultures. "Algunas palabras de bienvenida al cardenal Villeneuve," *Novedades*, 8 October 1945.

92 *Charros* are distinctive Mexican horsemen.

93 Ana Salado Álvarez, "Apoteótico recibimiento del cardenal Villeneuve," *Revista de Revistas*, 21 October 1945, Archives de l'archevêché de Québec

(AAQ), 14-12 Spicilège, 31-20 A, Cardinal Villeneuve: légation papale au Mexique, 1945.

94 *El Universal Gráfico*, October 9, 1945. AAQ, 14-12 Spicilège, 31-20 A, Cardinal Villeneuve: légation papale au Mexique, 1945.

95 Eduardo Tellez, "Se Desbordó el Fervor de México por la Virgen," *El Universal*, 12 October 1945.

96 *Gaceta Oficial del Arzobispado de México* vol. 37 (México, DF: 1945), 325. This publication can be found at the Archivos Históticos del Arzobispado de México (AHAM).

97 Brading, *Mexican Phoenix*, 297.

98 *Relations*, November 1945, 302.

99 "Recepción," *Acción* 10, nos. 11, 12 (November and December 1945).

100 Indeed, after Archbishop Villeneuve's visit to Mexico, Concepción Acevedo de la Llata (the infamous Madre Conchita) sent him a letter. AAQ, 14-12 Spicilège, 31-20 A, Cardinal Villeneuve: légation papale au Mexique, 1945. Jürgen Buchenau explains that José de León Toral's confession linked him to Concepción y de la Llata: "Based on interrogations under torture of Toral and other suspects, Calles concluded that Catholic radicals bent on avenging the campaign against the church had perpetrated the crime. Although Toral claimed to have acted on his own initiative, he formed part of a Catholic opposition group. An introverted mystic, he was an admirer of the martyred Father Pro. He had also engaged in secret gatherings of Catholic dissidents led by Concepción y de la Llata, better known as Madre Conchita, the Mother Superior of the Espíritu Santo convent." Buchenau, *Plutarco Elías Calles*, 145.

101 "Panorama general de las festividades" in Romero, SJ, ed., *Cincuentenario Guadalupano*, 22–36.

102 "Quebec Cardinal Named Papal Legate for Guadalupe Observance in Mexico," *Southern Messenger*, 4 October 1945.

103 *La Nación*, 11 October 1945.

104 Vértiz played a significant role in the foundation of *Universidad Iberoamericana* in 1943, collaborating with Rodulfo Brito Foucher in this endeavour. Contreras, *Rodulfo Brito Foucher*, 297.

105 Vértiz, SJ, *Gaceta Oficial del Arzobispado de México*, 335.

106 The statistic is for 1960, when the decline of the Catholic Church's power had begun in the province. Ferretti, *Brève histoire de l'Église catholique au Québec*, 142.

107 Vértiz, *Gaceta Oficial del Arzobispado de México*, 335.

108 Ibid., 336.

109 AGN, MAC, 547, 4/299, Denunciación Instituto Social Continental, 1945;
     MAC, 547, 5/24, Protesta celebración Virgen de Guadalupe, 1945.
110 The archives of Quebec City's diocese have a very good sample of the cov-
     erage generated by Cardinal Villeneuve's stops in the US.
111 Ibid., 34.
112 The archives of Quebec City's archbishopric has a copy of this film.
     Unfortunately, it has not yet been converted to a contemporary format to
     enable its viewing.
113 *Relations*, November 1945, 302.
114 "Québec rend hommage à la Vierge de la Guadeloupe," *Action
     Catholique*, 13 October 1945.
115 Romero, SJ, ed., *Cincuentenario Guadalupano*, 50.
116 Ibid., 51.

CONCLUSION

1   Curtis, "The 'Most Splendid Pageant Ever Seen,'" 58.
2   The case of the Cuban Revolution constitutes an exception here, as the
    model it provided for young radicals stirred passions. Moreover, the
    Trudeau administration supported the Revolution despite US aggravation.
    Wright, *Three Nights in Havana*.
3   Williams, *Marxism and Literature*.
4   Mace, "Les relations du Québec avec l'Amérique latine." Gratia O'Leary
    also told me that Walter, her husband, had directly influenced René
    Lévesque in his decision to open the *Délégation générale du Québec à
    Mexico*. Gratia O'Leary herself was René Lévesque's press secretary.
    Interview with Gratia O'Leary, conducted at her house in Montreal,
    14 February 2006.
5   Raymond Giroux, "Charest pourra rencontrer le président mexicain Fox,"
    Le Soleil, 13 October 2004.
6   Jean Chrétien, speech held at Windsor, Ontario, 28 April 1996. Quoted in
    Hedetoft, "Symbolic Politics and Cultural Symbols," 591–2.
7   This is a reference to a statement made by a member of External Affairs.
    Letter to N.A. Robertson from W.A.F. Turgeon, 19 June 1943, LAC,
    RG25-A-3-b, vol. 5753, Union culturelle des Latins d'Amérique.
8   Joseph, Rubenstein, and Zolov, "Assembling the Fragments," in *Fragments
    of a Golden Age*, 9.
9   Knight, "Rise and Fall of Cardenismo," 304.
10 Ibid., 302.

11 I put the words magnificent and persecuted in quotation marks because they were commonly used in the francophone press to describe the events unfolding in Mexico.

12 Comité de l'album, *Notre-Dame-de-la-Guadeloupe*, 23.

13 Harkness, "An Invasion by Request."

14 Voisine et al., *Histoire du catholicisme québécois*, 197.

15 LeGrand, "L'axe missionnaire catholique entre le Québec et l'Amérique latine." Foisy, "Des Québécois aux frontières." It is also important to acknowledge Yves Carrier's endeavour to preserve that memory.

16 Carrier, *Lettre du Brésil*. Considering the important contribution of Mgr Gérard Cambron to that project, this perspective seems promising.

Bibliography

ARCHIVES CONSULTED

Acervo Histórico Diplomático de la Secretaría de Relaciones Exteriores de
   México
   Fondos Documentales de la Dirección General de Asuntos Políticos y
   del Servicio Diplomático
Archives de l'Archevêché de Québec
   14, Fonds Cardinal Villeneuve
Archives de l'Université Laval
   P443, Fonds Paul Bouchard
Archives de l'Université de Montréal
Archives du Centre de recherche Lionel-Groulx
   P40, Fonds Dostaler et Walter O'Leary
   P7, Fonds Olivier Maurault
Archivo de la Acción Católica Mexicana
   Fondos Documentales de la Acción Católica Mexicana
   Newspaper and Magazine Collection
Archivo General de la Nación
   Fondos Documentales Manuel Ávila Camacho
   Newspaper and Magazine Collection
Archivo Histórico del Arzobispado de México
   Fondos Documentales Luis María Martínez
Archivo Histórico de la Provincia de México de la Compañía de Jesús
   Noticias de la Provincia de México
Archivo Histórico de la Universidad Nacional Autónoma de México
   3, 33, Fondos Documentales Rodulfo Brito Foucher
   Newspaper and Magazine Collection

Biblioteca Daniel Cosío Villegas
  Newspaper and Magazine Collection
Biblioteca Miguel Lerdo de Tejada
  Newspaper and Magazine Collection
Bibliothèque et Archives nationales du Québec (centre de Montréal)
  P97, Fonds Armour Landry
  Newspaper and Magazine Collection
Fototeca Nacional del Instituto Nacional de Antropología e Historia
  Fondo Casasola
Library and Archives Canada
  RG 25, Records of the Department of External Affairs
  RG 77, Records of the National Research Council
  RG 146, Records of the Royal Canadian Mounted Police
  Newspaper and Magazine Collection

NEWSPAPERS AND MAGAZINES
(REVIEWED FROM 1939 TO 1945)

Acción
Boletín de la Asesora de Grupos Internos de la JCFM
Boletín del Asistente Eclesiástico
Boletín Mensual de la Junta Central de la ACM
El Universal
Excelsior
Gaceta Oficial del Arzobispado de México
Juventud
L'Action Catholique
Le Devoir
La Patrie
La Presse
Le Soleil
Mandements des évêques de Québec
Novedades
Relations
Semaine Religieuse de Québec
The Gazette
The Star Weekly

Adelman, Jeremy. *Frontier Development: Land, Labour, and Capital on the Wheatlands of Argentina and Canada, 1890–1914.* Oxford: Clarendon Press, 1994.

Aguirre Cristiani, Gabriela. "Presencia de la Iglesia Católica en el Gobierno de Álvaro Obregón 1920–1924." In *Del conflicto a la conciliación: Iglesia y Estado en México, siglo XX*, edited by Franco Savarino and Andrea Mutolo, 65–82. Chihuahua: El Colegio de Chihuaha/ AHCALC, 2006.

Aillón Soria, Esther. "La política cultural de Francia en la génesis y difusión del concepto l'Amérique latine, 1860–1930." In *Construcción de las identidades latinoamericanas. Ensayos de historia intelectual, siglos XIX y XX*, edited by Aimer Granados and Carlos Marichal, 71–105. Mexico City: El Colegio de México, 2004.

Aird, Robert. *André Patry et la présence du Québec dans le monde.* Montreal: VLB Éditeur, 2005.

Albert, Jean-Pierre. "Sens et enjeux du martyre: de la religion à la politique." In *Saints, sainteté et martyre. La fabrication de l'exemplarité*, edited by Pierre Centlivres, 17–25. Neufchâtel, QC: Édition de l'Institut d'ethnologie, 2001.

Ampudia, Ricardo. *La Iglesia de Roma. Estructura y presencia en México.* Mexico City: Fondo de Cultura Económica, 1998.

Anderson, Benedict. *Imagined Communities: Reflections on the Origin and Spread of Nationalism.* London: Verso, 1991.

Armony, Victor. "Des Latins du Nord? L'identitée cuturelle québécoise dans le contexte panaméricain." *Recherches sociographiques* 43, no. 1 (2002): 19–48.

Armstrong, Christopher, and H.V. Nelles. *Southern Exposure: Canadian Promoters in Latin America and the Caribbean 1896–1930.* Toronto: University of Toronto Press, 1988.

Arrom, Silvia Marina. "Mexican Laywomen Spearhead a Catholic Revival: The Ladies of Charity, 1863–1910." In *Religious Culture in Modern Mexico*, edited by Martin Austin Nesvig, 50–77. Lanham: Rowman & Littlefield Publishers, Inc., 2007.

Assad, Carlos Martínez. "La rebelión cedillista o el ocaso del poder tradicional." *Revista Mexicana de Sociología* 41, no. 3 (1979): 709–28.

Avni, Haim. *Canada, Argentina and the Jews until World War II: the Impact of Immigration and Industrialization Policies on the Formation of Two Diasporas.* Jerusalem: Halbert Centre for Canadian Studies, 1996.

Axelrod, Paul. *Making a Middle Class: Student Life in English Canada during the Thirties*. Montreal: McGill-Queen's University Press, 1990.

Balthazar, Louis, Louis Bélanger, and Gordon Mace. *Trente ans de politique extérieure du Québec, 1960–1990*. Sainte-Foy, Quebec City: Centre québécois de relations internationales, 1993.

Bantjes, Adrian. *As if Jesus Walked on Earth: Cardenismo, Sonora, and the Mexican Revolution*. Wilmington: S R Books, 1998.

– "Religion and the Mexican Revolution: Toward a New Historiography." In *Religious Culture in Modern Mexico*, edited by Martin Austin Nesvig, 223–54. Lanham: Rowman and Littlefield Publishers, 2007.

Barajas Durán, Rafael. "Retrato de un siglo. ¿Cómo ser mexicano en el XIX?" In *Espejo mexicano*, edited by Enrique Florescano, 116–77. Mexico City: Fondo de Cultura Económica, 2002.

Baulu, Roger. "Actualités canadiennes: interviews avec Olivier Maurault, Dostaler O'Leary et Jacqueline Savard." *Radio-Canada*, 20 August 1944. http://archives.radio-canada.ca/emissions/1269/.

Beaudet, Pierre. *Une brève histoire de la solidarité internationale au Québec. Qui aide qui?* Montreal: Boréal, 2009.

Beaugrand, Honoré. "Anita: souvenirs d'un contre-guérillas." In *Mélanges. Trois conférences*. Montreal, [s.n.], 1888.

Becker, Marjorie. *Setting the Virgin on Fire: Lázaro Cárdenas, Michoacán Peasants, and the Redemption of the Mexican Revolution*. Berkeley: University of California Press, 1995.

Beezley, William H. *Judas at the Jockey Club and other Episodes of Porfirian Mexico*. Lincoln, NE: University of Nebraska Press, 1987.

Behiels, Michael D., Ramsay Cook, and Marcel Martel. *Nation, Ideas, Identities: Essays in Honour of Ramsay Cook*. Don Mills: Oxford University Press, 2000.

Bélanger, André-J. *L'apolitisme des idéologies québécoises: le grand tournant de 1934–1936*. Quebec City: Les Presses de l'Université Laval, 1974.

Bellavance, Marcel. *Le Québec au siècle des nationalités. Essai d'histoire comparée*. Montreal: V L B Éditeur, 2004.

Benessaieh, Afef, ed. *Transcultural Americas/Amériques Transculturelles*. Ottawa: Les Presses de l'Université d'Ottawa, 2010.

Berger, Carl. *The Sense of Power: Studies in the Ideas of Canadian Imperialism, 1867–1914*. Toronto: University of Toronto Press, 1970.

Bernard, Jean-Paul. *Les Rouges, Libéralisme, nationalisme et anticléricalisme au milieu du XIXe siècle*. Montreal: Les Presses de l'Université du Québec, 1971.

Bernd, Zilá and Michel Peterson, ed. *Confluences littéraires Brésil-Québec. Les bases d'une comparaison.* Candiac: Éditions Balzac, 1992.

Bidegain de Uran, Ana María. "La Organización de movimientos de juventud de Acción católica en América latina. Los casos de los obreros y universitarios en Brasil y en Colombia entre 1930–1955." PhD Diss., Université catholique de Louvain, 1979.

Blancarte, Roberto. *El pensamiento social de los católicos mexicanos.* Mexico City: Fondo de Cultura Económica, 1996.

– *Historia de la Iglesia Católica en México.* Mexico City: Fondo de Cultura Económica, 1992.

Bock, Michel. *Quand la nation débordait les frontières: les minorités françaises dans la pensée de Lionel Groulx.* Montreal: Hurtubise HMH, 2004.

Bonenfant, Jean-C., and Jean-C. Falardeau. "Cultural and Political Implications of French-Canadian Nationalism." *Report of the Annual Meeting of the Canadian Historical Association* 25, no. 1 (1946): 56–73.

Bouchard, Gérard. *Genèse des nations et cultures du nouveau monde: essai d'histoire comparée.* Montreal: Boréal, 2001.

– *Quelques arpents d'Amérique: population, économie, famille au Saguenay (1838–1971).* Montreal: Boréal, 1996.

Bourassa, Henri. *Hier, aujourd'hui, demain: problèmes nationaux.* Montreal: [s.n.], 1916.

– *Independence or Imperial Partnership?* Montreal: Imprimerie du Devoir, 1916.

– *La langue française au Canada: ses droits, sa nécessite, ses avantages.* Montreal: Imprimerie du Devoir, 1915.

– *Le Canada apostolique. Revue des œuvres de missions des communautés franco-canadiennes.* Montreal: Bibliothèque de l'Action française, 1919.

Bourdieu, Pierre. *Langage et pouvoir symbolique.* Paris: Éditions du Seuil, 2001.

Brading, D.A. *Mexican Phoenix. Our Lady of Guadalupe: Image and Tradition across Five Centuries.* Cambridge: Cambridge University Press, 2001.

Brand, Donald D. "United States-Mexican Scientific and Cultural Relations." *Annals of the American Academy of Political and Social Science* 255 (1948): 67–76.

Brown, Lyle C. "Mexican Church-State Relations, 1933–1940." *Journal of Church and State* 6, no. 2 (1964): 202–22.

Bruno-Jofré, Rosa. *The Missionary Oblate Sisters: Vision and Mission.* Montreal: McGill-Queen's University Press, 2005.

Buchenau, Jürgen. *Plutarco Elías Calles and the Mexican Revolution.* Lanham: Rowman & Littlefield Publishers, Inc., 2007.

Burke, Michael E. "The University of Mexico and the Revolution, 1910–1940." *The Americas* 34, no. 2 (1977): 252–73.

Butler, Matthew. *Popular and Political Identity in Mexico's Cristero Rebellion. Michoacan, 1927–1929.* Oxford: Oxford University Press, 2004.

Cabanel, Patrick, and Jean-Dominique Durand, eds. *Le grand exil des congrégations religieuses françaises, 1901–1914: colloque international de Lyon, Université Jean-Moulin-Lyon III, 12–13 juin 2003.* Paris: Editions du CERF, 2005.

Camp, Roderic Ai. *Mexican Political Biographies, 1935–1975.* Tucson: University of Arizona Press, 1976

Carrier, Yves. *Lettre du Brésil. L'évolution de la perspective missionnaire. Relecture de l'expérience de Mgr Gérard Cambron.* Louvain-la-Neuve: Academia Bruylant, 2008.

Casey, Clifford B. "The Creation and Development of the Pan American Union." *The Hispanic American Historical Review* 13, no. 4 (1933): 437–56.

Castellanos Pinzón, María de la O, and Arturo Curiel, eds. *Jalisco en el siglo XX. Perfiles.* Guadalajara: Universidad de Guadalajara/ACUDE, 1999.

Castillo, Richard Griswold del. "The Los Angeles 'Zoot Suit Riots' Revisited: Mexican and Latin American Perspectives." *Mexican Studies/Estudios Mexicanos* 16, no. 2 (2000): 367–91.

Ceballos Ramírez, Manuel. *El catolicismo social: Un tercero en discordia. Rerum Novarum, la cuestión social, y la movilización de los católicos mexicanos (1891–1911).* Mexico City: El Colegio de México, 1991.

– "La Conciliación, los Arreglos y la Reforma Constitucional: Tres Hitos en la Relación Iglesia-Estado en México." In *Del conflicto a la conciliación: Iglesia y Estado en México, Siglo XX*, edited by Franco Savarino and Andrea Mutolo, 113–24. Chihuahua: El Colegio de Chihuahua/AHCALC, 2006.

Chanady, Amaryll. *Entre inclusion et exclusion. La représentation de l'autre dans les Amériques.* Paris: Honoré Champion, 1999.

Chartier, Roger. "Texts, Symbols, and Frenchness." *Journal of Modern History* 57 (1985): 682–95.

Coerver, Don M., and Linda B. Hall. *Tangled Destinies: Latin America and the United States.* Albuquerque: University of New Mexico Press, 1999.

Coleman, William D. *The Independence Movement in Quebec 1945–1980.* Toronto: University of Toronto Press, 1984.

Collectif. *Vie illustrée du Prince de l'Église Son Éminence le Cardinal Jean-Marie-Rodrigue Villeneuve, Oblat de Marie-Immaculée, Archevêque de Québec.* Quebec City: [s.n.], [s.d.].

Comeau, Paul-André. *Le Bloc populaire, 1942–1948.* Montreal: Boréal, 1995.

Comeau, Robert. "Lionel Groulx, les indépendantistes de *La Nation* et le séparatisme (1936–1938)." *Revue d'histoire de l'Amérique française* 26, no. 1 (1972): 83–102.

– "Paul Bouchard." In *Histoire intellectuelle de l'indépendantisme québécois. Tome 1: 1834–1968,* edited by Robert Comeau, Charles-Philippe Courtois, and Denis Monière, 102–14. Montreal: VLB Éditeur, 2010.

Comité de l'album, ed. *Notre-Dame-de-la-Guadeloupe, 1945–1995.* Sherbrooke: Éditions Louis Bilodeau & Fils Ltée, 1994.

Conrad, Margaret, and Alvin Finkel. *Canada: a National History.* Toronto: Longman, 2003.

Contreras, Gabriela. *Rodulfo Brito Foucher (1899–1970). Un político al margen del régimen revolucionario.* Mexico City: IISUE, 2008.

Couillard, Marie, and Patrick Imbert. "Canada, Argentine et Amérique latine au dix-neuvième siècle." *International Journal of Canadian Studies/Revue internationale d'études canadiennes* 13, Spring/Printemps (1996): 1–23.

– *Les Discours du Nouveau Monde au XIXe siècle au Canada français et en Amérique latine: actes du colloque tenu du 29 septembre au 1er octobre 1994 à l'Université d'Ottawa dans le cadre de l'Accord d'échange entre l'Université d'Ottawa, Canada et l'Universidad Nacional de Rosario, Argentine.* Ottawa: Legas, 1995.

Cuccioletta, Donald. *L'américanité et les Amériques.* Quebec City: Les Presses de l'Université Laval, 2001.

Cuccioletta, Donald, Jean-François Côté, and Frédéric Lesemann, ed. *Le grand récit des Amériques: polyphonie des identités culturelles dans le contexte de la continentalisation.* Quebec City: Les Presses de l'Université Laval/IQRC, 2001.

Cueto, Marcos, ed. *Missionaries of Science: The Rockefeller Foundation and Latin America.* Bloomington: Indiana University Press, 1994.

Cuff, Robert D., and J.L. Granatstein. *Canadian-American Relations in Wartime: from the Great War to the Cold War*. Toronto: Hakkert, 1975.

Curtis, Bruce. "The 'Most Splendid Pageant Ever Seen': Grandeur, the Domestic, and Condescension in Lord Durham's Political Theatre." *The Canadian Historical Review* 89, no. 1 (2008): 55–88.

Danaux, Stéphanie and Nova Doyon. Dossier – "Enjeux et modalités des transferts culturels dans la vie artistique canadienne-française de la pre-mière moitié du XXe siècle." In *MENS: Revue d'histoire intellectuelle et culturelle*, 12:103–143, no. 2 (2012).

Darnton, Robert. *The Great Cat Massacre and Other Episodes in French Cultural History*. New York: Basic Books, 1984.

De Certeau, Michel. *La Prise de parole, pour une nouvelle culture*. Paris: Desclée De Brouwer, 1968.

De Certeau, Michel, and Luce Giard. *The Capture of Speech and Other Political Writings*. Minneapolis: University of Minnesota Press, 1997.

De Larrinaga, José A. "L'intervention française au Mexique vue par les principaux journaux canadiens-français du Québec (1861–1867)." MA thesis, Université d'Ottawa, 1976.

De la Tour Fondue, Geneviève. "Jean Désy." In *Interviews canadiennes*, 209–24. Montreal: Les Éditions Chantecler Ltée, 1952.

Delâge, Denys. *Le pays renversé: Amérindiens et Européens en Amérique du Nord-Est, 1600–1664*. Montreal: Boréal, 1991.

Delpar, Helen. *The Enormous Vogue of Things Mexican: Cultural Relations between the United States and Mexico, 1920–1935*. Tuscaloosa: University of Alabama Press, 1992.

Demers, Maurice. "Las fiestas guadalupanas de 1945 en la ciudad de México y la utilización del modelo conservador francocanadiense por la jerarquíra católica." In *Del conflicto a la conciliación: Iglesia y Estado en México, Siglo XX*, edited by Franco Savarino and Andrea Mutolo, 83–96. Chihuahua: El Colegio de Chihuahua/AHCALC, 2006.

Dominion Bureau of Statistics. *Report of the Eight Census of Canada, 1941. General Review and Summary Tables*. Ottawa: Dominion Bureau of Statistics, 1950.

Donneur, André. *Politique étrangère canadienne*. Montreal: Guérin Universitaire, 1994.

Dorion-Poussart, Nicole. "Le développement des relations Québec-Mexique sous l'administration du Parti québécois, 1978–1986." MA thesis, Université Laval, 1989.

Doyon, Nova. *Formation des cultures nationales dans les Amériques. Le rôle de la presse dans la constitution du littéraire au Bas-Canada et au Brésil au début du XIXe siècle.* Quebec City: Les Presses de l'Université Laval, 2012.

Dragon, Antonio, s j. *Au Mexique Rouge. María de la Luz Camacho, première martyre de l'Action catholique.* Montreal: L'Action Paroissiale, 1936.

– *Le Père Pro. Drame en trois actes.* Montreal: Librairie du Devoir, 1933.

– *Pour le Christ-Roi. Miguel-Augustin Pro de la Compagnie de Jésus. Exécuté au Mexique le 23 novembre 1927.* Montreal: Imprimerie du Messager, 1928.

– *Vida intima del padre Pro.* Mexico City: Editorial Buena Prensa, 1940.

– *Vie intime du père Pro.* Montreal: Atelier du Devoir, 1940.

Ducharme, Michel. *Le concept de liberté au Canada à l'époque des révolutions atlantiques, 1776–1838.* Montreal: McGill-Queen's University Press, 2010.

Dumont, Fernand. *Genèse de la société québécoise: essai.* Montreal: Boréal, 1996.

Dupont, Louis. "L'américanité québécoise ou la possibilité d'être ailleurs." *Le Québec et les francophones de la Nouvelle-Angleterre,* 187–200. Quebec City: Les Presses de l'Université Laval, 1991.

Durham, John George Lambton. *Lord Durham's Report: an Abridgement of Report on the Affairs of British North America.* Ottawa: Carleton University Press, 1992.

Edelman, Murray. "Political Language and Political Reality." *PS* 18, no. 1 (1985): 10–19.

– *Politics as Symbolic Action.* Chicago: Markham Publishing Company, 1971.

– "Symbols and Political Quiescence." *The American Political Science Review* 54, no. 3 (1960): 695–704.

Espinosa, David. "'Restoring Christian Social Order': the Mexican Catholic Youth Association (1913–1932)." *The Americas* 59, no. 4 (2003): 451–74.

– "Student Politics, National Politics: Mexico's National Student Union, 1926–1943." *The Americas* 62, no. 4 (2006): 533–62.

Faber, Sebastiaan. "'La hora ha llegado': Hispanism, Pan-Americanism, and the Hope of Spanish/American Glory (1938–1948)." In *Ideologies of Hispanism,* edited by Mabel Moraña, 62–104. Nashville: Vanderbilt University Press, 2005.

Fabre, Gérard. "Les passerelles internationales de la maison d'édition Parti pris," *Revue de Bibliothèque et archives nationales du Québec*, no. 2 (2010), 6–17.

Faucher de Saint-Maurice, Narcisse-Henri-Édouard. *De Québec à Mexico. Souvenirs de voyage, de garnison, de combat et de bivouac.* 2 vols. Montreal: Duvernay, Frères et Dansereau, Éditeurs, 1874.

– *Notes pour servir à l'histoire de l'Empereur Maximilien.* Quebec City: Côté, 1889.

Fein, Seth. "Everyday Forms of Transnational Collaboration: US Film Propaganda in Cold War Mexico." In *Close Encounters of Empire: Writing the Cultural History of US-Latin American Relations*, edited by Gilbert M. Joseph, Catherine LeGrand and Ricardo D. Salvatore, 400–50. Durham: Duke University Press, 1998.

– "Myths of Cultural Imperialism and Nationalism in Golden Age Mexican Cinema." In *Fragments of a Golden Age: the politics of culture in Mexico since 1940*, edited by Gilbert M. Joseph, Eric Zolov, and Anne Rubenstein, 159–98. Durham: Duke University Press, 2001.

Ferretti, Lucia. *Brève histoire de l'Église catholique au Québec.* Montreal: Boréal, 1999.

– *Entre voisins: la société paroissiale en milieu urbain: Saint-Pierre-Apôtre de Montréal, 1848–1930.* Montreal: Boréal, 1992.

Foisy, Catherine. "Des Québécois aux frontières: dialogues et affrontements culturels aux dimensions du monde. Récits missionnaires d'Asie, d'Afrique et d'Amérique latine (1945–1980). " PhD dissertation, Concordia University, 2012.

Foucault, Michel. "Nietzsche, la généalogie, l'histoire." In *Dits et écrits, 1954–1975,*1:1004–24. Paris: Éditions Gallimard, 2001.

– *Surveiller et punir: naissance de la prison.* Paris: Gallimard, 1975.

Fournier, Marcel. *Communisme et anticommunisme au Québec (1920–1950).* Laval: Les Éditions coopératives Albert Saint-Martin, 1979.

Galeana de Valadés, Patricia, ed. *Relaciones Estado-Iglesia: encuentro y desencuentros.* Mexico City: Archivo General de la Nación/Secretaría de Gobiernación, 1999.

García Canclini, Nestor. *Hybrid Cultures: Strategies for Entering and Leaving Modernity.* Minneapolis: University of Minnesota Press, 1995.

García Ugarte, Marta Eugenia. "Los católicos y el presidente Calles." *Revista Mexicana de Sociología* 57, no. 3 (1995): 131–55.

Garibi Tortolero, Manuel. *Histoire des apparitions de Notre-Dame de la Guadeloupe (en forme de catéchisme, par questions et réponses).* Quebec City: [s.n.], 1955.

Gauthier, Chantal. *Femmes sans frontières. L'histoire des Soeurs Missionnaires de l'Immaculée-Conception (1902-2007)*. Outremont: Carte Blanche, 2008.

Gauthier, Chantal and France Lord. *Engagées et solidaires: Les Soeurs du Bon-Conseil à Cuba 1948-1998*. Montréal: Carte Blanche, 2013.

Gay, Daniel. *Les élites québécoises et l'Amérique latine*. Montreal: Nouvelle Optique, 1983.

González González, Guadalupe. "México ante América Latina. Mirando de reojo a Estados Unidos." In *En busca de una nación soberana. Relaciones internacionales de México, siglos XIX y XX*, edited by Jorge A. Shiavon, Daniela Spenser, and Mario Vázquez Olivera, 463–508. Mexico City: Centro de Investigación y Docencia Económicas, 2006.

Goudreault, Henri. "Les missionnaires canadiens à l'étranger au XXe siècle." In *SCHEC, Sessions d'étude* (1983), 50:361–80.

Gougeon, Gilles. *Histoire du nationalisme québécois. Entrevues avec sept spécialistes*. Montreal: V L B Éditeur, 1993.

Granatstein, J.L. *Canada's Foreign Relations, 1919–1945*. Toronto: Ontario Institute for Studies in Education, 1974.

– *Canadian Foreign Policy since 1945: Middle Power or Satellite*. Toronto: Copp Clark Pub. Co., 1969.

– *A Man of Influence: Norman A. Robertson and Canadian Statecraft, 1929–1968*. Ottawa: Deneau Publishers, 1981.

– *The Ottawa Men: The Civil Service Mandarins 1935–1957*. Toronto: Oxford University Press, 1982.

Grandin, Greg. *The Last Colonial Massacre: Latin America in the Cold War*. Chicago: University of Chicago Press, 2004.

Granger, Serge. *Le lys et le lotus: les relations du Québec avec la Chine de 1650 à 1950*. Montreal: V L B Éditeur, 2005.

Greer, Allan, and Jodi Bilinkoff. *Colonial Saints: Discovering the Holy in the Americas, 1500–1800*. New York: Routledge, 2003.

Groulx, Lionel. "Le Canada français en Amérique latine." *Report of the Annual Meeting of the Canadian Historical Association* 40, no. 1 (1961): 13–27.

– *Le Canada français missionnaire: une autre grande aventure*. Montreal: Fides, 1962.

Gutiérrez Casillas, José, S J. *Jesuitas en México durante el siglo XX*. Mexico City: Editorial Porrúa, 1981.

Gutiérrez-Haces, Teresa. *Procesos de integración económica en México y Canadá. Una perspectiva histórica comparada*. Mexico City: Miguel Ángel Porrúa, 2002.

Hall, Linda B. *Álvaro Obregón: Power and Revolution in Mexico, 1911–1920*. College Station: Texas A&M University Press, 1981.

- *Mary, Mother and Warrior: The Virgin of Guadalupe in Spain and the Americas*. Austin: University of Texas Press, 2004.

- *Oil, Banks, and Politics: the United States and Postrevolutionary Mexico, 1917–1924*. Austin: University of Texas Press, 1995.

Handler, Richard. *Nationalism and the Politics of Culture in Quebec*. Madison: University of Wisconsin Press, 1988.

Harkness, Ross. "An Invasion by Request." *The Star Weekly*, 5 April 1951.

Hart, John M. *Revolutionary Mexico: the Coming and Process of the Mexican Revolution*. Berkeley: University of California Press, 1987.

Harvey, Julien, s j. "L'influence de la pensée sociale de l'Église au Québec." In *La question sociale hier et aujourd'hui: Colloque du centenaire de Rerum novarum, 12 au 17 mai 1991, Université Laval, Québec*, edited by Jean Richard and Louis O'Neill, 108–28. Sainte-Foy: Les Presses de l'Université Laval, 1993.

Harvey, Louis-Georges. *Le Printemps de l'Amérique française. Américanité, anticolonialisme et républicanisme dans le discours politique québécois, 1805–1837*. Montreal: Boréal, 2005.

Hedetoft, Ulf. "Symbolic Politics and Cultural Symbols: Identity Formation Between and Beyond Nations and States." In *The Cambridge Handbook of Sociocultural Psychology*, edited by Jaan Valsiner and Alberto Rosa, 691–507. Cambridge: Cambridge University Press, 2007.

Hernández García de León, Héctor. *Historia política del sinarquismo, 1934–1944*. Mexico City: Miguel Angel Porrua/Universidad Iberoamericana, 2004.

Hillmer, Norman, and J.L. Granatstein. *Empire to Umpire: Canada and the World to the 1990s*. Toronto: Copp Clark Longman, 1994.

Holloway, Steven Kendall. *Canadian Foreign Policy: Defining the National Interest*. Peterborough: Broadview Press, 2006.

Howe, George Frederick. "García Moreno's Efforts to Unite Ecuador and France." *The Hispanic American Historical Review* 16, no. 2 (1936): 257–62.

Hughes, Everett. *French Canada in Transition*. Chicago: University of Chicago Press, 1943.

Humphrey, John Thomas Peters. *The Inter-American System: a Canadian View. Issued under the Auspices of the Canadian Institute of International Affairs*. Toronto: Macmillan Co. of Canada, 1942.

Imbert, Patrick. *Trajectoires culturelles transaméricaines: médias, publicité, littérature et mondialisation*. Ottawa: Les Presses de l'Université d'Ottawa, 2004.

Imbert, Patrick, and Daniel Castillo Durante. *L'interculturel au cœur des Amériques*. Winnipeg: University of Manitoba, 2003.

Instituto Matías Romero de Estudios Diplomáticos and Secretaría de Relaciones Exteriores, ed. *Canadá y México: Los vecinos del vecino*. Mexico City: Secretaría de Relaciones Exteriores, 1997.

Jolivet, Simon. *Le vert et le bleu. Identité québécoise et identité irlandaise au tournant du XXᵉ siècle*. Montreal: Les Presses de l'Université de Montréal, 2011.

Jones, Richard. *Duplessis and the Union Nationale Administration*. Ottawa: Canadian Historical Association, 1983.

Joseph, Gilbert, and Daniel Nugent, ed. *Everyday Forms of State Formation: Revolution and the Negotiation of Rule in Modern Mexico*. Durham: Duke University Press, 1994.

Joseph, Gilbert, Anne Rubenstein, and Eric Zolov, ed. "Assembling the Fragments: Writing a Cultural History of Mexico Since 1940." In *Fragments of a Golden Age: The Politics of Culture in Mexico since 1940*, edited by Gilbert M. Joseph, Anne Rubenstein, and Eric Zolov, 3–22. Durham: Duke University Press, 2001.

Kennedy, James. *Liberal Nationalisms: Empire, State, and Civil Society in Scotland and Quebec*. Montreal: McGill-Queen's University Press, 2013.

Kirk, Betty. "Election Day, 1940." In *Revolution in Mexico: Years of Upheaval, 1910–1940*, edited by James W. Wilkie and Albert L. Michaels, 262–7. New York: Alfred A. Knopf, 1969.

Knight, Alan. *The Mexican Revolution*. Cambridge: Cambridge University Press, 1986.

– "Popular Culture and the Revolutionary State in Mexico, 1910–1940." *The Hispanic American Historical Review* 74, no. 3 (1994): 393–444.

– "Rise and Fall of Cardenismo, c. 1930–c. 1946." In *Mexico since Independence*, edited by Leslie Bethell, 241–320. New York: Cambridge University Press, 1991.

Krauze, Enrique. *La presidencia imperial: ascenso y caída del sistema político mexicano (1940–1996)*. Mexico City: Tusquest Editores México, 2002.

LaCapra, Dominick. "Chartier, Darnton, and the Great Symbol Massacre." *Journal of Modern History* 60 (1988): 95–112.

Lacasse, Robert. "L'intervention française au Mexique et l'opinion publique au Québec 1861–1867." MA thesis, Université de Montréal, 1975.

Lacombe, Sylvie. *La rencontre de deux peuples élus: comparaison des ambitions nationale et impériale au Canada entre 1896 et 1920*. Quebec City: Les Presses de l'Université Laval, 2002.

Lacroix, Michel. "Lien social, idéologie et cercles d'appartenance: le réseau 'latin' des Québécois en France, 1923–1939." *Études littéraires* 36, no. 2 (2004): 51–70.

Lamonde, Yvan. *Allégeances et dépendances: l'histoire d'une ambivalence identitaire*. Quebec City: Éditions Nota bene, 2001.

– "Dostaler O'Leary." In *Histoire intellectuelle de l'indépendantisme québécois. Tome 1: 1834–1968*, edited by Robert Comeau, Charles-Philippe Courtois, and Denis Monière, 123–31. Montreal: V L B Éditeur, 2010.

– *L'heure de vérité. La laïcité québécoise à l'épreuve de l'histoire*. Montreal: Del Busso Éditeur, 2010.

– *Histoire sociale des idées au Québec*. Saint-Laurent: Fides, 2000.

– *Louis-Antoine Dessaulles. Un seigneur libéral et anticlérical*. Montreal: Éditions Fides, 1994.

– *La modernité au Québec. La Crise de l'homme et de l'esprit, 1929–1939*. Montreal: Fides, 2010.

– *Ni avec eux ni sans eux: le Québec et les États-Unis*. Quebec City: Nuit blanche, 1996.

– *The Social History of Ideas in Quebec, 1760–1896*. Montreal: McGill-Queen's University Press, 2013.

Lamonde, Yvan, and Gérard Bouchard. *Québécois et Américains: la culture québécoise aux XIXe et XXe siècles*. Saint-Laurent: Fides, 1995.

Laperrière, Guy. *Les congrégations religieuses: de la France au Québec, 1880–1914*, 3 vols. Sainte-Foy, Quebec City: Les Presses de l'Université Laval, 1996.

"Le congrès eucharistique de Montréal en 1910: une affirmation du catholicisme montréalais." *Études d'histoire religieuse* 77 (2011): 21–39.

Lapointe, Marie, and Catherine Vézina. "El México rojo y la Cristiada en la mira de los diarios de Quebec 1926–1929." In *Las naciones frente al conflicto religioso en México*, edited by Jean Meyer, 265–88. Mexico City: Tusquests Editores, 2008.

Ledit, Joseph, S J. "Sinarquismo Victory in Tabasco." In *Revolution in Mexico: Years of Upheaval, 1910–1940*, edited by James W. Wilkie and Albert L. Michaels, 222–6. New York: Alfred A. Knopf, 1969.

LeGrand, Catherine. "L'axe missionaire catholique entre le Québec et l'Amérique latine. Une exploration préliminaire." *Globe. Revue internationale d'études québécoises* 12, no. 1 (2009): 43–66.

– "Cultural Approaches to Canadian-Latin American Relations: Catholic Missionaries, Dictatorship and Social Engagement in the Dominican Republic, 1935 to the Present." Lecture at the University of Manitoba, 2007.

– "Les réseaux missionnaires et l'action sociale des Québécois en Amérique latine, 1945–1980," *Études d'histoire religieuse* 79, no. 1 (2013): 93–116.

Le Moine, Roger. "L'aventure mexicaine de quelques Québécois." In *Les Discours du Nouveau Monde au XIXe siècle au Canada français et en Amérique latine*, edited by Marie Couillard and Patrick Imbert, 253–62. Ottawa: Legas, 1995.

Lesemann, Frédéric, and Jean-François Côté, ed. *La construction des Amériques aujourd'hui: regards croisés transnationaux et transdisciplinaires*. Quebec City: Les Presses de l'Université du Québec, 2009.

Lévesque, Andrée. *Éva Circé-Côté: libre-penseuse, 1871–1949*. Montreal: Les éditions du remue-ménage, 2010.

– *Virage à gauche interdit. Les communistes, les socialistes et leurs ennemies au Québec, 1929–1939*. Montréal: Boréal Express, 1984.

Levitt, Peggy, and Sanjeev Khagram, eds. *The Transnational Studies Reader: Intersections & Innovations*. New York: Routledge, 2008.

Linteau, Paul-André, René Durocher, and Jean-Claude Robert. *Histoire du Québec contemporain*, vol. 2. Sillery: Boréal Express, 1979.

Loaeza, Guadalupe. *Las niñas bien*. Mexico City: Oceano, 2004.

Loaeza, Soledad. *Clases medias y política en México: la querella escolar, 1959–1963*. Mexico City: El Colegio de México / Centro de Estudios Internacionales, 1988.

– "Los orígenes de la propuesta modernizadora de Manuel Gómez Morín." *Historia Mexicana* 46, no. 2 (1996): 425–78.

Lomnitz-Adler, Claudio. *Deep Mexico, Silent Mexico: An Anthropology of Nationalism*. Minneapolis: University of Minnesota Press, 2001.

Lynch, John. *New Worlds: A Religious History of Latin America*. New Haven: Yale University Press, 2012.

Mabry, Donald J. *The Mexican University and the State: Student Conflicts, 1910–1971*. College Station: Texas A&M University Press, 1982.

Mace, Gordon. "Les relations du Québec avec l'Amérique latine." In *Trente ans de politique extérieure du Québec, 1960–1990*, 221–49. Sainte-Foy: Centre québécois de relations internationales, 1993.

Mah, Harold. "Suppressing the text: The metaphysics of ethnographic history in Darnton's Great Cat Massacre." *History Workshop Journal* 31 (1991): 1–20.

Makabe, Tomoko. "The Theory of the Split Labor Market: A Comparison of the Japanese Experience in Brazil and Canada." *Social Forces* 59, no. 3 (1981): 786–809.

Mann, Susan. *The Dream of Nation: a Social and Intellectual History of Quebec*. Montreal: McGill-Queen's University Press, 2002.

Maurault, Olivier. *Le Mexique de mes souvenirs*. Montreal: Éditions des Dix, 1945.

– *Par voies et par chemins de l'air (les Amériques)*. Montreal: Éditions des Dix, 1947.

Martin, Lawrence. "Quebec Defines this Country." *The Globe and Mail*, 1 March 2007.

Martínez Assad, Carlos. *El laboratorio de la revolución. El Tabasco garridista*. Mexico City: Siglo Veintiuno, 1979.

Mayo, Carlos A., and David Matthew Khazanov Sheinin. *Es Igual pero Distinto: Essays in the Histories of Canada and Argentina*. Peterborough: Frost Centre for Canadian Heritage and Development Studies/Trent University, 1997.

McGowan, Mark G. *The Waning of the Green: Catholics, the Irish, and Identity in Toronto, 1887–1922*. Montreal: McGill-Queen's University Press, 1999.

McNair Jones III, Halbert. "'The War has brought Peace to Mexico': The Political Impact of Mexican Participation in World War II." PhD dissertation, Harvard University, 2006.

Melakopides, Costas. *Pragmatic Idealism: Canadian Foreign Policy, 1945–1995*. Montreal: McGill-Queen's University Press, 1998.

Melançon, Benoît. "La littérature québécoise et l'Amérique. Prolégomènes et bibliographie." *Études françaises* 26, no. 2 (1990): 65–108.

Mesli, Samy. "Le développement de la 'diplomatie éducative' du Québec." *Globe. Revue internationale d'études québécoises* 12, no. 1 (2009): 115–32.

Meyer, Jean. "Les Cristeros (1926–1929)." *La Révolution mexicaine, 1910–1940*. Paris: Éditions Tallandier, 2010.

– *La Cristiada. El conflicto entre la iglesia y el estado, 1926–1929*. Mexico City: Siglo Veintiuno Editores, 2004.

– *La Cristiada. La guerra de los cristeros*. Mexico City: Siglo Veintiuno Editores, 2004.

- *La Cristiada. Los cristeros*. Mexico City: Siglo Veintiuno Editores, 2004.
- *La cruzada por México. Los católicos de Estados Unidos y la cuestión religiosa en México*. Mexico City: Tusquests Editores, 2008.
- "An Idea of Mexico: Catholics in the Revolution." In *The Eagle and the Virgin: Nation and Cultural Revolution in Mexico, 1920–1940*, edited by Mary Kay Vaughan and Stephen E. Lewis, 281–96. Durham: Duke University Press, 2006.
- *El sinarquismo, el cardenismo y la iglesia: 1937–1947*. Mexico City: Tusquets Editores, 2003.

Meyer, Lorenzo. *Las raíces del nacionalismo petrolero en México*. Mexico City: Oceano, 2009.
- *Su majestad británica contra la revolución mexicana: el fin de un imperio informal*. Mexico City: El Colegio de Mexico, 1991.

Michaels, Albert L. "The Modification of the Anti-Clerical Nationalism of the Mexican Revolution by General Lázaro Cárdenas and its Relationship to the Church-State Detente in Mexico." *The Americas* 26, no. 1 (1969): 35–53.

Miller, Eugene H. "Canada and the Pan American Union." *International Journal* 3, (1948): 24–38.

Mills, Kenneth, William B. Taylor and Sandra Lauderdale Graham, eds. *Colonial Latin America: A Documentary History*. Lanham: S R Books, 2002.

Monette, Pierre. "Serie tango: el medio del tango en Montreal." In *El tango nómade: ensayos sobre la diáspora del tango*, edited by Ramón Adolfo Pelinski, 395–444. Buenos Aires: Corregidor, 2000.

Monière, Denis, and André Vachet. *Les idéologies au Québec*. Montreal: Bibliothèque nationale du Québec/Ministère des Affaires culturelles, 1976.

Moreno, Julio. *Yankee Don't Go Home! Mexican Nationalism, American Business Culture, and the Shaping of Modern Mexico, 1920–1950*. Chapel Hill: University of North Carolina Press, 2003.

Morisset, Jean. *L'identité usurpée. L'Amérique écartée*, vol. 1. Montreal: Nouvelle Optique, 1985.

Morisset, Jean, and Éric Waddell. *Amériques*. Montreal: L'Hexagone, 2000

Murray, D.R. "Canada's First Diplomatic Missions in Latin America." *Journal of Interamerican Studies and World Affairs* 16, no. 2 (1974): 153–72.

Napolitano, Valentina. "The Virgin of Guadalupe: a nexus of affect." *Journal of the Royal Anthropological Institute* (N.S.) no. 15 (2009): 96–112.

Nareau, Michel. "Coopération, réseautage et Liaison. 'Servir' la littérature
    québécoise par le recours à l'Argentine." *Mémoire du livre/Studies in
    book culture* 4, no. 1 (2012).
– *Double jeu. Baseball et littératures américaines.* Montreal: Le
    Quartanier, 2012.
– "La revue *Dérives* et le Brésil. Inscrire les mots d'autrui dans le récit
    québécois." *Globe, revue internationale d'études québécoise,* no. 1
    (2011): 165–84.
Nebel, Richard. *Santa María Tonantzin Virgen de Guadalupe.
    Continuidad y transformación religiosa en México.* Mexico City: Fondo
    de Cultura Económica, 1995.
Nelles, H.V. *The Art of Nation-Building: Pageantry and Spectacle at
    Quebec's Tercentenary.* Toronto: University of Toronto Press, 1999.
Nepveu, Pierre. *Intérieurs du Nouveau Monde.* Montreal: Boréal, 1998.
Newcomer, Daniel. *Reconciling Modernity: Urban State Formation in
    1940s León, Mexico.* Lincoln: University of Nebraska Press, 2004.
Niblo, Stephen R. *War, Diplomacy, and Development: The United States
    and Mexico, 1938–1954.* Wilmington: SR Books, 1995.
Noël, Mathieu. *Lionel Groulx et le réseau indépendantiste des années
    1930.* Montreal: VLB Éditeur, 2011.
Nye, Joseph, and Robert Keohane. "Transnational Relations and World
    Politics: An Introduction." *International Organization* 25 (1971):
    329–46.
Nykl, Alois Richard. "Summer School of the Universidad Nacional de
    Mexico." *Hispania* 8, no. 1 (1925): 52–5.
O'Dogherty, Laura. "Restaurarlo todo en Cristo: Unión de Damas
    Católicas Mejicanas, 1920–1926." *Estudios de Historia Moderna y
    Contemporánea de México,* 14 (1991): 129–58.
Ogelsby, John Charles Martin. *Gringos from the Far North: Essays in the
    History of Canadian-Latin American Relations, 1866–1968.* Toronto:
    Maclean-Hunter Press, 1976.
O'Leary, Dostaler. *Introduction à l'histoire de l'Amérique latine.* Montreal:
    Éditions latines, 1949.
– *Séparatisme, doctrine constructive.* Montreal: Jeunesses Patriotes, 1937.
Owram, Douglas. *Government Generation: Canadian Intellectuals and
    the State 1900–1945.* Toronto: University of Toronto Press, 1986.
Padilla Rangel, Yolanda. "Anticlericalismo carrancista y exilio católico a
    Texas, 1914–1919." In *El anticlericalismo en México,* edited by Franco
    Savarino and Andrea Mutolo, 449–71. Mexico City: Miguel Ángel
    Porrúa, 2008.

Paquin, Stéphane, ed. *Histoire des relations internationales du Québec.* Montreal: VLB Éditeur, 2006.

Pattee, Richard, and the Inter-American Committee, eds. *The Catholic Revival in Mexico.* Washington: The Catholic Association for International Peace, 1944.

Pérez Siller, Javier. *México Francia: memoria de una sensibilidad común, siglos XIX–XX.* Puebla: Benemérita Universidad Autónoma de Puebla/CEMCA, 1998.

Perin, Roberto. "L'Église et l'édification d'une culture publique au Québec." *Études d'histoire religieuse* 67 (2001): 261–70.

– *Ignace de Montréal: artisan d'une identité nationale.* Montreal: Boréal, 2008.

Platt, D.C.M. *Social Welfare, 1850–1950: Australia, Argentina and Canada Compared.* Basingstoke: Macmillan, 1989.

Platt, D.C.M., and Guido Di Tella. *Argentina, Australia, and Canada: Studies in Comparative Development, 1870–1965.* New York: St Martin's Press, 1985.

Podea, Iris S. "Pan American Sentiment in French Canada." *International Journal* 3, no. 4 (1948): 334–48.

Poole, Stafford. *Our Lady of Guadalupe: the Origins and Sources of a Mexican National Symbol, 1531–1797.* Tuscon: University of Arizona Press, 1995.

Quintanilla, Luis. *A Latin American Speaks.* New York: The MacMillan Company, 1943.

Racine, Claude. *L'anticléricalisme dans le roman québécois (1940–1965).* Montreal: Éditions Hurtubise HMH, 1972.

Radforth, Ian Walter. *Royal Spectacle: the 1860 Visit of the Prince of Wales to Canada and the United States.* Toronto: University of Toronto Press, 2004.

Rajotte, Pierre. "De Québec à Mexico de Faucher de Saint-Maurice: entre la fidélité à une tradition de lecture et la recherche d'originalité." In *Les Discours du Nouveau Monde au XIXe siècle au Canada français et en Amérique latine,* edited by Marie Couillard and Patrick Imbert, 263–75. Ottawa: Legas, 1995.

– "De Québec à Mexico de Faucher de Saint-Maurice: une tentative de voyage vers soi." *Canadian Literature,* nos. 144, 145 (1994): 77–96.

Rankin, Monica. "Mexico: Industrialization through Unity." In *Latin America during World War II,* edited by Thomas M. Leonard and John F. Bratzel, 17–35. Lanham: Rowman and Littlefield Publishers, 2007.

– *¡México, La Patria! Propaganda and Production during World War II.*
Lincoln: University of Nebraska Press, 2009.

Redinger, Matthew A. *American Catholics and the Mexican Revolution,*
1924–1936. Notre Dame: University of Notre Dame Press, 2005.

Reich, Peter L. *Mexico's Hidden Revolution: the Catholic Church in Law*
and Politics since 1929. Notre Dame: University of Notre Dame Press,
1995.

"Reportage no. 71." Canada: Office national du Film du Canada, 1944.
DVD, 7 min.

Robillard, Denise. *Aventurières de l'ombre. De l'obéissance au discerne-*
ment. Les missions des Soeurs de la Providence, 1962–1997.
Outremont: Les Éditions Carte Blanche, 2001.

Rocher, Guy, Guy Gaucher, and Suzanne Rocher. *Le Québec en mutation.*
Montreal: Hurtubise HMH, 1973.

Rochlin, James Francis. *Discovering the Americas: the Evolution of*
Canadian Foreign Policy Towards Latin America. Vancouver: UBC
Press, 1994.

Romero, José Antonio, SJ, ed. *Cincuentenario Guadalupano. México,*
1895–1945. Mexico City: Arzobispado de México, 1945.

Roy, Charles-Eugène. *La Vierge de Guadeloupe, Impératrice des*
Amériques. Montreal: Fides, 1957.

Rubenstein, Anne. *Bad Language, Naked Ladies, and other Threats to the*
Nation: a Political History of Comic Books in Mexico. Durham: Duke
University Press, 1998.

Rudin, Ronald. *Making History in Twentieth-Century Quebec: Historians*
and their Society. Toronto: University of Toronto Press, 1997.

Rumilly, Robert. *Maurice Duplessis et son temps.* Montreal: Fides, 1978.

Ryan, Pascale. *Penser la nation: la Ligue d'action nationale, 1917–1960.*
Montreal: Leméac, 2006.

Sariñana, Fernando. "Amar te duele." Mexico: Lionsgate, 2002. DVD,
104 min.

Savarino, Franco. *Pueblos y nacionalismo, del regimen oligárquico*
a la sociedad de masas en Yucatán, 1894–1925. Mexico City:
Instituto Nacional de Estudios Históricos de la Revolución
Mexicana, 1997.

Schiavon, Jorge A., Daniela Spenser, and Mario Vázquez Olivera. *En*
busca de una nación soberana: relaciones internacionales de México,
siglos XIX y XX. Mexico City: Centro de Investigación y Docencia
Económicas, 2006.

Schuler, Friedrich E. *Mexico between Hitler and Roosevelt: Mexican Foreign Relations in the Age of Lázaro Cárdenas, 1934–1940*. Albuquerque: University of New Mexico Press, 1998.

Section canadienne de l'Union Culturelle des Latins d'Amérique, ed. *Rapport complet: Journées d'Amérique latine, 1943*. Montreal: [s.n.], 1943.

Sherman, John W. *The Mexican Right: The End of Revolutionary Reform, 1929–1940*. Westport: Praeger, 1997.

Shore, Marlene Gay. *The Science of Social Redemption: McGill, the Chicago School, and the Origins of Social Research in Canada*. Toronto: University of Toronto Press, 1987.

Shumway, Nicolas. "Hispanism in an Imperfect Past and an Uncertain Present. " In *Ideologies of Hispanism*, edited by Mabel Moraña, 284–99. Nashville: Vanderbilt University Press, 2005.

Silva Herzog, Jesús. *Una historia de la Universidad de México y sus problemas*. Mexico City: Siglo Veintiuno Editores, 1974.

Smith, Peter H. *Talons of the Eagle: Dynamics of US-Latin American Relations*. New York: Oxford University Press, 2000.

Soares de Souza, Licia. *Utopies américaines au Québec et au Brésil*. Quebec City: Les Presses de l'Université Laval, 2004.

Solberg, Carl E. *The Prairies and the Pampas: Agrarian Policy in Canada and Argentina, 1880–1930*. Stanford: Stanford University Press, 1987.

Stevenson, Brian J.R. *Canada, Latin America, and the New Internationalism: a Foreign Policy Analysis, 1968–1990*, edited by Centre d'études des politiques étrangères et de sécurité (Université du Québec à Montréal). Montreal: McGill-Queen's University Press, 2000.

Stoler, Ann Laura. "Matters of Intimacy as Matters of State: A Response." *The Journal of American History* 88, no. 3 (2001): 893–7.

Subrahmanyam, Sanjay. "Connected Histories: Notes Towards a Reconfiguration of Early Modern Eurasia." In *Beyond Binary Histories. Re-imagining Eurasia to C 1830*, edited by V. Liberman, 289–315. Ann Arbor: University of Michigan Press, 1997.

Super, John C. "'Rerum Novarum' in Mexico and Quebec." *Revista de Historia de América*, no. 126 (2000): 63–84.

Tenorio-Trillo, Mauricio. *Mexico at the World's Fairs: Crafting a Modern Nation*. Berkeley: University of California Press, 1996.

Thériault, Joseph Yvon. "Chronique des Amériques: l'américanité comme effacement du sujet québécois." *Argument* 3, no. 1 (2000-01): 136–44.

– *Critique de l'américanité. Mémoire et démocratie au Québec*. Montreal: Québec-Amérique, 2002.

– "Mais qu'a bien pu vouloir nous dire Robert Lepage?" *Nuit blanche, le magazine du livre*, no. 114 (2009): 10–13.

Torres Septién, Valentina. *La educación privada en México (1903–1976)*. Mexico City: El Colegio de México/Universidad Iberoamericana, 1997.

Trudeau, Pierre Elliott. *Federalism and the French Canadians*. Toronto: Macmillan of Canada, 1968.

Vaughan, Mary Kay. *Cultural Politics in Revolution: Teachers, Peasants, and Schools in Mexico, 1930–1940*. Tucson: University of Arizona Press, 1997.

Vaughan, Mary Kay, and Stephen E. Lewis. *The Eagle and the Virgin: Nation and Cultural Revolution in Mexico, 1920–1940*. Durham: Duke University Press, 2006.

Voisine, Nive, Jean Hamelin, Nicole Gagnon, and Philippe Sylvain. *Histoire du catholicisme québécois*. Montreal: Boréal express, 1984.

Wade, Mason. *The French Canadians, 1760–1945*. Toronto: Macmillan, 1955.

Warren, Jean-Philippe. "Le corporatisme canadien-français comme 'système total.' Quatre concepts pour comprendre la popularité d'une doctrine." *Recherches sociographiques* 45, no. 2 (2004): 219–38.

Wilkie, James W. Statistics and National Policy: Supplement 3 (1974) Statistical Abstract of Latin America. Los Angeles: University of California, 1974.

Williams, Raymond. *Marxism and Literature*. Oxford: Oxford University Press, 1977.

Wright, Dean. "For Greater Glory." Santa Monica: Arc Entertainment, 2012. DVD, 150 min.

Wright, Robert A. *Three Nights in Havana: Pierre Trudeau, Fidel Castro and the Cold War World*. Toronto: HarperCollins, 2007.

Yankelevich, Pablo. "América Latina en la agenda diplomática de la revolución mexicana." In *En busca de una nación soberana. Relaciones internacionales de México, siglos XIX y XX*, edited by Jorge A. Shiavon, Daniela Spenser, and Mario Vázquez Olivera, 277–312. Mexico City: Centro de Investigación y Docencia Económicas, 2006.

Young, Julia G. "The Calles Government and Catholic Dissidents: Mexico's Transnational Projects of Repression, 1926–1929." *The Americas* 70, no. 1 (2013): 63–91.

Index